WITHDRAWN

the teaching ministry of the pulpit

the teaching ministry of the pulpit

ITS HISTORY, THEOLOGY, PSYCHOLOGY, AND PRACTICE FOR TODAY

Craig Skinner

BAKER BOOK HOUSE
Grand Rapids, Michigan

46973

Copyright © 1973 by
Baker Book House Company

ISBN: 0-8010-7981-0
Library of Congress Card Catalog Number: 72-9334

Printed in the United States of America

First printing, April 1973
Second printing, September 1973

Dedicated to the congregations of
    Calvary Baptist Church of Chicago,
    Fortified Hills Baptist Church, Atlanta,
    and *Blakehurst Baptist Church,* Sydney, Australia,
and to my wife, *Betty,*
    all of whom were subjected to an incredible number of homiletic
    experiments by me in the interest of this study, and *still*
    encouraged me;
and to *Guy and Ann Thomason* of Atlanta whose hospitality made much of it
    possible.

CONTENTS

CONTENTS

PART I
perspective from history

PART IV
practice

FOREWORD

I know this quality book on preaching is backed by years of hard work, unfailing courage, sheer determination, and high dedication. Craig Skinner's single volume covers more territory and makes more useful contributions than any other book on preaching I have read in a long, long time.

This Australian pastor-teacher unfolds and supports his main thesis — that good preaching always has been, is now, and ever must be strong in the teaching element. He discriminatingly surveys the whole field of relevant human endeavor (except that of public entertainment) for confirming materials. Drawing on the history of preaching, the history of education, the fields of ecclesiology, pastoral care, theology, psychology, public address, semantics, modern salesmanship, motivational research, evangelism, and homiletics, Craig Skinner comes up with exciting applications.

No reader, however, must think that he is headed into an unorganized jumble or a mere rehash of stale ideas. Rather, this is a well-organized, creative, free-flowing, interest-sustaining, and highly profitable study. Like the author himself, the book breathes warmth, openness, evangelical concern, Biblical loyalty, and constructive purpose, all supported by sound scholarship. I have known this author both as a former graduate student and a friend. Only a mature person such as he is with broad training and varied experiences in both business and the ministry could produce writing like this. This book is a must for all preachers and theological students, who would find fresh inspiration to preach the Word and upgrade their pulpit performance.

Faris D. Whitesell
Winfield, Illinois

Dr. Faris D. Whitesell, MA., BD., ThD., DD., is emeritus-professor of preaching, Northern Baptist Theological Seminary, Illinois; contributing editor, *Christianity Today*; author of *The Art of Biblical Preaching, Power in Expository Preaching, Variety in Your Preaching, Great Expository Sermons*, etc.

PREFACE

The Bible declares that the Spirit of God moves out into the lives of persons via the preached Word and the listening ear. The Barthian crisis-theology has lifted preaching to a new significance today with its demands for a proclamation approach that issues in genuine confrontation of man with God. Others are so concerned about preaching relevance that they want us to delete vast areas of the Biblical revelation in order to increase effective communication.

This study is cognizant of these areas, and it often refers to them, but it does not base itself on such concepts. Here is material which centers rather on the practical purposes for which preaching is intended, factors in the preaching situation which have had all too little attention from theologians in recent days. Ample scholarly support has been found for concepts which can be operative within the most pragmatic applications, within history, theology, and psychology.

No attempt to lay down an arrangement of prepackaged sermon plans has been made. This discussion is rather a serious endeavor to guide the reader into more effective sermon design for himself, but along lines that harmonize with both contemporary insights and the standard theories of preaching.

A conservative theological view will be apparent, particularly as it relates to the conversion experience. Many today who are classified as church members are finding new lives of assurance, and spiritual understanding, through the public confession of a personal relationship with Christ and possession of the benefits of His atonement, in such services as those being conducted internationally by men like Evangelist Billy Graham.

This study begins with the assumption of such a commitment to discipleship, and centers on the pulpit task of the Christian educator in bringing his hearers to spiritual maturity. We begin with the new man in Christ, seeking to lead him on, rather than with the old man in sin, seeking to lead him to Christ. The true child of God has a new nature, a new desire for truth, and a new willingness to follow in God's ways. The presence and resources of the indwelling Holy Spirit give a new motivation for Christian living and a new power to perform.[1] Whether personal faith is discovered within the family testimony, as with Timothy, or as the fruit of a long search for truth, as with Apollos and the eunuch from Ethiopia, or in a dramatic experience, as with Saul of Tarsus, the fact remains that the pastoral task is to take the newborn lambs of God and shepherd them to maturity. The only imperative in the great commission of Matthew 28:19-20 is the direct command to *disciple.* All other aspects of ministry are dependent on this cardinal imperative.[2]

The theological focal point chosen is that of the preacher as the *voice of the body of Christ,* as this is a Scriptural concept which forms a natural nucleus around which these truths collate themselves effectively.

I gladly acknowledge the interest and courtesy of librarians,[3] professors,[4] and an uncounted multitude of pastors and others who, since this research was first projected in late 1963, have helped with suggestions and shared insights in response to many inquiries addressed to them in these matters.[5]

Thanks is most due to some initial guidance in several areas from Dr. Lois E. LeBar, professor of Christian Education in the graduate school of Wheaton College, Illinois; and Dr. Faris D. Whitesell, of Northern Baptist Theological Seminary, Oakbrook, Illinois (who has also graciously consented to write the foreword). I owe more to these two teachers than I can ever fully acknowledge.

There will always be some unacknowledged persons who should be noted. For such it is hoped that Kipling's word on the

---

1. See Findley B. Edge, *Teaching for Results* (Nashvile: Broadman, 1956), pp. 22-27.

2. As the Greek tenses in this passage show.

3. Particularly those at Columbia Theological Seminary, Decatur, Georgia (Presbyterian), and Candler School of Theology at Emory University, Atlanta, Georgia (Methodist).

4. The Freeman thesis was discovered through the personal interest in the project of Dr. Samuel Millar, dean of Harvard Divinity School, and the Reid thesis was likewise found through the counsel of Dr. Halford Luccock, Jr., of Boston University.

5. Many of the executive personnel of the Sunday School Board of the Southern Baptist Convention have also been most helpful.

matter will be sufficient —

> When 'Omer smote 'is bloomin' lyre,
> 'E'd 'eard men sing by land and sea;
> An' what 'e thought 'e might require,
> 'E went an' took—the same as me!

> The market-girls an' fishermen,
> The shepherds an' the sailors too,
> They 'eard old songs turn up again,
> But kep' it quiet—same as you!

> They knew 'e stole; 'e knew they knowed,
> They didn't tell, nor make a fuss;
> But winked at 'Omer, down the road,
> An' 'e winked back—the same as us![6]

Craig Skinner
Queensland Baptist Theological College
Brookfield, Australia

6. Rudyard Kipling, *Rudyard Kipling's Verse*, inclusive edition, 1885-1926 (New York: Doubleday, 1928), p. 403.

WANTED: Baptist Minister for Growing Church

A real challenge for the right man! Opportunity to become better acquainted with people!

Applicant must offer experience as shop worker . . . office manager . . . educator (all levels, including college) . . . artist . . . salesman . . . diplomat . . . writer . . . theologian . . . politician . . . Boy Scout leader . . . children's worker . . . minor league athlete . . . psychologist . . . vocational counselor . . . pyschiatrist . . . funeral director . . . wedding consultant . . . master of ceremonies . . . circus clown . . . missionary . . . social worker. Helpful but not essential: experience as butcher . . . baker . . . cowboy . . . Western Union messenger.

Must know all about problems of birth, marriage, and death; also conversant with latest theories and practices in areas like pediatrics, economics, and nuclear science.

Right man will hold firm views on every topic, but is careful not to upset people who disagree. Must be forthright but flexible; returns criticism and back-biting with Christian love and forgiveness.

Should have outgoing, friendly disposition at all times; should be captivating speaker and intent listener; will pretend he enjoys hearing women talk.

Education must be beyond Ph.D. requirements, but always concealed in homespun modesty and folksy talk. Able to sound learned at times, but most of time talks and acts like good-old-Joe. Familiar with literature read by average congregation.

Must be willing to work long hours; subject to call any time day or night; adaptable to sudden interruption. Will spend at least 25 hours preparing sermon; additional 10 hours reading books and magazines.

Applicant's wife must be both stunning and plain; smartly attired but conservative in appearance; gracious and able to get along with everyone, even women. Must be willing to work in church kitchen, teach Sunday school, baby-sit, run multilith machine, wait table, never listen to gossip, never become discouraged.

Applicant's children must be exemplary in conduct and character; well behaved, yet basically no different from other children; decently dressed.

Opportunity for applicant to live close to work. Furnished home provided; open-door hospitality enforced. Must be ever mindful the house does not belong to him.

Directly responsible for views and conduct to all church members and visitors; not confined to direction or support from any one person. Salary not commensurate with experience or need; no overtime pay. All replies kept confidential. Anyone applying will undergo full investigation to determine sanity.

From the *Crusader* (Valley Forge, Pa.: American
Baptist Convention, March 1962)

1

Introduction: Background
to Homiletics

Preaching is the heart of all Christianity, and is central to all of its evangelism, theology, and spiritual life. It is a function of worship, an agency for Christian education, and a vehicle for promoting change. It has therefore been long recognized as a powerful force in the shaping of human culture. The practice of preaching can be defined as an *art*—the art of verbal communication by a human personality through which God is pleased to reveal Himself.

Preaching is an art, as its practice assumes the existence of basic principles which govern its operation. Man has the ability to create new objects, develop new ideas, and cultivate new relationships because he is made in the image of a creating heavenly Father. He uses the raw materials in the world which God has given him, including the natural talents with which he has been endowed. He expresses the results of his creation through the vocal, graphic, and literary arts.

The quality of all such human creation depends directly on the individual's gifts and the extent to which he has trained himself to use them. God given abilities are released to a fuller activity through a mastery of the ideas which make them work and improve the quality of their operation. Good practice in every human art is a direct product of inherent talent, plus a thorough knowledge of the techniques which make such aptitudes function best.

Homiletics is the *science* of which preaching is the art, and such study digs in a field with no fences. Preaching theory cannot be contained within one or two simple academic disciplines. We may begin by an exploration of exposition, only to find a dozen fresh lines of investigation sprouting in adjoining acreages. Concern for a good theology of preaching will underline the need for an in-depth understanding of the pastoral role and of the nature and needs of persons. Desire for effective communication will highlight the demand for a thorough understanding of learning theory, educational psychology, logic, and a multitude of other elements all clamoring for valid attention within a right comprehension of good preaching.

These factors are best systematized via an overview of values gleaned from the confluent streams of Biblical and classical tradition in history. The Bible gives motive, content, and inspiration for Christian preaching, while forms and rules for effective public discourse come from the highly developed Greek and Roman *rhetoric* (theory) and *oratory* (practice) of the ancient world. We must begin with a survey study of these twin sources which are still the foundation of the contemporary art of preaching. Christian preaching always remains both a spiritual function in the encounter with God which it engenders, and a secular exercise in the creation of the form which that revelation assumes in its verbal communication.

THE BIBLICAL FOUNDATION

While there is much preaching throughout the Bible, is there any homiletics? Not if by this we mean a formal set of rules for the composition and delivery of religious discourse; but there are some elements of theory which do appear, as well as some hints and suggestions inherent in the Biblical record which are well worthy of attention.

Prophetic Style

The great strophēs of the prophetic records, particularly those of Isaiah and Jeremiah, show an intimate acquaintance with the majesty and power of right language. There is deep drama and biting force in almost every line of the originals. These men knew how to make their messages live for their hearers through apt illustration and telling metaphor. Their competence in these areas seems inexplicable unless we accept the probability of literary studies in such teaching communities as the "schools of the prophets."

Literary Detail

Another prominent element that is evident in every period of Hebrew history is the emphasis on literary exactness. The preservation of the correct forms of the divine revelation was regarded as primary, with careful attention being paid to every word of the sacred writings. The learners were expected to copy and repeat these without the smallest deviation. The exacting textual demands of the scribes, and of the synagogue, seem the more valid when undergirded by the concept of such a theory about the value of words and of their selection.

What is general among prophets and scribes becomes specific in the wisdom literature. A definite rhetorical culture here becomes explicit as writers discuss a sense of expressive arts theory. The author of the Book of Proverbs reveals the aims of his work, informing us that his words have been chosen for the purposes of instruction and wisdom, and that they might create an insight which will develop moral values and improve character (1:1-4). The great passage in Ecclesiastes 12 reveals a commitment to principles of word selection and of the choice of figures of speech, all of which are specifically designed to communicate, clarify, and motivate (vv. 9-12).

The artist who wrote that "a word fitly spoken is like apples of gold in a framework of silver" (Prov. 25:11) was deeply aware of the power of words. He enunciates a clear rhetorical principle— the power of a right word as being a medium of communication in motion (literally "a word spoken on his wheels"), giving the sense of a truth smoothly rolled into place without force, adapted to its context and circumstance, and enhanced by them. "Apples of gold" (a common poetic name for oranges in the East) is thought to set this fruit, mature and sweet, against a network of orange blossom in its silver hue, the whole forming a picture of balance and beauty beyond description.

Jesus' Teaching

Jesus' teaching appears to be the absolute of quality in the Hebrew tradition. All the major elements of argument, explanation, logic, and illustration are evident in His presentations, and He was sufficiently aware of the value of words to teach human responsibility concerning them (Matt. 12:36-37).

He spoke with a divine dynamic that had such force that the crowds often burst into excited comment. However, the force of this impact came not from His declaration of deity, but from the manner of His revelation of truth. His command came most from the use of apt illustration, in the truly prophetic manner, in distinction from the command of the current religious teachers, who depended on arguments based on the legal minutiae of Scripture.

Synagogue Practice

A standard synagogue tradition of narrative address is shown in both Stephen's sermon (Acts 7) and Peter's at Pentecost (Acts 2). Each preacher used much of the same factual material, but Peter also shows a definite balance of argument and illustration around a central proposition that "Jesus Christ is Lord." The elements of form are discernible in the sermons of Paul, and he clearly indicates his determination to speak without oratorical trickery, and with restraint and reasonableness (I Cor. 1:17; 2:1-5, 13). The characteristic public speech of that age was full of bombastic eloquence and common vulgarities. Paul, on the other hand, spoke clearly, concisely, and with directness. The style of his Athenian address is faultless, and shows evidence of most careful and controlled expression (Acts 17:22-33).

Direct Instruction

The apostle Paul's blessing rests clearly on the essence of good homiletical theory throughout the epistles, particularly in those addressed to Timothy. While there is no formal treatment of the subject, there is constant endorsement of it and encouragement to the young preacher to pay attention to it. In II Timothy 2:2, 24, a premium is placed on teaching ability; and in verses 15 and 16 of the same chapter Paul affirms the necessity of selecting the best of words for preaching. In II Timothy 1:13 he again emphasizes precision in word selection for the most effective gospel communication.

According to I Timothy 3:2, skill as well as an understanding of content is required from the preacher. In I Timothy 4:13-16 the young preacher is advised to give careful attention to preparation, delivery, and the art of communicating so as to motivate response. He is told that such "teaching for results" should be both thorough and practical. In I Timothy 5:17 such teaching and discourse is said to require hard labor.

THE CLASSICAL CONTRIBUTION

As far back as 466 B.C. Korax of Syracuse presented a treatise that gave rules for the art of speaking, revealing how much this function was intrinsic to the Greek ideals of society. The establishment of a democracy after the overthrow of the tyrant Thrasybulus in that same year had brought many cases to be tried before the popular courts, and the lack of skilled pleaders for these tasks inspired Korax to offer his material.

The Contribution of Aristotle (384-322 B.C.)

By far the greatest Greek contribution was Aristotle's well-known *Rhetoric,* thought by many to be the gathered notes of his pupils, who studied with him during long afternoon walks while he taught discursively. It was an attempt to gather all the elements of speech theory of his day, and place them in relation to his own teachings and reflections.

Aristotle discusses argument, diction, and order, and defines the art of persuasion. His work is full of sound counsel about communication, and his division of the parts of a speech into the introduction of a proposition and its proof remains still the most practical and concise division possible. This study is all the more remarkable when we realize that it came, not from a professional rhetorician, but rather from an all-around philosopher. It is significant as the supreme treatment of the subject in its age, and is rich with luminous suggestions.

The Works of Quintilian (A.D. 150-220)

Formal instruction in Greek and Latin literature began in Rome about 1000 B.C. Both Cicero (106-43 B.C.) and Julius Caesar (102[?]-44 B.C.) wrote literary treaties which discuss speech principles from a variety of perspectives, each drawing heavily on Aristotelean ideas. The definitive Roman work was that of Quintilian, whose twelve-volume *Institutes of Oratory* form a highly elaborate professional analysis of rhetorical theory into which he condensed the study and practice of a lifetime.

The contrast between Aristotle and Quintilian is strong. The first wrote out of the profundity of his thought, in the prime years of Grecian culture, and as an all-around academic and philosopher. The second wrote some four hundred years later, in the early years of the Roman decline, and as a cultivated specialist in a specific area. Aristotle's work is original and unpolished. Quintilian's is a highly elaborate refinement produced by one who had given all of his life to the task. Together these two great works provide a summary of all that is best in the Graeco-Roman heritage, and, surprisingly, contain most of the elements of rhetorical theory still enunciated today.

THE CHRISTIAN APPLICATION

The early Christian preachers moved out as evangelists across a world to which conquered Greece had given many elements of culture, including the grammar schools and universities.

In that ancient world the seven "liberal arts" of education were generally listed in the order of *grammar, dialectic* (logic), and *rhetoric,* as a primary group. The group most approximating today's emphases was quite secondary to the former three, usually listed as *arithmetic, geometry, astronomy*, and *music.* Thus there was an emphasis on the humanities and literary skills, and this emphasis held educational sway in the first five centuries of the Christian era. Within this emphasis rhetoric was principal.

Thus the early missionaries found themselves proclaiming the gospel to a generation in which public speaking was popular, and in which its theory and practice were central to all government, society, and culture. The Graeco-Roman rhetoric operated on well-defined principles which were easily captured for Christian ends. Thus the smaller stream of Biblical prophecy and preaching flowed forth in new power as it blended with the classical homiletic tradition, surging along the currents of the times. The classical context affected the church most during the first fifteen hundred years of its life, reaching an all-time significance through the revival of letters in the fifteenth and sixteenth centuries.

The Patristic Age (A.D. 100-600)

By the end of the first century the New Testament canon had been formed and preachers were giving attention to the presentation of its teachings in the best of terms. The Biblical and classical impulses, which we have already traced, continued to work as parallel forces in shaping the theory of preaching. An educated man in the ministry had mastered the construction and delivery of a secular discourse through his standard schooling, and such factors influenced his sermons and their delivery. There was also, however, an attitude of criticism toward oratorical extremes among the church fathers, which made them cautious about the wholesale adoption of secular ideas. Thus Paul, in Corinthians, set himself to avoid "the persuasive words of man's wisdom."

The early church built its illustrations of spiritual truth on the lives of Biblical characters; and there was a historical, ethical, and moral foundation to their preaching, all Scripturally based. Preaching itself was gradually recognized as primarily the interpretation and explanation of Scripture. The New Testament documents replaced oral tradition, and preaching became much more an exposition of Biblical passages for the edification of the hearers. This whole movement lies behind Paul's demands that local churches elect the kind of leader who would work hard at the tasks of teaching and pastoring people via a genuine ministry of the Word.

Origen (185-284). The greatest of the Alexandrian theologians combined spiritual and secular values into an effective theory, and for the first time in Christian history revealed the importance of a teaching ministry for the pulpit. Origen left no formal treatise on preaching, but many valuable perspectives show clearly through his voluminous writings.

Origen knew his Bible well, and gave himself unreservedly to the task of its interpretation, encouraging a formal structure for the sermon. He was deeply concerned about real spirituality in the preacher, and he urged attention to personal character, as well as to Biblical fidelity.

Before Origen's time the "homily" in the church had been a rather loosely connected set of comments on a given passage. He advocated analysis and interpretation as the basis of a cohesive exposition. He believed that each passage of Scripture held three foundational meanings—the historical, the doctrinal, and the spiritual. He thus spoke first of the surface or face meaning of the text, next of its practical application, and finally of its mystical and symbolic significance.

Unquestionably Origen gave undue prominence to the third area of interpretation, taking allegorical truth to unwarranted extremes. However, as his was the first genuine breakthrough in hermeneutics, it was this also in homiletics. His overemphasis on imaginative application did promote an imbalance, but it also served to underline the need for an inspirational perspective to preaching.

Chrysostom (347-407). Chrysostom, the great preacher of Antioch and Constantinople, has left us some six hundred homilies. Undoubtedly these form the greatest body of sermonic literature extant from those early days, and the most significant. He exhibits a great variety of approach, as well as much attention to exegesis and exposition.

Chrysostom insisted that every discourse must be founded on the Word of God, and that spiritual edification must come before oratorical display. A moral earnestness characterized his whole ministry, and emphasis is laid on the literal teachings of Scripture and their authority for the believing Christian. He also underlined the needs for listener involvement and vital communication, with a great attention to introductions and their significance.

A number of scattered hints about preaching theory appear in others of the early Fathers, showing clearly the synthesis of the Biblical and classical traditions. However it is not until well into the fifth century that these principles were clearly distilled by the great Augustine.

Augustine (354-430). The great theologian who, in many senses, ultimately fathered the Reformation, was himself a preacher plain in style, and Biblical and spiritual in method. For most of his secular life Augustine was a teacher of rhetoric, and it was therefore to be expected that he would apply these values within his new faith after his conversion in 387. As bishop of Hippo, in North Africa, his influence was powerful and wide; and he clearly viewed the preaching ministry as the teaching function of Christian leadership within the church assembled for worship. Thus his great four-volume study centered on the public teaching and interpretation of the Bible, and was aptly titled *De Doctrina Christiana (On Christian Teaching)*.

His first three volumes present clear principles of exposition, and the fourth deals with homiletics proper. He defends the Christian adaptation of secular rhetoric, and applauds the natural eloquence which accompanies real wisdom. He has much to say about the preacher's personal life and attitudes, and urges dependence on the Holy Spirit. He advocates clarity of diction, and shows great insight into the relation of lucid aims to the successful motivation of hearers into action. In all it is a masterly treatment for that age.

Two great summations still stand as abridgments of Augustine's thought having contemporary value. About the preacher's objectives he said, *"Non solum docere ut unstruat, et delectare ut teneat, verum etiam flectere ut vincat"* ("Not only to teach that he may instruct him, and to please that he may hold him, but also to move that he may overcome him"). About the relevance of style to the subjects discussed he advised, *"Parva submisse, modica temperate, magna granditer"* ("Little things humbly, ordinary things moderately, great things grandly").

Thus, in such passages and others, Augustine grasped the fundamental elements of preaching theory, matching the rules of rhetoric with the attitudes of spirituality. He regarded the right character of the preacher, together with his proper understanding of the spiritual nature of his preaching task, as essential, and felt that the careful preparation of the sermon was Biblically valid, and that it ought to draw its whole authority only from Scripture.

This, then, is the first formal treatise in which the Biblical and classical elements combine with solid scholarship and spiritual insight. Its clear emphasis is on preaching as a teaching function of the ministry.

The Middle Ages (600-1500)

During this period preaching entered a wilderness from which it did not emerge until the Reformation era. There were some homiletical productions, but what was written was mundane, repetitious, and of minimal interest. *Rabanus Maurus* (776-856), the Frenchman, later archbishop of Mainz, rehashed Augustine's *On Christian Teaching*, grouping it with his own comments and discussions of clerical duties. His work *De Clericorum Institutione* (*On the Institution of the Clergy*) was a kind of text for parish ministers in which he not only borrowed Augustine's ideas, but often (quite shamelessly) his very words as well.

With the rise of scholasticism *Guibert of Nogent* (1053-1124) and *Bonaventura* (1221-1274) wrote small works relevant to preaching, as did some others; but during this period there is little of any real homiletical consequence despite the revival of preaching itself under the Dominicans and the Franciscans. One work ascribed to *Thomas Aquinas* (1227-1274) reveals a knowledge of sermons as being either topical, textual, or expository in nature. This is the first time that such a clear distinction is recognized.

The Fifteenth and Sixteenth Centuries

Following the fall of Constantinople in 1453, the new life in art and literature darted arrows of intellectual fire in many directions. A widespread quickening of thought, accuracy in scholarship, and upgrading of culture was accompanied by a revival of the study of classical rhetoric. Cicero, Aristotle, and Quintilian again came into their own, and the study of their approaches created much dialogue with the dry scholasticism which was advocated by most contemporary preachers.

Desiderius Erasmus (1466-1536). In 1504 *John Reuchlin* (1455-1522) published a collection of rules relative to preaching, which awakened a new interest in homiletics. This was further stimulated by the publication of Erasmus' famous *Gospel Preacher* in 1535. Although ill arranged and verbose, this work is undoubtedly the most significant since Augustine. In it the writer summarizes most that could be gleaned of value from all the preceding centuries, making observation, application, and illustration of its worth to his own day and time.

Philip Melanchthon (1497-1560). Two Latin works by Melanchthon, Luther's close associate, should be mentioned. The first is a voluminous treatise on rhetoric (*Elementorum Rhetorices Libri Duo*), and the second a brief summation of preaching method (*Ratio Brevissima Concionandi*). There is nothing in these that is at all new, and the style of both is scholastic and dry. Melanchthon was known, however, as a theologian whose lectures on preaching were popular while he served on the faculty at Wittenberg. Like Augustine, he sought to ally the theological and rhetorical understandings of preaching into a single discipline.

Andrew Hyperius (1511-1564). All that had developed during the first fifteen hundred years of the church's understanding of homiletics was again summarized by one Andrew Gerard, later known as Andrew Hyperius (taken from his birthplace at Ypres in Flanders). After work at the University and the Sorbonne in Paris, and being influenced by Reformation ideas while teaching in England, he settled as a teacher at Marburg. A fine, all-around scholar, his work *De Formandis Concionibus Sacris* (*On the Making of Sacred Discourse*), published in 1522, advanced beyond others in that it suggested a "scientific" approach to preaching theory.

Hyperius has much to say about aims and needs of those who preach, and of those who listen. He argues for the centrality of propositions, and outlines facets of communication. Here was a distinct pinnacle in preaching theory. The humanists (including Melanchthon) had taught rhetoric as applied to preaching, rejecting the dry and academic extremism of the scholasticism that held sway at that time. Hyperius launched truth from a fresh perspective, teaching preaching as it related to rhetoric. His nucleus was theological in distinction to that of his contemporaries, which was often so secular. This new departure marked an epoch in the history of homiletics, and his original and significant work is full of lively thought.

From II Timothy 3:16 and Romans 15:4 he deduced a quintet of approaches to preaching which he defined as the Doctrinal, the Argumentative, the Institutive, the Corrective, and the Consolatory. He was deeply concerned about his hearers as individuals and with the right motivation of their feelings for genuine response. The second half of his work, often published separately and titled *Theological Topics*, is a detailed application of the principles expounded in *On the Making of Sacred Discourse*. The entire work is saturated with worthy Biblical example and exposition.

In the preface to his work Hyperius states that it arose out of the oft expressed needs of his ministerial candidates for such practical information. His whole approach was vitally linked to needs and introduced a fluidity until then absent in the rigid traditional perspectives of those who antedated him.

Reformation Period

At the Reformation stage of history, preaching was regarded as a natural and permanent element in the worship and ministry of the Christian faith, and as an eternal revelation of the mind and will of God. It was also seen as being vitally related to the art of oratory and to the science of rhetoric. The rise of scholasticism had added an analytical method to preaching, and the refinement of excesses in all these areas was continuing.

With the advent of Luther, Zwingli, Calvin, and Knox, there grew a greater respect for preaching as the God given method of Christian instruction in truth and practice. Thus preaching began to assume a greater significance than other elements of worship in the church service. The mass and the ritual had crowded out the sermon; the reformers put it back in the center. Preaching became more polemic and doctrinal as they sought to refute the errors of the day.

Reformed preaching was also Biblical preaching. The Bible was recognized as the supreme authority in faith and practice, and was therefore given a better interpretation than before, with emphases on clarity and essential grammatical meanings. *Calvin* took up consecutive exposition of the Scripture as a plan for preaching. *Luther* was the master of forceful, popular eloquence. He introduced a great variety in his preaching style and form with earnestness and warmth which quickly won the hearts of his hearers. He was particularly noted for his homely, practical illustrations. *Zwingli* began his work as pastor in Zurich with an exposition of the Gospel of Matthew and was known for the classic style of his discourses, a reflection of his wide humanistic studies in previous years. *Knox* was a fiery and direct challenge to the formalism of his day. He preached extemporaneously and with great intensity, after thorough preparation. There arose, therefore, a real revival of Biblical authority, with preachers amply concerned for their hearers. In that way their sermons took on a more instructive character. The people now had the Bible in their own language, and longed for deeper understanding of its truths.

None of the four great Reformation leaders mentioned above left a formal treatise on preaching, but their practice and writings reveal a greater emphasis on aims as well as content in preaching. The Bible was the content, and the aims of all preaching were didactic. Thus the Reformation era restored the teaching ministry of the pulpit, long ago propounded by Augustine, but forgotten during those dark ages when it was not uncommon to hear sermons full of wild fables about saints and martyrs, or dull passages read from the church fathers, or tedious arguments on fine points of doctrine far above the grasp of those listening. In that way the Bible was preached, and in that way the people were taught. [1]

The Last Three Hundred Years

A general increase in the quantity, if not the quality, of material about homiletic theory is evident in the seventeenth and eighteenth centuries, tapering off in the latter century with the rise of historical criticism. A sharp upsurge in the 1850s launched into a full flood tide in the years that followed, and before that century had closed the output of how-to-preach books was well beyond the demand. These, apart from a few classics,[2] can be found today only on the musty shelves of some of the older theological libraries. This is as it should be, as the same ground was

---

1. Much more detail can be ferreted out from the various histories of preaching, especially from E. C. Dargan's two-volume work, *A History of Preaching*, now reprinted (Grand Rapids: Baker Book House, 1954, and F.R. Webber's three--volume *A History of Preaching in Britain and America* (Milwaukee: Northwestern 1957). The best of homiletic development is to be found in Dargan's masterpiece (still out of print), *The Art of Preaching in the Light of Its History* (Nashville: Sunday School Board of the Southern Baptist Convention, 1922).

2. See bibliography, especially Phelps, Garvie, Broadus, and so forth.

flow of preaching comment seemed to stimulate much more from every quarter. Everywhere the breadth and scope of preaching was discussed as writers took basic concepts as old as Augustine and gave infinite detail to their definition and application. With the twentieth century came an increase in studies about human personality, and in the past twenty years a return to a more Biblical theology. The application of pragmatic educational theory burst forth in the first half of this century, forming a context for the contemporary demands for communication and brevity that stands as a backdrop to the current revival of preaching. The pulpit has assumed a new power as part of a total ministry to persons within the scope of the pastoral relationship.

The English language development of homiletic theory is surveyed and collated in the concepts that form the major part of the study that follows. There is little point, therefore, in taking our historical survey further at this stage. It must be noted, however, that the concept of the teaching ministry of the pulpit has been a Christian conviction from the earliest of times; and its virility is apparent right through the ages. Our present study stands not so much as a new departure in preaching theory as it does as a restatement of ancient truth. The whole man was challenged by the early New Testament preachers who sought to reach man's intellect, emotions, and will for Christ. Our current theory expands and clarifies many significant aspects of preaching, but the logical and motivating sequence of action—which is the objective of all true preaching—is still our major concern.

The function of personality. From this overview of preaching history and theory we may confidently affirm a philosophy that views preaching not only as an exposition of the Biblical revelation, but also as a function of the human personality, which may be learned and which constant study and practice may improve. The adaptation of learned techniques for the improvement of preaching must be made in relation to the individual personality. In addition, a constant spiritual fitness for the task is paramount, and an ever deepening response to the power of the Holy Spirit is essential.

Nowhere is this better summarized than in Paul's advice to the young Timothy. His two epistles to Timothy are full of counsel to the young preacher to take heed to himself and to doctrine (teaching).[4] In this sense Paul anticipates Phillips Brooks's famous statement that preaching is the communication of truth through personality, and he does it by emphasizing that the personality of the preacher is his personal responsibility and that the communication of God's truth to others is his function. It is the preacher's responsibility to take the truth of revelation and discover the most suitable and effective means for its delivery. It is his holy obligation to capture and utilize every human art and science to such ends.

List of Significant Preachers

A survey of important preachers follows. This list is not meant to be exhaustive and could be expanded infinitely according to personal preference. Those mentioned have been major preachers or homileticians who have made a direct contribution to theory by their publications or by their good practice.

Apostolic Fathers (Those born before A.D. 150)
1. Polycarp
2. Clement of Rome
3. Ignatius
4. Barnabas
5. Hermas
6. Papias
7. Irenaeus
8. Justin Martyr
9. Tertullian

Preachers 150-430
1. Origen (185-254)
2. Basil (330-379)
3. Gregory of Nazianzen (330-390)
4. Gregory of Nyssa (335-369)
5. Chrysostom (347-407)
6. Augustine (354-430)

---

4. This is the word in I Tim. 4:16. Verses 11–16 amplify Paul's awareness of these two aspects of preaching as involving both truth and personality.

Early Medieval Preachers 430-1095
1. Patrick (372-465)
2. Leo I (390-461)
3. Columbia (521-597)
4. Gregory the Great (540-604)
5. Augustine of Canterbury (566-607)

Scholastic Preachers 1095-1361
1. Peter the Hermit (1050-1115)
2. Bernard of Clairvaux (1091-1153)
3. Dominic (1170-1221)
4. Francis of Assisi (1182-1226)
5. Anthony of Padua (1195-1231)
6. Bonaventura (1221-1274)
7. Thomas Aquinas (1227-1274)
8. John Tauler (1290-1361)
9. Henry Suso (1295-1366)

Reformation Preachers 1361-1572
1. Wycliffe (1320-1384)
2. Huss (1369-1415)
3. Savonarola (1452-1498)
4. Hubmaier (1480-1528)
5. Luther (1483-1546)
6. Zwingli (1484-1531)
7. Latimer (1490-1555)
8. Knox (1505-1572)
9. Calvin (1509-1564)

Modern Preaching
French
1. Claude (1619-1687)
2. Bossuet (1627-1704)
3. Bourdaloue (1632-1704)
4. Fenelon (1651-1715)
5. Massillon (1663-1742)
6. Saurin (1677-1730)
7. Vinet (1797-1847)
8. Lacordaire (1802-1861)
9. Monod (1802-1856)

German
1. Spener (1635-1705)
2. Franke (1663-1727)
3. Bengel (1687-1752)
4. Zinzendorf (1700-1760)
5. Schleiermacher (1768-1834)
6. Tholuck (1799-1877)

7. Helmut Thielicke (1908-   )

British
1. John Knox (1505-1572)
2. Richard Hooker (1563-1600)
3. John Donne (1573-1631)
4. Jeremy Taylor (1613-1667)
5. Richard Baxter (1615-1691)
6. Vavasor Powell (1617-1671)
7. John Bunyan (1628-1688)
8. Matthew Henry (1662-1714)
9. Joseph Butler (1692-1752)
10. Phillip Dodderidge (1702-1751)
11. John Wesley (1703-1791)
12. George Whitefield (1714-1770) (also U.S.A.)
13. Rowland Hill (1745-1833)
14. Andrew Fuller (1754-1815)
15. Charles Simeon (1759-1836)
16. William Carey (1761-1834)
17. Robert Hall (1764-1831)
18. Christmas Evans (1776-1838)
19. Thomas Chalmers (1780-1847)
20. F. W. Robertson (1816-1853)
21. Alexander Maclaren (1826-1910)
22. R. W. Dale (1829-1895)
23. Joseph Parker (1830-1902)
24. C. H. Spurgeon (1834-1892)
25. Alexander Whyte (1836-1921)
26. J. D. Jones (1847-1906)
27. F. B. Meyer (1847-1929)
28. P. T. Forsyth (1848-1921)
29. G. Campbell Morgan (1863-1942)
30. John Henry Jowett (1864-1923)
31. Charles Silvester Horne (1865-1914)
32. Frank W. Boreham (1871-1960) (Australia)
33. James S. Stewart (1896-   )
34. D. Martyn Lloyd-Jones (1896-   )
35. W. E. Sangster (1900-1960)

American
1. Jonathan Edwards (1703-1758)
2. Francis Asbury (1745-1718)
3. Lyman Beecher (1775-1863)
4. Thomas H. Skinner (1791-1871)
5. Charles G. Finney (1792-1875)
6. Horace Bushnell (1802-1876)

7. Henry W. Beecher (1813-1887)
8. Austin Phelps (1820-1890)
9. John A. Broadus (1827-1895)
10. W. M. Taylor (1829-1895)
11. T. DeWitt Talmage (1832-1902)
12. Phillips Brooks (1834-1893)
13. A. J. Gordon (1836-1895)
14. A. T. Pierson (1837-1911)
15. D. L. Moody (1837-1899)
16. E. C. Lorimer (1838-1904)
17. R. H. Conwell (1843-1925)
18. C. I. Scofield (1843-1921)
19. A. B. Simpson (1844-1919)
20. Sam P. Jones (1847-1906)
21. R. H. Torrey (1856-1928)
22. J. Wilbur Chapman (1859-1918)
23. Charles E. Jefferson (1860-1937)
24. Billy Sunday (1863-1945)
25. George W. Truett (1867-1944)
26. H. A. Ironside (1876-1951)
27. H.E. Fosdick (1878-1969)
28. Clarence E. Macartney (1879-1957)
29. A.W. Blackwood (1882-1966)
30. W.A. Maier (1893-1950)
31. Billy Graham (1918-   )

2

The Nature of Nurture

God reaches out through preaching to confront men with truth. Thus the divine action operates within a human function, which is, itself, most complex. From the manward side preaching has a dual character. It is (1) the recital of facts and insights revealed by God, and (2) their presentation in words, forms, and orders that will best allow for human reception. It is therefore essential for the preacher to be aware of educational philosophy and methodology.

No scholarship, however broad, can ever substitute for spiritual unction. There have always been men who lacked formal educational understanding who were nevertheless mightily used of the Lord. We do not challenge such ministry by the advocation of a formal "science of teaching" within preaching; but it is affirmed that where knowledge and unction go together, the quality and effectiveness of preaching will be enhanced. An understanding of the natural ways in which men learn will help supernatural elements of communication to be more effective. Such preaching skill merely adds rational effectiveness to its art. We may assert that the sermon most likely to be used by the Holy Spirit to help a soul will probably be the one most likely to help a soul if there was no Holy Spirit.[1] The man who is both Spirit filled and educationally apt will be the most effective preacher because he will meet both spiritual and intellectual needs. The Bible clearly commends the teaching art as essential.[2]

A study of educational history helps give dimension, perspective, and proportion to human thought and activity. The complexity of the individual and of society is revealed, and the link between good educational practice and the genesis and development of man's greatest ideas about himself and his world is shown. A composite and eclectic approach to contemporary need is possible when we see the relationships between preaching and the disciplines of philosophy, psychology, and sociology.

Many good elements of learning entered into the early church from both the Greek and Hebrew cultures. The heritage of Judaism gave ways of teaching which tended to give Christianity the aspect of a Hebrew sect. Consequently the early church was under a constant tension as it strove to emerge as a faith that was to be universal and not controlled by its Hebrew roots. Most of life, for the Jews, centered around the local synagogue and its teachers, the rabbis. Even after the dispersion some remnants remained, held together by the law and by sentiment, and strengthened by their synagogue school system.

Christ is called a teacher thirty-one times in the Gospels, and it is simple as well as profitable to trace how He used the methods of the story, the dialogue, the disputation, and the teaching of a select few who in turn would teach others. The Jews taught through the everyday experiences of the family, and by the use of the great feast days and temple rites. Ritual and symbol were vehicles for the propagation of truth, as well as were the more standard forms of public address. Thus Jesus was quite at home using object lessons in His teaching.

---

1. This statement has been attributed to Charles Haddon Spurgeon, but it cannot be traced.

2. II Tim. 2:2.

ALEXANDRIAN SCHOOL TO HUSS

In A.D.190 the earliest schools for the training of Christian leaders began in Alexandria. These *catechetical* institutions prepared great scholars such as Clement and Origen for their Christian service, and followed the much earlier established *catechumenal* schools, which, beginning early in the second century, rapidly became characteristic elements of local church life in which converts were prepared for Christian baptism. This system continued to the fifth and sixth centuries, when postbaptismal instruction became more prevalent.[3]

The following centuries placed Christian education more within a monastic context as illiteracy prevailed among the common people and the clergy. Liturgy, pageantry, drama, and similar forms of symbolic communication carried the Christian message. In the eighth century the interest of the great Frankish king Charlemagne resulted in the establishment of the University of Paris, under the auspices of the church; and, as feudalism declined, intellectual interests arose. In these "dark ages" the church assumed the teaching functions of society; but, as the emphasis settled more and more on theory than on the practice of the faith in vital Christian living, educational method became more and more transmissive. Scholasticism purposed to bring reason to the support of faith and to overcome all difficulties by argument and logic.

Knowledge therefore became systematized and was viewed as a purely intellectual discipline. *Thomas Aquinas* (1227-1274) insisted that reason was the interpreter of revealed truth, and thus the whole movement fell far short of meeting human spiritual needs. The discussion of Christianity seemed to have little reality in the world of everyday life.

With the rise of humanism and the renaissance ideal there arose a protest against authoritarianism in the intellectual and social aspects of life. Educational aims were redefined in relation

---

3. J. Donald Butler, *Religious Education: The Foundations and Practice of Nurture* (New York: Harper, 1962); William Barclay, *Train Up a Child* (Philadelphia: Westminster, 1959); and Lois E. LeBar, *Education That Is Christian* (Westwood, N.J.: Revell, 1958). These all cover highlights of Christian education and its interrelation with secular concepts.

to the freedom of the individual to mature as one who needed practical and aesthetic development, as well as intellectual. *John Wycliffe* (1320-1384) and his English followers wrote and distributed popular tracts defending their views. These frequently dealt with the right for individual convictions based on the Bible rather than on the teachings of the church. *John Huss* (1369-1415) and his followers in Germany stressed purity in Christian conduct and other practical applications of Biblical truth.

ERASMUS TO PESTALOZZI

Erasmus (1466-1536), the most famous of the Reformation leaders in learning-theory, recognized the role of individual talents and differences among scholars, and acted as spokesman for the more person-related educational ideas which were developing in his age.

The sixteenth century humanist and religious educators cannot be separated. The affinity between secular and Christian education theory was almost complete as religious leaders generally seized on education as a basic means to institute reform. *Martin Luther* (1483-1546) redefined concepts of the nature of education, and *Philip Melanchthon* (1497-1560) implemented his reforms. Melanchthon's whole application was in the field of preparing men for civil and ecclesiastical offices. The Society of Jesus, emerging in 1540 as the basic counter-Reformation movement, gathered into it many of the Reformation values, seeking, through its schools, to hold Catholic converts and to educate people into submission.

The Jesuits gave themselves unreservedly to the task of teaching the truth, as they saw it, and often engaged in arduous research to accomplish their ends. A small handful of priests, bent on enlisting China's millions, spent years soaking up the principles of Chinese art, philosophy, language, and literature, until their expertise in these areas made them acceptable to the Chinese intellectuals.

Inner tensions and local social changes prohibited final success, but experiments such as these proved that the interest for prospective pupils lies at the place where teachers and pupils share common concerns.

The modern era begins with the rise of realism and naturalism in education. Natural phenomena and social institutions, rather than languages and literature, received much attention in the seventeenth century. *Rabelais* (1488-1553), *Milton* (1608-1674), and *Michel de Montaigne* (1533-1592) all contended for realism in education, asserting that knowledge comes basically through the senses. Educational methodology was therefore moving away from intellectual memorization to training in sense perception. All of this led to the introduction of the inductive method of teaching as being the most practical. As a result a priori speculations were abandoned, as the foundations for modern scientific method were laid through the new method of reasoning from the particular to the general. *Francis Bacon* (1561-1626), *René Descartes* (1596-1650), and *Peter Ramus* (1517-1572) amplified the social and pragmatic values of the new logic in the years that followed.

The most important representative of the new realism for educational theory was the Moravian bishop *John Amos Comenius* (1592-1670). He believed that the purpose of all education was to bring man into right relationship with God. Fallen man was viewed as redeemable, and education was regarded as the means whereby a true humanity could be forged into the ideal social context. He therefore assumed, and promoted, an identity between the Christian faith and the ideal secular culture. His work had great acceptance since it viewed human nature as having a greater inherent potential for good than did the works of Luther or Calvin.

Comenius brought the Baconian inductive method into the everyday school. He called for an independent human knowledge gained by individual pupil observation and investigation. Learning was to be gained via the senses, and instruction should therefore be in harmony with the ages, interests, and abilities of the pupils. Most of his principles grew directly out of his own teaching practice. He wrote five school books, texts, and Latin grammars, and summarized his educational ideals in his *Great Didactic*, published in 1657.

Among those directly influenced by Comenius were *John Locke* (1632-1704), who believed that experience was the source of all knowledge, and *August Hermann Francke* (1663-1727). Francke sought to combine practical preparation for life, Christian training, and an integration of knowledge with piety. His movement was primarily a reaction against the formal and rational emphases of the schools of his day.

French theorists set up a national system of schools in 1763 on the wave of humanism which affected all education of that age, *Jean Jacques Rousseau* (1712-1778) was one who advocated a naturalistic approach to education, rejecting all artificial elements. He sponsored an educational process that sought to follow the natural stages of development through which children reach maturity. His concepts were worked out into a practical methodology by *Basedow* (1724-1790) and *Pestalozzi* (1746-1827).

HERBART TO DEWEY

It was *John Friederich Herbart* (1776-1841) who took these principles to their logical end with his philosophy of associationism. His work became the foundation for all secular and religious education for the following century.

Herbart based his educational philosophy on some of the growing understandings of human personality. Social environs were primary in his thinking, and he believed that ideas grouped themselves in "apperceptive masses," according to similarities between them. He felt that it is the teacher's task to direct the process of discovery of that similarity for each pupil. He devised a five-step methodology which, for the first time, gave teachers in all areas of life a foundation on which to build curriculum. His ideas may be listed as follows:

1. *Preparation*, or preparing the student's mind for the assimilation of the new idea
2. *Presentation* of the new idea
3. *Association*, or assimilation of the new idea by the old
4. *Generalization*, or the general idea that comes from the combination of the old and new ideas
5. *Application*, or the use of the new knowledge in solving problems [4]

---

4. Francesco Cordasco, *A Brief History of Education* (Totowa, N.J.: Littlefield, Adams, and Co., 1967), p. 102.

His five steps became very mechanical in their later application by his followers, and by 1900 they were being used as a fairly rigid structure around which all methodology was constructed in teacher-training institutions across the world.

The Sunday school, best known of all the organizations created for the teaching ministry of the church, arose in the eighteenth century as a simple movement among many other charitable agencies. Like them, it was spawned by the growing social conscience of the age. So remarkable was this movement that only thirty-one years after its birth nearly half a million children were enrolled in its activities in the British Isles alone.[5] It was misunderstood by the clergy and opposed by the church, and thus never had full maturity in the land of its birth. It was not until well into the nineteenth century that the churches of the United States took hold of the Sunday school, and, applying its scope to a full age range, exercised the major teaching function of the church through it.

The Sunday school movement has now embraced most of the insights into educational processes which history has furnished. As it began in the Herbartian period there was in the early years of Sunday school outreach great emphasis on child study. By 1908 this had reached a pitch sufficient to produce great criticism of the Uniform Lessons, and to motivate the implementation of a much more closely graded curriculum.

Horace Bushnell (1802-1876) was concerned that children should grow into natural Christian experience, and not be forced into it through the emotional revivalism of his era. His 1847 publication, *Christian Nurture*, drew heavily on the Herbartian associationism. His attempt was to bring Christian commitment into focus as a natural result of Christian education within the family and the church. Butler challenges Bushnell's approach with the comment that faith discovered in this way may become

> a shield or protective device that shelters the child from facing his own religious crises for himself. They have the outward pattern of the life of the Christian without having gone through the crises of belief and commitment which are at the heart of being a Christian.[6]

---

5. Butler, p. 62.
6. Butler, p. 103.

With *John Dewey* (1859-1952) there came a new era which has influenced the whole educational world since that time. The biological and physical sciences, as applied philosophically by such as *Herbert Spencer* (1820-1903) and *Thomas Huxley* (1825-1895), began to influence all thought and educational practice. *Charles Darwin*'s monumental *Origin of Species,* published in 1859, was foundation for much that followed.

By 1900 serious attempts were being made in many quarters to transform the process of education into a more meaningful experience for the learner. It was seen that all the *knowing,* or theory, provided by the older transmissive methods did not necessarily create a true *feeling* and *doing.* A revolt against formal and authoritarian methods of instruction was in progress. It was believed that real understanding of truth would issue in practical actions; and, where these did not evolve, the knowledge discovered was not genuine.

Dewey and his friend *William James* (1842-1910) enunciated this philosophy of practical values, giving it the name of "pragmatism." This they defined as the view that the truth about any subject can only be stated in relation to its practical workability. Thus the functional use of every idea determines its value. They believed that the truth in any concept made it "work," and if it would not so work, then this was a measure of its error. Because man is so related to his society and to the material world in which he lives, there was a great deal of truth inherent in this philosophy.

Much of Dewey's work was his own; much was also simple common sense plus values gleaned from good educational techniques, proved over the many years of the American educational experience.[7]

The progressive education movement (as it became known) sought to give the pupil a greater freedom in self-discovery.

---

7. Conservative evaluations of the worth of Dewey which deserve attention, in addition to the comments in Butler and LeBar, are J. Donald Butler, *Four Philosophies and Their Practice in Religious Education,* rev. ed. (New York: Harper, 1957); and Warren C. Young, *A Christian Approach to Philosophy* (Grand Rapids: Baker Book House, 1962), especially pp. 38-40, 53-55, 126-30, 173-76, 187-88.

Violent reaction against the authoritative transmission of information meant that curriculum was much more vitally related to pupil needs, and all kinds of mental and physical activities were encouraged while pupils were learning. The child was led to explore his world through programs of self-involvement, and to mature through the experiences of everyday situations. In some extreme applications of this perspective, pupils' schedules were limited only by their felt needs or curiosities.

Dewey focused attention on the centrality of the pupil in all educational experience. He challenged the bland assumptions of his age which equated learning with simple exposure to truth and memorization of certain facts concerning it. Educators sought to produce a real maturity grown from an expanding understanding, rather than a mechanical surface knowledge produced by a transmissive authoritarianism. The whole movement was born out of a profound, and valid, respect for the independence of the individual personality.[8]

The major challenge to Dewey is at the point of his naive naturalism. Because of his adherence to Darwinian concepts, Dewey had an unwarranted trust in the competence of human intelligence. However, human nature, being subject to the pressures of evil forces, intrinsically lazy, and (in the Biblical view) fallen to a state of sin in every aspect, cannot be trusted to educate itself through wisely chosen experiences alone. Dewey's humanism had few, if any absolutes; and he therefore regarded education as very fluctuant, and in total response to changing needs.

Dewey's idea of God is simply accommodation to cultural concepts, and it is shaped by our emotional needs. Most of the values he advanced, therefore, belong to the field of human relationships rather than to the spiritual or the intellectual. His idea of being is completely humanistic; and, since he holds that there is no other world than this present material one, the only real values for him are those which grow directly from the experiences of life.

---

8. Butler, *Four Philosophies*, and Young.

The two major world wars, the economic depression, and other oscillating factors in twentieth century life have brought the weaknesses of these perspectives into open view. Men seem to be simply unable to improve themselves by human choices alone. Humanistic optimism has disappeared in the wake of the selfish applications of capitalism, the unethical extremes of nazism, fascism, and communism, and amid the contemporary racial and social problems of Western culture. The animal nature of man has bared its fangs in the past half century for all to see, and its roar has frightened off the egocentric realism of the naturalistic philosophers.

Although Dewey's concepts were based more on Grecian philosophy than on Biblical theology, seeking to create social rather than spiritual efficiencies, they have not by any means ceased to have relevance. The influence of Deweyan pragmatism remains as the greatest philosophical force in general American culture and across the world, next to that of the standard Christian realism.[9]

DENOMINATIONAL DEVELOPMENTS

This instrumental philosophy has seriously influenced the theory and practice of much Christian education. Growth, via environmental reaction, has often taken priority over the exposition of the Biblical revelation. The controlling unit in some Christian education has become the finite, fallen, human self. Thus a humanistic context became the normal for many curricula. James D. Smart, a former editor involved in one of these departures, has clearly enunciated the tragic results of such extreme applications.[10]

Freeman has also detailed the Presbyterian failure. His study centers around the "Faith and Life" curriculum, a progressive approach which became the foundational influence on many other

---

9. Butler, *Four Philosophies*, and Young.

10. James D. Smart, *The Teaching Ministry of the Church* (Philadelphia: Westminster, 1964), pp. 46-107.

similar denominational adjustments of the period.[11] The curriculum aimed to use both the Biblical revelation of truth as it is in Christ, and the contemporary revelation of Christian discipleship found in congregational fellowship. Freeman is convinced that both of these purposes failed. The naturalistic orientation and humanistic philosophy of most of its writers forced applications which made the material violate its own foundational goals. The pragmatic demands of contemporary life overshadowed all other influences.[12]

The curriculum was set totally within life-situation needs, in direct reflection of the Deweyan concepts; and its results were tragic for Presbyterians. Independent surveys taken by others[13] confirm Freeman's contention that the end was chaos. Procedures used created attitudes so humanistic that the end product was a church whose members were preoccupied with human relationships, family problems, and other self-centered needs. Their religious life developed mainly in relation to the competitive secular society to which they belonged. The goals sought degenerated into those linked with personal comfort and success in social adjustments.

These family values captured the church members' primary loyalties; and the entire curriculum was revealed, by these studies, to be far removed from the Biblical ideas of maturity in discipleship. Foundation aims of the curriculum were not only never achieved, but also violated so severely that goals exactly the opposite to those selected were the ones that were reached![14]

Such results were so provoking that James D. Smart, the major leader involved in the curriculum operation, was forced to

---

11. Roger Maclement Freeman, *The Inviability of Two Basic Principles in the Christian Faith and Life Curriculum* (Cambridge, Mass.: Unpublished Ph.D. thesis, Divinity School, Harvard University, December 1963).

12. Freeman.

13. Roy W. Fairchild and John Charles Wynn, *Families in the Church: A Protestant Survey* (New York: Association Press, 1961); see also Freeman, pp. 118-40.

14. Some of the effects are also discussed in Martin E. Marty, *New Shape of American Religion* (New York: Harper, 1958).

reevaluate the whole program and its bases in a most critical perspective.[15] In his assessment he advocated a return to a more conservative approach, stressing Biblical theology as needed more within the functions, as well as the form, of all Christian education curricula.[16]

The Methodists have had similar troubles. Their adaptation of progressive educational techniques has also dictated a real divorce from New Testament teachings. This has been recorded by one of those involved in the Methodist production. He believes that their similar failures in the results of new curricula have their roots in the humanism and naturalism so characteristic of the pragmatic philosophy.[17]

The largest denominational group in the world, the eleven-and-one-half-million-member Southern Baptist Convention, seems to be the one major group least affected. Southern Baptists emerged as a virile evangelical association of churches born in the revival spirit of the early American frontier years, and with direct roots in the earlier "Great Awakening" and its genesis in the Wesley-Whitefield evangelical upsurge.[18] They consequently had a predisposition toward a conservative theological position, plus a missionary passion. When the Dewey techniques came into prominence they were therefore able to apply them, but all the while insisting on a Biblical theology as foundation to their use. The humanist philosophies have been deleted, as their current guides to curriculum show.[19] The theological foundations and

---

15. Dr. Smart's work was *Basic Principles: Christian Faith and Life, A Program for Church and Home* (Board of Christian Education, Presbyterian Church in the U.S.A., 1948).

16. Smart, *The Teaching Ministry of the Church.*

17. James Earl Sellers, *The Church and Mass Communication* (Nashville: Unpublished Ph.D. thesis, Vanderbilt University, 1958), pp. 291-97.

18. See W. W. Sweet, *The Story of Religion in America* (New York: Harper, 1930), p. 220, and chap. 10.

19. This, the most remarkable and complete expression of philosophy and practice in evangelical Christian education available, is reproduced as appendix B, at the end of this study.

teaching and training objectives reveal an educational program which undergirds all evangelism and extension.

The convention was organized in 1845 as a separate Southern association of Baptist churches in protest against deficiencies in Home Missions development of the South and West under the national programs operated by the Northern-centered denominational boards. The slavery issue was catalyst, but not cause, for the separation from Northern direction. In 1845 there were only 4,126 Baptist churches in the South, with some 351,951 members.[20] By 1971 the number of churches had risen to a staggering 34,441, with a total membership of 11,826,463. There are also many independent Baptist churches in the South, following similar programs, spawned by the parent body.

The vast denomination has been built almost solely on a movement of Christian education for all ages, which began with the official formation of their Sunday school board in 1891. Riding the crest of the wave of new progressive educational methods in the years that followed, they now enlist a Sunday school enrollment of 7,141,453 (1971), in an age range from nursery babies through senior adults. A large leadership-training organization enlists 2,106,855 in Sunday evening preservice study each week. 76.3 percent of their churches hold vacation Bible schools. 39.4 percent operate a men's brotherhood organization, 62.8 percent a women's missionary organization. 55.6 percent have an age graded music training program; and the convention supports 2,222 home, and 2,501 foreign, missionaries. All of these agencies of Christian service are fully supported with strong educational curricula and materials which reflect the most pragmatic methodologies. The convention operates hospitals, homes for the aged and for children, enrolls 82,129 students in its 44 accredited senior colleges and universities, 11 junior colleges, 12 Bible schools and academies, and 7 graduate schools of theology. Southwestern Baptist Theological Seminary, the largest theological institution in the world, is a fully accredited graduate

---

20. J. Allen, ed., *Encyclopedia of Southern Baptists* (Nashville: Broadman, 1958), 2 vols., pp. 201-2. Updated membership figures are from Research Services Dept., Sunday School Board of the Southern Baptist Convention, June 12, 1972.

school enlisting 2,171 students, and offers programs through to doctoral levels in music, education, and theology.[21]

Vast literary resources produced by an army of competent scholars undergird every program, and the immense training plans also reflect the pupil-related procedures suggested by Dewey. The convention is continually active in deep research and self-evaluation processes also in these areas, recently redrafting its entire curriculum approaches and organizational relationships in order to mesh with contemporary needs.

The American (Northern) Baptist Convention has also made significant progress in the development of progressive educational methods without the liberal penchant so characteristic of the nonconservative denominations. The less extreme among the conservatives whose activities center around Chicago, and the National Association of Evangelicals, have also absorbed Deweyan concepts without harm to either the virility of their spiritual life or their Biblical convictions.[22]

LEARNING-THEORY TODAY

Pragmatic principles have had a more general absorption into contemporary Christian education theory than their humanistic origins would suggest they warrant.[23] They were introduced at a time when educators were seeking new concepts which were more practically workable than the old ideas. This approval now remains

---

21. These, and the following statistics, are summarized from Martin E. Bradley, ed., *The Quarterly Review* (Nashville: Sunday School Board of the Southern Baptist Convention, July 1969), 29:3. Membership figures updated June 12, 1972. The 55.6 percent figure is for churches having a music program of some type. It cannot be said that all music training programs are totally age graded.

22. See J. Edward Hakes, ed., *An Introduction to Evangelical Christian Education* (Chicago: Moody Press, 1964); also Clarence J. Sahlin, *A Comparison Between the Pragmatic and Conservative Christian Approach to Education* (Chicago: Northern Baptist Theological Seminary, unpublished Th.M. thesis, 1956).

23. The applications of worker training, prospect enlistment, and general organization for reaching and teaching evident in the well-known Graham evangelistic crusades have vital roots in the Southern Baptist applications of pragmatic method. Graham was converted under Southern Baptist preaching, and remains an ordained minister with them today.

in many areas despite the convalescence of theology toward a more conservative view in our generation. We may summarize the generally accepted aspects of progressive learning-theory today as follows:

1. *We learn what is transmitted.* An important place for content still exists if it has significance for the business of living. Pupil action can be influenced by simple transmission of information, but this must include an application of its relevance to specific needs.

2. *We learn what is rehearsed.* Habit may also influence action. The pupil who is trained to react to a specific set of circumstances in a particular way, and who is given reasons to structure that action, may learn better than the one who has merely had information transmitted to him. The immature will often lack the necessary experience to exercise a right choice over things which he is to learn, and the teacher may give his main attention to guiding the pupil through role-rehearsal experiences which will train him.

3. *We learn what we discover.* Experience that is personally chosen gives stronger insight than any other. The child who burns himself on the hot stove, because he chose to touch it himself, will be taught not to do it again. This kind of learning is deeper than that which is transmitted or accepted via role-rehearsal.

4. *We learn most what is discovered through choices made within problem situations in which we are personally involved.* When a life-situation encounter faces us with the demand for deliberate decision among a number of live alternates, learning is at its deepest. The wise teacher will therefore endeavor to guide the learner through natural experiences of a problem-solving character.

Butler believes that learning-theory, in the Christian connotation, is an inclusive concept.[24] The Christian context of church and community provides, for him, a *field*, and the relative nature of the instruction offered provides a *dynamic*, which together build the learning experience. They are incomplete without the transmission of subject matter and the experiences of action such

---

24. Butler, *Religious Education*, pp. 234-37.

as role-rehearsal, which he views as *channels* for learning. He sees the confrontation of the learner with live alternates in a problem situation as the *focal center* for the educational process at any given point in it. The critical factor in learning is, for him, the resolution of tension by a decisive action.[25]

LeBar has a good statement about Christian education in her study, describing it as simply "guiding experience, and declaring truth."[26]

From such concepts has come a growing significance of the place of the pupil, and his experience, in self-education. Movement from a posed problem to a Biblical answer has replaced the transmissive exposition of Scriptural truth with a tacked-on application. Attempt is made to have the teacher do only what the hearer cannot more profitably do for himself. From such values has grown the developing science of group dynamics.

It has been shown that progressive, democratic elements usually provide a responsible freedom in any group, and that authoritarian or laissez-faire approaches inhibit this.[27] As far back as the 1930s it was shown that significant achievements and balanced conclusions within a group become prominent in proportion to the democratic emphases of its leadership.[28] Such empirical evidence has moved social scientists to study group processes as an extension of the problem-situation approach to vital learning.[29]

EFFECT ON HOMILETICS

It is most interesting to see how all this has affected homiletics. While many would not care to insist, with Dewey, that

---

25. Butler, *Religious Education.*

26. LeBar, p. 168.

27. See Micheal S. Olmstead, *The Small Group* (New York: Random House, Studies in Psychology series, 1959), pp. 34-38; and Herbert A. Thelen, *Dynamics of Groups at Work* (Chicago: University of Chicago Press, 1954).

28. An interesting application of these ideas to evangelism has been made by Paul M. Miller in *Group Dynamics and Evangelism: The Potential of Christian Fellowship* (Scottdale, Pa.: Herald Press, 1958).

29. Thelen, pp. 32-68, 129-78.

man never thinks seriously or learns completely unless he is faced with a problem situation, all will admit that, where such an element enters in, the learning experience takes on a dynamic until then unknown. Preachers soon discovered this technique as a valuable preaching tool, and its application became known as "life-situation preaching."[30]

The greatest exponent of this method was *Harry Emerson Fosdick*, of Riverside Church, New York, whose impress in this area remains as, perhaps, his most lasting contribution. Fosdick was, however, an extreme liberal in theology. By his own testimony this was a result of some twisted juvenile perspectives of God, and from reaction to unbalanced "hellfire and brimstone preaching,"[31] from a brand of evangelism the antithesis of that practiced by D. L. Moody, whom he greatly respected.[32]

Personal counseling insights led Fosdick to the discovery that the pulpit ministry was, in part, simple personal counseling on a group scale. He emphasized the need for sermons to be cooperative enterprises between the preacher and his congregation, and advised a thinking through of the points made by both preacher and congregation together.[33] He said he wanted preaching to be "a co-operative dialogue in which the congregation's objections, doubts, and confirmations are fairly stated, and dealt with."[34] He urged an enlistment crisis to promote an active conduct response as an essential part of the sermon itself.

But again, however, the humanist foundations of pragmatic principles created perils and perversions in life-situation preaching, evils of which Fosdick himself had warned.[35] McCracken, Fosdick's successor, has acknowledged it in these words:

---

30. Halford E. Luccock, *In the Minister's Workshop* (New York: Abingdon, 1944), pp. 50-72.

31. Harry Emerson Fosdick, *The Living of These Days* (New York: Harper, 1956), pp. 33-36.

32. Fosdick, p. 35.

33. Fosdick, p. 96.

34. Fosdick, p. 97.

35. Fosdick, pp. 98-99.

Life-situation preaching is often criticised because the temptation besetting many who specialise in it is that they become wholly pre-occupied with issues of the hour. That is what accounts for the secular and indeed shallow aspect of much contemporary preaching. Its primary sources are the newspaper, the weekly magazine, the digests, and only secondarily the Word of God. What is said in church on Sunday frequently has the character of an editorial comment with a mild religious flavour. It lacks any distinctive Christian insight and emphasis.[36]

What began as a movement sincerely seeking to commence with the needs of persons, relating these needs to God's revelation, has in most instances become mere topical preaching and general discussion of contemporary problems of culture and society. Fosdick insisted that these methods did not have to minimize Biblical content in the sermon, but rather that they ought to strengthen each other.[37] With Biblical theology to the fore again today, criticism of the abuses in most life-situation preaching is increasing.[38]

All of our western culture has been touched by Dewey's influence. Consequently, the same humanistic sympathies and naturalistic presuppositions entered into American preaching, driving it away from Biblical exposition, just as they had similarly affected its Christian education. They came from the same sources and, when applied outside of a basic evangelical, conservative, and Biblical framework, had tragic results. Luccock traces a clear line back to Dewey in his discussion of life-situation approaches:

Spiritual truth is brought to bear at the point in experience where a particular need is felt. It is all wrapped up in the dictum of the Dewey pedagogy, that thinking begins with a felt difficulty.[39]

The truth which has been revealed in our survey of the history of nurture, and of its philosophy as enunciated by Dewey,

---

36. Robert J. McCracken, *The Making of the Sermon* (New York: Harper, 1956), p. 62.

37. Fosdick, p. 95.

38. See Ilion T. Jones, *Principles and Practice of Preaching* (New York: Abingdon, 1956), pp. 39-43.

39. Luccock, p. 52.

is that of the vital association of the learning experience with *the needs of the congregation*. We also see that *listener involvement is critical* if the learner is to find the experience relevant and if the sermon is to produce results. Our criticism of the extremes of its application must not blind us to these discoveries, and our responsibility is to use these insights within an acceptable—and Biblical—approach.

Dewey's steps of reflective thinking moved through five stages. He began with a felt need, moved to the statement of a problem to be solved, then to the collation of hypothetical solutions, and the assimilation of data pointing to a probable solution, and on to the verification of the solution via experimental testing. There is an affinity provided by such a cycle, which gives a high identity to the three concepts of *reflection, science,* and *research*.[40]

This "scientific method," applied to educational theory, can result in a properly constructed science of teaching. This may then be represented as an educational cycle. The steps of ordered progress will be as follows:

1. *The needs of the learners* (often obtained through survey and problem analysis)
2. *Clear aims arising* (chosen to meet the discovered needs)
3. *Planned programs* (designed to reach the goals that have been selected)
4. *Useful methods* (chosen for pupil centrality in the learning experience, and to aid self-discovery)
5. *Selected materials* (chosen as suitable for the program and the methods)
6. *Adequate organization* (practical detail planning for the efficiency of the learning experience)
7. *Effective administration* (creative and efficient supervision of the learning experience)
8. *Realistic evaluation,* which will, in turn, lead to the discovery of *revised needs,* thus reactivating a continuous cycle of educational activity.[41]

---

40. Frederick Lamson Whitney, *The Elements of Research,* 3rd ed. (Englewood Cliffs, N.J.: Prentice-Hall, 1950), pp. 1-27.

41. Dr. Lois E. LeBar has been most helpful in bringing this perspective of Dewey's concepts as an educational cycle to this writer's personal attention. Fig. 1, "The educational process" (p.58), represents such a process as is envisaged.

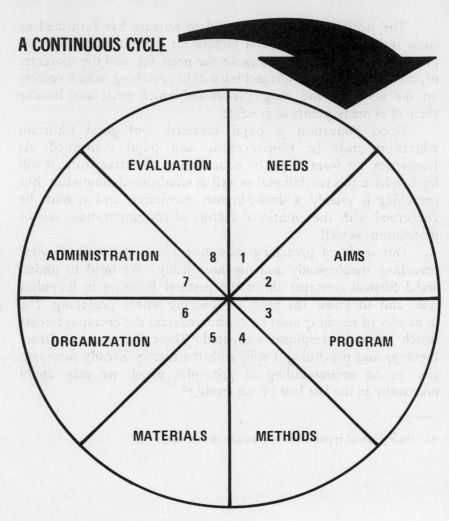

A CONTINUOUS CYCLE

EVALUATION   NEEDS

ADMINISTRATION   8   1   AIMS

7   2

6   3

ORGANIZATION   5   4   PROGRAM

MATERIALS   METHODS

FIGURE 1: *The educational process.*

The history of homiletics and of nurture has furnished us some insights that are critical factors for the minister's effective pulpit function. We can recognize the need for, and the character of, an efficient science of teaching within preaching, which centers on the needs of the congregation and which must also involve them at as many points as possible.

Good education is pupil centered, but good Christian education must be *Christocentric* and pupil concerned. As homiletics is a form of public education in Christian truth, it will have to have this revelational as well as educational dimension. But preaching is mainly a divine-human encounter, and it must be concerned with the emotional factors of communication, and of motivation, as well.

Our study of preaching must now move, therefore, to view preaching theologically and psychologically. We need to understand Biblical concepts about the pastoral function in its pulpit role, and to know the place of teaching within preaching. The dynamics of reaching must be considered, and the encouragements which promote response evaluated. These perspectives (from theology and psychology) will, with the history already surveyed, give us an understanding of principles which we may apply practically in the last half of our study.[42]

---

42. These practical applications form part IV of this study.

PART II

perspective from theology

3

The Minister and the Ministry

The New Testament insists that the church is not simply one organization among many in our overorganized society. It defines the church as the one earthly association which exists within an eternal framework, and which finds a temporal expression in our world. No Biblical reference is ever made to a local group as *a* church, but always as *the* church in a local situation.

THE CHURCH AND ITS MINISTERS

Such a view of the church is endorsed by the Epistle to the Ephesians, which regards the *ecclesia* (ἐκκλησία) as an ultimate gathered reality in eternity, and as the consummate kingdom of God in its absolute and eternal expression. Each congregation is considered throughout the Bible to be a local expression of the eternal *ecclesia* in that particular place. Such a "local church," having Christ in the midst, is the proximate expression in time of the ultimate reality which is in eternity. Thus the individual congregation is not a unit within an aggregate total which, with the redeemed of all the ages, makes up the *ecclesia.* It is rather the real, direct, and local manifestation of the kingdom of God in our earthly society.[1]

As such the church is a reservoir of divine life in the world. Its members, indwelt by God's Spirit, have the responsibility to fulfill His will. In practice, however, we fail to apply this high view of the church's nature, and tend to organize ourselves as a group gathered around one or more specialists who are responsible to see that the work of God is effectively fulfilled through *their* service.

The concept of such a limited ministry is well illustrated through an "advertisement" carried in a religious news magazine some time ago. A university teacher, who was also a Christian layman and head of the technical writing division of an automobile manufacturer, presented this advertisement to reflect congregational attitudes he felt were retarding ministerial recruitment. His challenging and revealing job description is reproduced on page 18 in this study. It would be humorous if it was not so often tragically true. The New Testament completely shatters any idea of such a one-man ministry with its many comments about the multiple ministry inherent in every local congregation.[2]

The Believer a Priest

Every reference to priesthood in the New Testament that does not designate a specific relation to the old Jewish priestly order or to the high priesthood of Christ through some contextual statement, includes the entire believing community. I Peter 2:9-10 refers to the corporate priesthood of all, and tells us the purpose of such a total function is for the ministry of the pardoning grace of God to be declared by all.

This priesthood of all believers, as a natural corollary of our Lord's high priestly function,[3] involves us all in the role of representation. When a believer prays, worships, serves, or otherwise acts, he is always a member of Christ's body. He is not simply involved as an individual alone, but is always representatively acting, speaking, or doing, identifying his ministry with that of Christ, and, through Him, with all the other members of His body.

---

1. Eph. 1:20-23; Heb. 2:12; 12:23.

2. See Heb. 13:15-19; I Peter 2:4-10; Rev. 1:5, 6; 5:9, 10.

3. Heb. 4:4-16.

There is nothing, therefore, that the minister does in his public function that every believer does not also have the right to do. He may lead publicly in such functions at any time, *at the call and commission of the church.* The ordained person is simply one member of the congregation, the one authorized by the others to give full attention to the various functions of the body which it is more expedient for him to fulfill. He is one priest, set apart among many priests, to act in their behalf. Ordination is the outward sign of such congregational recognition of divine gifts in that member which make him suitable to perform such functions. Essentially this is little different to the election of any other person to a position of specific responsibility—such as clerk or treasurer—within the local congregation. Wherever the word *ordain* is used in the New Testament it has the sense of appointment, commission, election, or choice;[4] and its context carries ideas of representation and endorsement. The laying on of hands was a physical acknowledgment of the church's association with the calling by the Spirit of such a one into specific service, *and of identification of all members in that service.*

A variety of ministry within the early church is now widely accepted. Some denominations who have traditionally opposed a multiple ministry, and drawn hard distinctions between clergy and laity, have gone on record in recent days as now aware of the falseness of these distinctions.[5]

One of the most outstanding contributions to the doctrine of the ministry was that of J. B. Lightfoot, Cambridge Professor of Divinity and bishop of Durham, who appended his essay to the famous Philippian commentary. This was direct challenge to some episcopalian applications.[6] He was adamant that the oversight exercised by early church leaders was not the extravagant

---

4. Mark 3:14; John 15:16; I Tim. 2:7; Acts 14:3.

5. The fourth regional conference of the Protestant Episcopal General Convention, meeting in February 1964, went on record as insisting that all Christians are ministers of Christ, and that the division between priest and layman is false. Those involved in this statement included National Episcopal Council leaders. (Reported in the *Christian Century,* 4 March 1964, p. 302.)

6. J. B. Lightfoot, "Dissertation on the Christian Ministry," in *Saint Paul's Epistle to the Philippians,* rev. ed. reprint (Grand Rapids: Zondervan, 1953), pp. 180-269.

exaltation of power and monopoly of authority shown in the records of men like Ignatius, Irenæus, and Cyprian. He found his greatest support for episcopal government in the pressures demanded by the substantial threat of schisms of the early second century, and from assumed sanctions by the apostle John.[7]

When Bishop Phillips Brooks, the famous Boston leader, read Lightfoot he wrote a friend that he considered that it "finished the Apostolic Succession theory completely."[8]

Lightfoot wrote of the contrast between some current practices and the New Testament revelation of ministerial function, and that

> the priestly functions and privileges of the Christian people are never regarded as transferred or even delegated to these officers. They are called stewards, or messengers of God, servants or ministers of the Church, and the like; but the sacerdotal title is never once conferred on them. The only priests under the Gospel, designated as such in the New Testament, are the saints, the members of the Christian Brotherhood.[9]

And again, after reference to I Corinthians 12:28 and Ephesians 4:11 as describing the true ministry, he says:

> There is entire silence about priestly functions; for the most exalted office of the church, the highest gift of the Spirit, conveyed no sacerdotal right which was not enjoyed by the humblest member of the Christian community.[10]

In discussing the rise of sacerdotal views of the ministry Lightfoot affirms that its origin is outside of the New Testament[11] and is an entirely new principle.[12] He argues that unless the terms *bishop* (ἐπίσκοπος) and *elder* (πρεσβύτερος) are interchangeable, the word *for*, in Titus 1:5-7, is out of place.[13] He declares:

---

7. Lightfoot, pp. 227-44.

8. Raymond W. Albright, *Focus on Infinity: A Life of Phillips Brooks* (New York: Macmillan, 1961), p. 150.

9. Lightfoot, pp. 184-85.

10. Lightfoot, p. 186.

11. Lightfoot, p. 24.

12. Lightfoot, p. 24.

13. Lightfoot, p. 95.

The episcopate was formed, not out of the apostolic order by localization, but out of the presbyterial by elevation: and the title (bishop) which was common to all, came at length to be appropriated by the chief among them.[14]

Acts 20:17-28 describes the Ephesian elders as bishops, and also charges them with the pastoral function. Greek and Syriac usage supports this interchangeability,[15] and the acceptance therefore of three standard orders of ministry among certain episcopalians is viewed by some as not necessarily in conflict with the total priesthood of believers.[16]

Ministry had been a multiple responsibility in some areas in the synagogues of Judaism. Jesus and Paul thus read, preached, and shared in prayers and services, as opportunities arose, and as every male Jew had the right to do. The ministerial functions were not the monopoly of any privileged class.

The Minister a Priest?

Among the first actions of the European reforms of the early sixteenth century was the substitution of the word *minister* for *priest.*[17] The English Puritans also demanded this change, along with other reforms calculated to stress the unmediatory work of the one who led the church in its communion at the Lord's table.[18] Traditional European liturgies bear more evidence of a heart return to these Reformation principles than the Anglican, although the English *revisions* do show some greater understandings.[19] All this was valid protest against the abuse of a word with Old Testament overtones that was felt to be out of place

---

14. Lightfoot, p. 196.

15. See George Johnson, "Constitution of the Church" in *The Twentieth Century Encyclopedia of Religious Knowledge,* ed. L. A. Loetscher (Grand Rapids: Baker Book House, 1955), p. 252.

16. T. W. Manson, *Ministry and Priesthood: Christ's and Ours* (London: Epworth, 1958), p. 35.

17. Ilion T. Jones, *An Historical Approach to Evangelical Worship* (New York: Abingdon, 1954), p. 125.

18. Jones, p. 125.

19. Jones, pp. 133-47.

within a New Testament church.

Nevertheless there is a sense in which every pastor of a local congregation is priest, and in a special way. The right of every believer to direct access to God through Jesus Christ ought not to be limited to the function of representation in which the congregational pastor always is involved. Manson says: "The function of the minister who celebrates is to be the representative and spokesman of God through Christ to the congregation, and of the congregation to God through Christ."[20] While he is speaking mainly of the communion table, and in this taking a high and sacramental view, his comment is right in principle and inherent truth. Nonconformists will want to challenge the extremism, but ought to support the emphasis. Lightfoot, as usual, comments most explicitly:

> The minister's function is representative without being vicarial. He is priest, as the mouthpiece, the delegate, of a priestly race. His acts are not his own, but the acts of his congregation. Hence, too, it will follow, viewed on this side, as on the other, his function cannot be absolute, and indispensable. It may be a general rule, it may be under ordinary circumstances a practically universal law, that the highest acts of congregational worship shall be performed through the principal officers of the congregation. But an emergency may arise when the spirit, and not the letter, must decide. The Christian ideal will then interpose, and interpret our duty. The higher ordinance of the universal priesthood will overrule all special limitations. The layman will asume functions which are otherwise restricted to the ordained minister.[21]

Such a view of the minister as a priest does not suggest the offering of sacrifices to effect atonement. It is rather the setting apart of one member of the body as a deputy to approach God publicly for men, and as God's special ambassador to approach men publicly for Him with the gospel. In each case the function bases on an identification where the appointed representative simply fulfills a role that is more expedient for an individual than for a group to take. He does not "interpose between God and man in such a way that direct communion with God is superseded on

20. Manson, p. 71.

21. Lightfoot, p. 268.

the one hand, or that his own mediation becomes indispensable on the other."[22]

Lightfoot was frank in his recognition of errors and abuses to which the episcopalian tradition was suspect. Some will feel that the very history which Lightfoot unfolds well illustrates the futility of a pattern of government, however expedient, which does not foundation its detail *practice* firmly on the theocratic nature of the local assembly, and give room for regular ministry in numerous areas by *all* the members. Hudson believes that the voluntary principle in religion needs an open emphasis and encouragement for its best expression, and that the lack of consistent application in contemporary church life lies at the heart of some of our weakness.[23]

However, our discussion here is not concerning the degree of value in any particular system of church organization, but rather the New Testament concept of ministry. No denomination has ground for "unchurching" another on this basis; for, provided the two-way representative function of the ministry in relation to both God and the congregation is recognized, the ministry is Biblically valid. No matter how secular, prosaic, or expedient our views of the ministry may be, *its representative character is its major essential.*

Therefore, in differing forms, both the episcopalian and the congregational traditions of church organization place emphasis on the total priesthood of all believers, as well as on the ambassadorial function of the pastoral office. They both emphasize the ministry's representative function in terms of the declaration of divine revelation and in the sharing of congregational needs through a representative approach to God. They both view the preacher as the one who verbalizes the congregational belief and understanding.

So when the minister preaches to the world he is bringing both God's Word and the testimony of Christ's body to them. When he speaks to the church the body is teaching itself through him, *who is its mouth. We may, then, regard the pulpit function of*

---

22. Lightfoot, p. 267.

23. J. Winthrop Hudson, *The Great Tradition of the American Churches*, rev. ed. (New York: Harper, 1963).

the pastoral role as the voice of the body of Christ.

THE CHURCH AND ITS MINISTRY

The task of the preacher, as the voice of the body, is to enlist the unordained into a fulfillment of their own ministry. His nonsacerdotal function is often expressed by the cliché–*all Christians are laymen.* This can often be the badly worn side of a coin used in the currency of congregational government when it becomes necessary to limit the pastor's leadership or control his power. The Scriptural perspective is higher than this, teaching that *all Christians are ministers.* We each participate in the ministry of a living Lord, through His living body, the church.[24] The preacher has the task of developing the ministry of all the members into a unified wholeness of witness and service. Roy Pearson expresses this significantly: "The professional minister is the minister of a ministering community. He is a preacher to other preachers, a priest to other priests, a pastor to other pastors, and a prophet to other prophets."[25]

It is evident that, within the general call to the ministry for all disciples, there are some specific ministries. Ephesians mentions some of these callings, suggesting them as particular gifts.[26] They may be such that the possessors are immediately recognized and set aside for service within that special field. One man may even have a variety of gifts. Certainly evangelism in the New Testament expected both a gifted divine ability in some, as well as an implied human responsibility in all. Acts 8 indicates that, while the gifted apostles waited at Jerusalem (v. 1), every believer was evangelizing (v. 4); and a simple deacon was so faithful, and successful, in this task that he later became known as Philip, the evangelist (vv. 5-8, 26-40; with Acts 21:8). Evangelism was evidently both the gift of individuals and, at the same time, the expected function of all the members.

Paul speaks of such various ministries as gifts when he says, "And he gave some, apostles; and some, prophets; and some,

---

24. See Franklin M. Segler, *A Theology of Church and Ministry* (Nashville: Broadman, 1960), pp. 75-85.

25. Roy Pearson, *The Preacher: His Purpose and Practice* (Philadelphia: Westminster, 1962), p. 85.

evangelists; and some, pastors and teachers; for the perfecting of the saints for the work of the ministry for the edifying of the body of Christ."[26] The context affirms that differing gifts come from the ascended Lord to meet the needs of the church. These verses declare that all four roles (apostle, prophet, evangelist, and pastor-teacher) are fulfilled on the basis of a divine gift so to function, and that *these gifts are to promote the total growth and total ministry of the total church.* Those who exercise these gifts act in behalf of God and in behalf of the body of Christ, the church. If a message is delivered by the evangelist to the lost, it is both the revelation of God and the testimony of the congregation concerning the gospel. The pastor-teacher who speaks to the congregation does so only with the call and authority of Christ, and of the assembly itself.

In his pulpit role, then, the pastor-teacher is the voice of the body, as well as of its Head. He verbalizes the divine revelation, articulates the congregation-held truth, displays it in liturgy, and focuses it in application. His basic task is exposition and communication. He interprets, guides, and teaches in patient, authoritative proclamation to all.[27] He is a minister to the ministry, seeking to build the body of Christ to maturity.

A Supervising Ministry

It was these same Ephesian pastor-teachers who were earlier urged to feed the flock of God, and were then called "bishops" (Acts 20:17, 28). *Episcopos* (ἐπίσκοπος) means a responsibility for oversight, or supervision, just as *poimen* (ποιμήν) points to the shepherding relationship of such leaders. Where there is a variety of gifts and functions there must be cohesion and leadership. The pulpit role of the pastor-teacher is to be *a voice of leadership within a multiple ministry.*

Apostles were special representatives with unique commissioning direct from Christ. This was a ministry that was limited to those who knew Him in the flesh, and one which Ephesians 2:20

26. Eph. 4:11 ff.

27. Eph. 4:11 ff.

declares as being foundational and noncontinuous. It was the base on which other ministry was erected.

Prophets were annunciators of God's revelation.[28] They often brought comfort as well as challenge; and their ministry seems to have passed into that of *evangelists*, who delivered the message of salvation. The *pastors and teachers* appear as the group in permanent ministry, serving the needs of the congregation in distinction to evangelists who served unbelievers with the gospel of grace. After evangelism comes growth. The pastor's task was to teach truth in its influence on life and conduct.

Evidently Paul served with success in all the functions described in this listing. A young pastor, timid and therefore apparently ungifted in evangelism and prophetic utterance, was urged both to evangelize the unsaved and exhort his people (II Tim. 4:5; I Tim. 4:13). Today's pastor may serve both the world and the church, the one with the gospel and the other with its exposition and application to living. He may emphasize either aspect of ministry, as he may be more gifted in one area than the other; but he dares not ignore his total responsibility to both.

Literally the *bishop,* or pastor-teacher, is an overseer, a supervisor, one who has a *super*vision and sees over the whole task from a perspective above that of the individual. Bishops were plural in individual congregations at times, and this seems to indicate that they formed a board of local leadership in the assembly.[29] The preaching bishop must remember that he is but part of such spiritual oversight, his deacons, elders, or other similar leadership officers working with him. But as the preaching bishop, his oversight will be worked out in his teaching. As the voice of the body it will be normal for others in leadership to look to him to be the leader of the leaders in the church.

To supervise the leadership of the church, a bishop is required to manage and administer his own family well (I Tim. 3:4). He is expected to be one who feeds others (I Peter 5:1-4), and those who fulfill the office are commended if they toil at the

---

28. This term may also be applied to those who give direct revelation from God, under special Spirit guidance. Cf. the description in I Cor. 14:3.

29. Phil. 1:1; James 5:15; etc.

task of teaching (I Tim. 5:17). Teaching and encouragement are listed as important elements in all his service (Rom. 12:8; I Thess. 5:12, 13).

One of the most illuminating words relative to the supervising ministry of local church leadership is found in a similar listing of gifts and functions in I Corinthians 12:28. "Governments," *kubernayseis* (κυβερνήσεις), is better rendered as "administrators" or "organizers." It is related to *kubernaytays* (κυβερνήτης), the "pilot" or "steersman" of Revelation 18:7, and the "master" of Acts 27:11, where the form is *kubernaytay* (κυβερνήτη). The kind of supervision which is required from those leaders whom God places in the church is one that gives direction and mastery over a total ministry, one that guides the church toward chosen objectives.

The bishop is also called a "pastor," the word being *poimen* (ποιμήν): literally, a "shepherd." This also endorses the guidance and organizational functions of the local supervisor. Christ is called the good pastor, the great pastor, and the chief pastor,[30] and His pastoral care is also linked with His supervisory function.[31]

So then what Christ is to pastors as the chief shepherd, pastors are to members of the local congregation. Paul longed for the maturity of those whom he shepherded, and his constant prayer was that they would grow in Christ.[32]

The modern concept of supervision, as it applies within industry and society, is the multiplication of the abilities of the executive through the services of many. The leader in any program of education or production must give himself to *management*—the segmenting of a total program into individual areas, the distribution of responsibilities, and detail planning to meet discovered needs. He must also give himself to *training*—the enlistment, teaching, mobilization, and development of persons, and the provision of resources to enable them to fulfill their responsi-

---

30. John 10:11; I Peter 2:25; I Peter 5:4.

31. I Peter 5:4.

32. See Eph. 1:15-23 and 2:14-19.

bilities. The third element of good supervision is *promotion*—the active development of a climate for growth which is created by guidance, counsel, publicity, and warm personal relationships. All these secular concepts ally with the Biblical patterns of supervision also.

Christ, our chief pastor, was well aware of such needs. Of course it was possible for Him to feed five thousand persons with bread in any manner He chose. There could have been greater impact through a more dramatic miracle than the one which He did choose. He decided to work in association with His disciples, segmenting the responsibility for distribution and organizing the whole event in order to enable them to participate in His ministry, and in this manner be trained for theirs. The entire experience is a model of good supervision, even to the efficient collection of scraps left over. In this kind of shepherding and supervising relationship the disciples learned far more than they ever would have, had Christ simply made bread appear in the hands of those who were needy.

Wise administration is not so much the doing of things as it is the growing of persons. Good organization and detail planning means the way is opened for adequate supervision. If the local pastor is such a supervisor, then the church will be a growing fellowship. A monopolized ministry will not only hamper efficiency, it will also hinder systematic expansion. The minister is the voice of leadership within a multiple ministry; he is *supervisor.*

A Teaching Ministry

The second broad theme of Ephesians 4:11-12 is a deeper underscoring of the pastor's teaching function. The "pastors and teachers" of verse 11 appears to be a collective description of a single function in which both guidance and instruction are paramount. This concept is followed immediately by words which enlarge on this aspect of the leadership task. We are told that God gives gifts, particularly the gifts of pastors and teachers, "for the perfecting of the saints, for the work of the ministry." Leaders are not chosen to lift the load of responsibility from the shoulders of others, but to help them discharge their individual responsibilities more effectively. The first comma in verse 12 in our English translations can be challenged on the ground of Paul's change of pronouns from *pros* ("for") to *eis* ("unto") here; and this gives greater support, grammatically, for what is clearly evident in the thrust of Paul's thought.[33]

As a teacher, then, the minister in the local congregation is *the voice of leadership toward unity in fellowship and purpose.* He is to be a coordinator, teaching and training others to whom he ministers, so that the total ministry will have harmony, balance, and shared objectives. The word "saints," *hagioi* (ἅγιοι), suggests a separation of members from other goals to unite under the purpose of serving God.

From this perspective baptism is an ordination rite into the ministry. Ritschl observes: "The church does not have a mission, but the church is a mission, and it is performed by all members with their gifts of grace, which are given for the edification of the church, and the service to unbelievers."[34]

Kraemer says that the missionary nature of the church is not a volitional choice but rather a direct function of its essential nature. The church *is* mission, and it *is* ministry.[35] Biblical terminology for "laity" indicates a worshiping community totally committed to these ideas;[36] and a study of New Testament teaching clearly indicates that the laity have "a full, responsible share in bringing the nature and calling of the Church to expression."[37]

Pentecost gives us good illustration of this essential concept in the New Testament doctrine of the church. First, a foundational preparation was laid for the program outlined by Christ. The field was divided, by Him, into Jerusalem, Judea, Samaria, and the regions beyond. Second, the disciples organized for action,

---

33. See Francis Foulkes, "The Epistle of Paul to the Ephesians," in *Tyndale Bible Commentaries*, ed. R. V. Tasker (Grand Rapids: Eerdmans, 1963), p. 20; and Dale Moody, *Christ and the Church* (Grand Rapids: Eerdmans, 1963), p. 94.

34. Dietrich Ritschl, *A Theology of Proclamation* (Richmond: John Knox Press, 1960), p. 117.

35. Hendrik Kraemer, *A Theology of Laity* (Philadelphia: Westminster, 1958), pp. 135-55.

36. Kraemer, pp. 155-64.

37. Kraemer, p. 161.

replacing the lost Judas and waiting on God in prayer for power to proceed. Third, with the coming of the Spirit the gospel message was proclaimed, and it was proclaimed in a special way.

Peter preached the formal message; but, as Acts 2:1-13 clearly shows us, *this public sermon was only the culmination of a prior witness by all the disciples.* The whole church witnessed to the wonders of redemption. This informal testimony was brought by Galileans to men of a multitude of races, each in his own language, as the disciples spoke under the power of the Spirit. Peter's word was interpretation and explanation of the "wonderful works of God" (v. 11) which these men had heard, and of the divinely given language ability of the many witnesses. It brought to a climax all that had been informally presented by a Spirit-filled church, and culminated in a formal invitation to respond for a like experience (v. 38). Peter stood up with the eleven to declare his message; but Acts clearly indicates that those who were all with one accord in one place when the Spirit came, and who were filled and witnessed, included the whole company of the disciples, of whom the men numbered one hundred and twenty (1:14, 15; 2:1 ff.).

The pattern of private witness, which promotes to a later public climax of proclamation and response, is repeated again and again through the early church history.[38] It is expressly noted that the whole body functioned in this natural manner, often while the leadership was elsewhere.[39] The pastor's task then is to so teach and train his people that this kind of natural evangelism will be a normal program characteristic.

The word in Ephesians 4:12 for "perfecting," *katartismon* ($\kappa\alpha\tau\alpha\rho\tau\iota\sigma\mu\grave{o}\nu$), suggests equipment for usefulness. Jesus encountered James and John "perfecting"[40] their nets; that is, mending, repairing, and equipping their nets for service. The pastor's task is to make his congregation useful, to fit each

---

38. Even Paul usually reasoned and discussed with small groups and private individuals before proceeding to public proclamation of the gospel in the cities in which he ministered.

39. Acts 8:1 ff.

40. Mark 1:19, *katartizontas* ($\kappa\alpha\tau\alpha\rho\tau\acute{\iota}\zeta o\nu\tau\alpha s$)

member for his appropriate place in the program of Christian service.

Each church will therefore need a well-planned program to train people to exercise their gifts and to discharge their functions. Special callings within the church are to develop the workers, and all these minister to each other within the fellowship. The teaching pastor will help shape the entire development as he coordinates this activity into a unity.

Our Lord's prayer in John 17, "that they all might be one, even as *we* are one," suggests that the unity of the body of Christ is like that of the Trinity. It is a unity built through the relationship of persons, and one that is compatible with variety. Fellowship, *koinonia* (κοινωνία) , is simply a sharing partnership. Peter and John were called *koinonoi* in the fishing business.[41] It is the minister's function to teach so that this sense of working together at a total task will be enthusiastically present. He is to be the voice of leadership toward such a unity of fellowship and purpose. He is teacher.

A Building Ministry

The final concept here is that of leadership as building. A careful study of the prepositions and constructions in Ephesians 4:11-13 yields a literal translation which can be freely expressed thus:

. . . and, indeed, he gave the apostles,
        and the prophets,
        and the evangelists,
    and the shepherds and teachers,
toward
the complete fitting of the saints into
their work of service;
toward
a building up of the body of Christ;
    (until we all attain to the unity of the faith,
    and to the knowledge of the Son of God,
    into a mature manhood);

---

41. Luke 5:10.

toward
a complete and fully developed body of Christ.[42]

The emphasis on a forward movement is inescapable. The thrust of argument is for the need to give Christ a fully developed body. The church was not the body of Christians for Paul, as he once thought it was when he persecuted them. It was now for him the body of Christ, since he had realized that it was but the earthly expression of the one single Person whose Spirit indwelt it. Paul's greatest concern was now for the maturity of that body, both in quality and quantity. Spiritual gifts and skillful leaders were all given, along with ministering saints, to help that body to grow.

Consequently the minister will function as *the voice of leadership encouraging growth to a maturity of faith and knowledge.* He is to be a builder. Where the local church leadership is such, the membership will no longer be characterized by the immaturity, instability, and gullibility which he mentions in verse 14. Believers who are weak, wayward, and able to be deceived are such because the ministry has not encouraged growth.

Growth in Christ is linked with speaking the truth in love (v. 15). The section concludes with a picture of the fitted completeness that comes with maturity. An increasing faith and knowledge restores disjointed and dislocated members to a harmony of usefulness with dividends for all (v. 16). While ultimate maturity awaits our identity with Christ in the life to come, here we are taught that the gifts we have in the church are given to help us along the road to this objective. We may thus proceed in a growing development, assured that we will ultimately be like Him in the life everlasting.[43]

A Christian who demands that he be spiritually served by others, without himself contributing to the ministry by his own service, has missed the whole meaning of his calling. Each is to serve, and all are ministering to each other.

---

42. My free rendition.

43. I John 3:1-2. See D. Martyn Lloyd-Jones, *The Basis of Christian Unity* (London: Inter-Varsity Fellowship, 1962), an exposition of Eph. 4 and John 17 which summarizes problems faced by evangelicals in the current ecumenical dialogue, but with some excellent exposition of true Christian maturity.

The minister's function is to build the body through his leadership of all the members in their multiple ministry. Administration dynamics for such a pastoral relationship have been enunciated by several writers.[44] There is a glory to come when we finally are fully identified with Christ and made into His image; *but there is also a glory in the growing!* Nothing exalts the pastor's spirit higher than the realization that his people are growing. As the spiritual muscles build, the weak hands of service take up their tasks, the congregational tongue begins to articulate, and the body of Christ rises and begins to walk worthily of its calling. This is the pastor's joy and crown. The glory of a congregation of upward reaching saints will offset many other discouragements.

We have seen that the concept of the church and its ministry in the New Testament includes leadership, supervision, teaching, and building. The pastor-teacher must function as a voice of leadership within a multiple ministry, toward unity in fellowship and purpose, and encouraging maturity of faith and knowledge. His preaching must reflect the over-view, the interpretive-view, and the development-view. In all this we see the teaching ministry of the pulpit as cardinal for the effective work of the minister. In our next chapter we will study the New Testament *practice* of this responsibility as an integral whole.

---

44. See Gaines S. Dobbins, *A Ministering Church* (Nashville: Broadman, 1960); Edgar N. Jackson, *The Pastor and His People* (Manhassett, N.Y.: Channel Press, 1963); Ilion T. Jones, *The Pastor: The Man and His Ministry* (Philadelphia: Westminister, 1961).

4

Preaching and Teaching

The contemporary distinction between teaching and preaching elements within the pastoral pulpit ministry also has its roots in the history of New Testament criticism. In 1845 Baur queried the Pauline authorship of some epistles, and assumed an antagonism between the Petrine and Pauline views of the gospel. From this context a critical perspective developed in theology which held sway across the world for over half a century.[1]

Baur's extremes were corrected through the forceful work of Harnack, Ritschl, Lightfoot, and others, who pointed out that his imposing arguments were erected "by neglecting all sources except Galatians and Corinthians, and then by misinterpreting these."[2]

The critical approach was later extended by Albert Schweitzer. He rigidly excluded all value from the kingdom teachings of Jesus, except as "interim ethic," and saw little therefore in Paul's interpretation of the gospel beyond the

---

1. See information under "Paulinism," "Jesus and Paul," etc., in any standard Bible encyclopedia, or similar.

2. J. Gresham Machen, *The Origin of Paul's Religion* (New York: Macmillan, 1921), p. 125.

influences of Jewish eschatology.[3] It was Harnack, however, who, reacting from the Baur extremism, popularized the claim that Paul took the concept of the kingdom of God as presented by Christ and placed in into such entirely fresh perspective that he altered its spirit and changed its emphasis. For Harnack, these unconscious modifications of the gospel by the apostle proved the existence of a distinctive Pauline theology, far beyond the revelation made in the life and ministry of the Son of Man Himself.[4]

Most theologians were prepared to admit the obvious Semitic influences on the interpretation of Jesus' teachings within the early church, but felt that such strong criticism was unjustified. One well-known conservative scholar dramatized the alternatives:

> Paulinism was not based on a Galilean prophet. It was based either on the Son of God who came to earth . . . or else it was based on colossal error. But if the latter alternative be adopted the error is not only colossal, but also unaccountable.[5]

THE CONTRIBUTION OF C. H. DODD

In 1935 the English theologian C. H. Dodd produced the most significant study relative to the Pauline teaching and preaching of the gospel.[6] One authority classifies Dodd's work as the most influential theological writing since the First World War, comparable in quality and significance only to the more recent offerings of Karl Barth and Rudolf Bultmann.[7]

Dodd discerned a clear difference through the entire New Testament between the primitive *preaching* and the primitive *teaching* of the early church. He saw the former as a simple

---

3. See note 1.

4. See note 1.

5. Machen, p. 169.

6. C. H. Dodd, *The Apostolic Preaching and Its Development* (Cambridge: At the University Press, 1935).

7. Floyd V. Filson, *Three Crucial Decades: Studies in the Book of Acts* (Richmond: John Knox Press, 1963), p. 29.

declaration of essential gospel facts with a view to the evangelization of the hearers, and the latter as theological and ethical application of this basic for the edification of believers.

Therefore, the preaching, *kerygma* (κηρύγμα), can be defined as "an irreducible core of New Testament preaching which may neither be ignored nor diminished lest the Christian message be destroyed."[8] Dodd reconstructed this *kerygma* from the Pauline letters and the sermons reported in Acts, using as keys such recurrent phrases as "preaching the kingdom of God," "preaching Christ," and "preaching Jesus." In that way he came to feel that the simple declaration of the facts concerning the death, burial, and resurrection of Christ, declared to those from whom a salvation commitment was desired, constituted preaching.

Dodd viewed teaching, *didache* (διδαχῇ), in the New Testament as totally different than preaching. This was mainly to be found in the epistles, and constituted the balance of apostolic exposition argued from the Gospel facts.

Thus, in his concepts, Dodd emphasized a basic and New Testament authenticated witness, first to the passion details, and then to their implications. He clarified concepts that gave a new wholeness to New Testament interpretation, as had never been done before.[9]

THE CHALLENGE TO DODD

Serious challenge ought to be made to some of Dodd's assumptions. While the *kerygma* and *didache* can be distinguished as varying emphases within the New Testament, they still remain as facets of one homogeneous ministry. A complete division, into either form or function, is just not totally possible. Dodd's major contribution lies in his insistence that the Pauline teaching was a valid exposition of the meaning of the gospel. As such it expanded the approach laid down by Christ Himself, in both His work and His words. But the very point that Dodd supports, links these two together in a program which denies the possibility of their separation.

---

8. Claude H. Thompson, *Theology of the Kerygma* (Englewood Cliffs, N.J.: Prentice-Hall, 1962), pp. 1-2.

9. His "realised eschatology" also has homiletic implications. See Thompson.

There is no truth in the assertion that the apostles *either* preached the gospel *or* taught the church. In Jesus' own *teaching,* as well as that of the early church, the *preaching* element is very prominent, often linked together within the same passages. Passages that clearly show this include Matthew 4:23; 9:35; Luke 20:1; Acts 5:42; 15:35; 28:31. Mark (in 1:39) and Luke (in 4:44) consider that the word "preaching" is sufficient to describe what Matthew calls "preaching and teaching" (in 4:23). This included teaching in the synagogue. Again Mark (in 1:21, 22, 27) describes the Capernaum ministry in the synagogue as "teaching"; yet in a few verses beyond this he calls that same synagogue ministry in towns of Galilee "preaching." Unbelieving Jews are the context of some uses of *didasko* (διδάσκω) in John 6:59 and 7:14. Pharisees and others were taught in John 8:20; yet the message here much more concerns redemption than instruction in doctrine. A variety of authorities now therefore challenge Dodd's exclusivism.[10]

Dodd may not have intended to draw as hard a line as he did, but the overwhelming consensus of those who read him is in criticism of his extremism.[11] Mounce sums up the contemporary view well when he says that *kerygma* is foundation and *didache* is superstructure, and that a complete building needs both.[12] They are not mutually exclusive but inclusive. James D. Smart has also summarized the position of modern New Testament criticism in relation to Dodd,[13] and his work merits special attention as it places the problem within the total Christian education context and relates it to some liberal trends of recent theology.

---

10. See Robert L. Mounce, *The Essential Nature of New Testament Preaching* (Grand Rapids: Eerdmans, 1960), p. 4.: Alan Richardson, ed., *A Theological Word-Book of the Bible* (New York: Macmillan, 1962), pp. 171-72.

11. In addition to Mounce, Filson, and Thompson, see also Grady H. Davis, *Design for Preaching* (Philadelphia: Muhlenberg Press, 1958), pp. 120-26; Charles W. F. Smith, *Biblical Authority for Modern Preaching* (Philadelphia: Westminster, 1949), p. 108; and Donald Gordon Stewart, *Christian Education and Evangelism* (Philadelphia: Westminster, 1963), pp. 47-54.

12. Mounce, pp. 42-43.

13. See James D. Smart, *The Teaching Ministry of the Church* (Philadelphia: Westminster, 1954), pp. 11-23; and *The Rebirth of Ministry* (Philadelphia: Westminster, 1960), especially pp. 84 ff.

From such a perspective we may affirm that *there is always a didactic element implicit within the apostolic evangelistic preaching.*

The terms "prophet," "teacher," and "pastor" appear to be interchangeable. The Corinthian list of functions omits that of evangelists, suggesting an accepted understanding that the other terms covered this task. We are clearly informed that doctrine *(didache)* was involved in the conversion of Sergius Paulus, and Paul's proclamation of resurrection truth records that this preaching was hailed as a new teaching by the Athenian hearers.[14]

Filson's evaluation is helpful.[15] He has shown that Dodd almost ignores the preaching of the gospel to the Gentiles. He studies the addresses at Lystra and Athens, and concludes that the basic teachings about monotheism and man's moral responsibility formed a part of Paul's gospel preaching, necessary in order to clear away the polytheistic and idolatrous presuppositions of his listeners.[16] Paul is often found indulging in prolonged debate and argument when preaching, to both Jews and outsiders. These were the then accepted methods, as shown in Acts 6:9 and 17:2.[17]

That gospel proclamation involves a most thorough dialogue and discussion is demonstrated by the use of *katagellomen* (καταγγέλλομεν) , "to tell thoroughly," in Colossians 1:27-28, a word also often used in relation to unbelievers. Philippians 1:15-17 displays this word as a synonym for *kerussousin* (κηρύσσουσιν) in its appropriate form, *katagellousin* (καταγγέλλουσιν) , suggesting complete interchangeability. The model participles *nouthetountes* (νουθετοῦντες), "admonishing," and *didaskontes* (διδάσκοντες), "teaching," again appear in Colossians 1:27-28, explaining methods for the proclamation of Christ.

---

14. Acts 13:12 and 17:18-19 with context.

15. See note 7.

16. Filson, pp. 39 ff.

17. Acts 6:9 and 17:2 seem to illustrate a norm. Acts 4:2 and 21:28 also refer to a *didache* process of gospel preaching.

Paul taught thus in the synagogue,[18] the marketplace,[19] and within the philosophical schools.[20] In his discussion with Felix he argued.[21] All of this intensive teaching had evangelism as both its aim and atmosphere. He shared much more material than the simple recital of facts about the passion of Christ when he was evangelizing.

We must also affirm that *there is always a kerygmatic element implicit within the apostolic teaching to Christians.*

Whenever we enter into Christian *didache* we find it naturally rooting back to a foundational *kerygma.* It is just not possible to interpret the meaning of Christian life without reference to the history of redemption. Knox affirms that this fact alone supports the interpenetration of preaching and teaching.[22] What is so constantly surprising is the explicit manner in which the Pauline teaching exhibits this. Again and again the matters expounded in all the epistles are given their total life and meaning by a distinct relation to the norms of conversion, or by a direct association with grace and the facts of the atonement.[23]

RESULTANT CONCEPTS

Any attempt to teach ethic without the soteriological structure spells ruin to the didactic purpose, because the strength to obey is only discovered in response to the divine love which gives justification. The supreme example of this interrelationship is shown in I Corinthians 15:1-11, which begins with a simple statement of the basic facts of the evangel, and follows with a whole chapter of argument and illustration indicating the significance of these facts for the disciple, in relation to the afterlife.[24]

---

18. Acts 18:4.

19. Acts 18:19.

20. Acts 19:19.

21. Acts 24:25.

22. John Knox, *The Integrity of Preaching* (New York: Abingdon, 1957), pp. 47-56.

23. See Rom. 6; II Cor. 4:1-3; Eph. 2:8-10; I John 4:11.

24. Illustrated again in Gal. 3:1-4 and 4:9.

Such passages do not move from the *kerygma* facts to new ideas, but relate these facts to the resultant doctrine in an association which makes each thoroughly dependent on the other. The whole Roman epistle carries a similar flavor. The first half stresses the nature of salvation as being righteousness *imputed* to the believer, the second half discusses how it is practically *imparted* to him. Justification is first taught as arising directly from the atonement and as linked with it, and sanctification is likewise related. Without such close relation the doctrines concerned could not stand alone.

The New Testament knows nothing of idealistic ethics without such firm bases. All of its instruction arises from the application of a dynamic gospel and its meaning. Christianity is never, therefore, taught as *being* (in the sense of its raw existence), as a code of conduct, an attitude of character, or even a moral standard or truth. Christianity is revealed as *possessing* these things, but as *being* a way of salvation, a personal relationship with the Son of God as Savior, through faith. Christianity cannot therefore be defined in terms of its ethic alone. If discussion is limited to what Christianity has, or teaches, in isolation from what it essentially is, we have departed from Biblical fulness.

To teach the precepts of the Sermon on the Mount without proclaiming the dynamics of the incarnation, atonement, and resurrection, will mean that both the motive to fulfill such ideals and the power to achieve them will be missing. The only adequate foundation for obedience is the forgiveness which comes by grace, and the personal involvement with the will of God so created. Christian behavior is rooted in redemption experience.

Perhaps it is the lack of clarity concerning this interpenetration of redemption and behavior that is responsible for so many pulpit discussions of moral truth and idealistic ethic which pass for sermons today. It is not the pulpiteer's responsibility to create little christs by imitation. It is his task to clear away the ignorance, prejudice, and uncommitment which blocks the reproduction of the new nature already implanted within the believer, a new nature which is the life of the Holy Spirit Himself.[25] Paul anchors

---

25. II Peter 1:4; II Cor. 5:17.

the development of this new nature to the clarity of our vision of the revelation in the Word.[26] Without an understanding of what God has revealed, and of the vital association of this doctrine with the salvation experience, our attempts to teach will always be frustrating and ineffective.

Karl Barth has supported this by his insistence that the preacher's proclamation of facts is to expose the hearer into a direct and critical confrontation with God. He also affirms the necessity of setting ethical instruction within the redemptive act,[27] and this is considered by some as the most significant contribution of neo-orthodoxy to homiletics.[28]

Others, such as Farmer, consider that Barth has too strong a distinction between preaching and teaching in his attempt to support evangelism as gospel annunciation. Farmer's word is adequate summary of the whole point at issue:

> If it [the preaching element] be used in such wise as to exclude from the sermon what may be called in a broad sense instructional matter then it is misleading: it unduly narrows the context of preaching. Everything depends upon what the containing context, and what the focal point, of the sermon, are. If the context is always God's saving activity through history in Christ, and if the focus is the encounter of that saving activity with those who listen, then nothing that does not fog that context, or blur that focus, must be excluded.[29]

We see that the interrelation of kerygmatic and didactic elements means that, while the preacher publishes facts, *he is committed to the publication of these in dialogue with the needs and reactions of his listeners.* He may give prominence in his ministry to evangelizing, or to teaching, but even the "simplest" preaching of the gospel must carry doctrine and follows suitable

---

26. II Cor. 3:18.

27. Karl Barth, *God in Action* (his "little dogmatics") (New York: Round Table Press, 1963), pp. 73-81, where he declares that "following after righteousness" means keeping the resurrection in remembrance, doing the work of an evangelist, etc.

28. See David Edward Kline, *A Study of Contemporary Neo-orthodox Philosophy of Preaching* (Chicago: Northern Baptist Theological Seminary, 1959, unpublished B.D. thesis).

29. Herbert H. Farmer, *The Servant of the Word* (New York: Scribner's, 1942; Fortress Edition, 1964), pp. 16-17.

teaching method. Likewise, the most involved instruction and the deepest Christian ethic must root back to the redemption history continually in order to find strength and motive for its application.

From this perspective we gather the truth that he who fulfills the preaching role must always function as a teacher, and in this functioning he must never turn aside from the vital dynamic of the gospel message.

PART III

perspective from psychology

5

Preaching, Teaching and Reaching

One of the greatest dangers in all public utterance is the bland assumption that truth shared means truth communicated. We too easily equate telling with teaching, and listening with learning, often so anxious to cover a given amount of material that we are unconcerned about how much actually is received.

Unless a genuine rapport is first established, the proclamation of truth is ineffective; for real communication depends both on listener and on speaker. Again, facts may be transferred from speaker to listener as he views his congregation as a kind of mental sponge, able to receive these elements of truth and to return them when prodded, but genuine communication may still be missing if the impact of this theory does not issue in its practical application within the individual.

A small army of highly skilled personnel, together with millions of dollars, daily create commercial appeals to eye, ear, and heart, issuing them through the mass media of our secular society. These often unethical, and even immoral, communicators condition our whole culture. The average listener, who has little understanding of how to evaluate truth, can easily fall victim to techniques of persuasion and mistake his emotional responses for rational decisions. The freedom of man, said Christ, is bound up with the knowledge of the truth,[1] and this knowledge is bound up with a right hearing of it.[2]

Communications-theory is related to linguistics, sociology, and psychology; and it is by no means an exact science. There are, however, several key studies, with significant areas of agreement, which reveal some basic principles.[3] Likewise the creative process involved in sermon preparation cannot be reduced to a simple formula which will ensure success; but some principles can be defined, and some techniques must always be sought and applied.

There is a communications power inherent in the Holy Spirit's ministry,[4] and the use of the best possible tools and methods is not a refutation of this dynamic but a creation of such conditions as will make this more effective. An audience of several thousands needs public-address equipment in order to hear the speaker's words satisfactorily. Unless the technician hooks up the microphone, amplifier, and speakers, the good news simply will not be heard. Similarly, the art of preaching ability is always dependent on the technique which carries God's Word to the inner ears of those listening. Effective communications depend on valid media.

Communication is blocked by differences and by disunity.
Communication is aided by interest and by involvement.

COMMUNICATION BARRIERS

Differences in Mental Images

Part of the difference between personalities is the contrast

---

1. John 8:32.

2. John 8:32; Rom. 10:13-17.

3. A general and comprehensive treatment is given by Eugene A. Nida, *Message and Mission: The Communication of the Christian Faith* (New York: Harper, 1960); a simpler study for the preacher in a practical context is that by Reuel L. Howe, *The Miracle of Dialogue* (Greenwich, Conn.: Seabury Press, 1963), especially pp. 18-35; also Hendrik Kraemer, *The Communication of the Christian Faith* (Philadelphia: Westminster, 1956); Halford E. Luccock, *Communicating the Gospel* (New York: Harper, 1953); and James L. Sellers, *The Outsider and the Word of God* (New York: Abingdon, 1961).

4. See Leslie W. Sargent, "Communication and the Spirit," *Christianity Today*, 1 February 1963, pp. 15-17.

between each person's background, education, and environment. Concepts are common, only in so far as these elements are. Every congregation will have wide dissimilarities because of these factors, and the preacher's position will be often shaped by experiences quite different than those of his audience. Homiletic approach must, therefore, be cognizant of such a variety of attitudes and understandings that can block good communication.

The preacher will be speaking with many who are ignorant of the specific knowledge he possesses. He may address those whose views of religious truth may differ from his, or who may be opposed to him. Any speaker who assumes that his audience thinks and feels exactly as he does will always be wrong.

A Biblical preacher, beginning with the Christian understanding of God as Father, may cross a confusion of ideas in the minds of his hearers. Some will see God as an ineffective and benign creator, others as a stern tyrant, and some as mere impersonal force. Unless the preacher discerns such problems and plans for them in his presentation, his communication of truth will be obstructed by them. Our responsibility is to begin where people are, not where we assume them to be.

The great gulf that yawns between the Bible world and the twentieth century demands bridging. Some, like Bultmann, would have us rephrase the revelation by the exclusion of all elements except the familiar and those whose truth and value are scientifically demonstrable. The more conservative feel that a depth interpretation is preferable to such excision. The revelation of God in history has been set within a Hebraic context, amid a supernaturalism that must be retained for the expression of its full meaning. "Demythologizing" always reduces the message.

Because, however, we refuse to reduce the revelation of God is no excuse for ignoring the need to interpret it. We must combine an intimate knowledge of Biblical truth with a thorough familiarity with the environment and attitudes of twentieth century man as he is found in the local congregation. F. W. Dillistone comments:

> This is no easy task. To wrestle with three histories simultaneously—my own history within its social context, my brother's history within its social context, and the history of Jesus the Saviour of mankind within its social context—and

then to relate these histories to one another in such a way that a meaningful redemption and a relevant hope begin to be formed: here is a task hard enough to tax the resources of the strongest. Yet nothing less is involved in a comprehensive communication of the Gospel of Jesus Christ.[5]

If the speaker is rejected as a person, so is his message. Barriers can be created by poor enunciation, weak delivery, and bad physical mannerisms. An impersonal presentation, devoid of empathy, can encourage disinterest. The warm-voiced speaker, with his open personality, friendly smile, and constant eye contact with his audience may actually *be* no more in a deep relationship with them than is his absentminded, introspective, and note-bound brother. However, because he appears to be so, the audience may feel that he *is* more involved with them. Such feelings are open doors for the increase of communication.

There may be envy, or criticism, or other negative attitudes arising in an audience as reaction to a speaker — attitudes of which he may be unaware. If he holds a doctrine opposed to theirs and which they therefore consider erroneous, this can distort the ideas he presents, as they are filtered through prejudice and suspicion. Truths can be twisted into unrecognized caricatures of the proposed originals as they are received through such warped ideas. A speaker discussing social reform will need extraordinary care in his word choices if, for example, he is suspected of Communist sympathies. Innocent ideas and expressions can confirm prejudicial judgments unless he plans specifically to avoid them.

Communicator and receptor must participate in a common quest for truth. The natural defense mechanism of the listener's will may be stimulated if the speaker functions in a strongly authoritative and dictatorial role. Mental resistance to such technique is just as normal as the desire to return a physical punch to the one who assaults us. When a listener feels that his freedom to think and respond is being restricted, he can rationalize away the most constructive argument, often unaware that his reaction is based mainly on emotional grounds. He may be convinced that he is motivated by facts, when it may be by feelings. Even the

---

5. F. W. Dillistone, *Christianity and Communication* (New York: Scribner's, 1956), pp. 107-8.

minority who always blindly follow a strong leader carry an unconscious measure of rejection and annoyance, which may come out in later tensions.[6]

Differences in Verbal Symbols

The verbalization of our ideas reveals various factors that inhibit good communication.

Words are symbols. They are communications units, which are first discovered in the family relationships of the early years of life. Two persons, parent and child, agree that certain sounds will stand as symbols for objects or ideas. The audible word thus comes to represent the material unit or the concept being considered or communicated. As the child develops so does his vocabulary, and he senses some variety of meaning within certain words. It is only when the word symbol used stirs up the *exact* object or idea in the mind of the hearer as exists initially in the mind of the speaker, that we may say communication truly has occurred.

Words can be so badly chosen that they do not convey the true meaning as it is born in the mind of the originator. Words may be well chosen to convey their meaning as fully as possible and yet fail because, as they are filtered through the hearer's own understandings, their original weight of meaning may be limited or distorted.

The child who has an unhappy home life may respond to the word *father* out of the subconscious fears of his emotional associations. *Teacher* is a word that can stir feelings of resentment because of harsh discipline or other unpleasant memories. The shallow Christian can respond to the word *religion* as a comfortable habit; the committed Christian may respond to it with a sense of challenge. The unchurched may associate the concept of religion with fanaticism and irrelevance in a secular world. *Happiness* will have overtones of material affluence to most, of family and social bliss to many, and of sensual satisfactions to some. In this way personal emotional contents can rule out the basic Biblical ideas we often take for granted in the use of such

---

6. This dynamic has been shown in the studies of group behavior referred to in an earlier chapter.

words in preaching and teaching. Fatherly care, growth by guided experience, and joy in a personal relationship with God — the Biblical import of the first three italicized words above — can all be lost because they are not communicated clearly, although they may be clear in the communicator's own mind. The contentment of faith, entirely independent of circumstances, which is the Scriptural context of "happiness,"[7] is seldom if ever conveyed without detail exposition.

Just as the word *fast* can be a symbol for the idea of a speedy rate of physical transport, or for a dishonest way of making a smooth profit, or for a firm anchorage, or for a period of abstinence from food, depending on its context, so all meaning depends on emotional as well as grammatical surrounds. The simple hearing of words is not necessarily the same as the communication of the ideas which are involved.

Words are actually symbols of abstraction. They relate differences, and similarities. The total reality of one human personality has so many insubstantials that a full description cannot be completely reduced to words. *Woman* is a word which indicates a division of humanity. *The woman* gives individuality to the concept, and reveals to us that the subject under discussion is of adult age and feminine gender. An adjectival list added gives more distinction of the one concerned, marking her off from all others, such as *"the fine, educated, tall, smiling woman in the red dress."* We must keep adding more word-symbols to be aware of her disposition, family, interests, abilities, and all the other matters that fill out personality. But the only way to do complete justice to the human personality is to bring the woman into a face to face encounter with the listener. Yet even such a relationship gives no full revelation, immediately. The knowledge of another's personality is constantly enlarged over the years as a relationship develops and as understandings grow.

A material object, such as the book, the table, the chair, the house, and so forth, is easiest to understand; for each exists as a concrete and visible entity. The world of ideas is even more abstract than either the world of persons or the world of things,

_____

7. Phil. 4:11-13.

and communication at these levels is therefore the most difficult. It is most interesting to note how often ideas are communicated in Scripture through their identity with human experience. Biblical biographies link the intangible truths and principles of revelation with their outworkings in human personalities and relationships. The gap between abstract ideas and concrete realities is therefore bridged as the life situations of characters presented to us in Scripture make truth live in our minds with a greater force than is possible through any other medium. This is why some of the strongest points made in our sermons are often the simple illustrations of truth which come as we share our own personal experiences or segments of the life histories of others.

The tyranny of words as symbols also appears strongly in the church in some specialized vocabularies. Pious expressions, such as "washed in the blood," and technical descriptions of theological concepts such as being "born again," or looking for the "second advent," can also be confusing. These all have their proper place among the initiated; but, unless explained, they are mystifying to outsiders. This is where many traditional confessional creeds and liturgies break down. What may often have been good colloquial expression of truth centuries ago can be a communications barrier for the contemporary mind.[8]

Disunity Through Unclear Objectives

Disunities in discussion can hinder communication as much as differences in mental images and verbal symbols. Unless the listener can discern a clear progression of thought toward distinct objectives, it will be difficult for him to have much interest in the argument. The illogical and the unreasonable, in argument, are communications barriers.

The last words of Christ's great commission to the church, in Matthew 28, relate to the duty of teaching others *to observe* the things which He has commanded. Our discipleship responsibility remains unfulfilled unless motivation issues in direct application of

---

8. Good tradition can be simple escapism from relevant issues. Liturgy is valuable as the church's memory in a fixed form, but it needs constant revision and interpretation.

truth into right actions. Fosdick has summarized the need for preaching goals to be specific:

> The preacher's business is not merely to discuss repentance but to persuade people to repent: not merely to debate the meaning and possibility of the Christian faith in the lives of his listeners; not merely to talk about the available power of God to bring victory over trouble and temptation, but to send people out from their worship on Sunday with victory in their possession. A preacher's task is to create in the congregation the thing he is talking about.[9]

A pulpiteer may air a subject; this is lecturing. The greatest need is to aim a sermon; this is preaching.

While all preaching will have general objectives of instruction and inspiration, each sermon needs a specific goal and must be planned to lead toward its achievement. Andrew Blackwood recalls that the great Bible expositor G. Campbell Morgan insisted, to Princeton students, that preaching differed from teaching in that the former sought a movement of the will into action.[10] There is an analogy between sermon creation and human existence. Like men, sermons must have *skeletons.* These, though largely unseen, must be firm and strong to structure the body, and to correlate and unify its members. Warm, living *flesh* must clothe the physical man, just as art, imagination, and illustration will weave a covering to make the sermon's inner skeleton of truth presentable. Yet when all this is done, the man is still inanimate. He must now *live!* And so must the sermon! The whole point of physical creation is not for the beauty of a symmetrically designed, mechanically sound, well-organized, and unified production, but that this creation may *live!*

Our sermons then must take their place in society. Unless launched into the broad stream of life, proving their worth against the crosscurrents of evil that drag against them, they are something less than sermons. As Fosdick again affirms:

> A good sermon is an engineering operation by which a chasm is bridged so that spiritual goods on one side—"the unsearch-

---

9. Harry Emerson Fosdick, *The Living of These Days* (New York: Harper, 1956), p. 99.

10. Andrew W. Blackwood, *Biographical Preaching for Today* (New York: Abingdon, 1954), pp. 38-39.

able riches of Christ"—are actually transported into personal lives upon the other.[11]

The only objective in some preaching appears to be to occupy the traditional period in the worship service with the traditional function. Some endeavor a simple sharing of truth, aiming to cover a given curriculum of factual content. But preaching, by its nature, is never truly preaching unless these facts are presented with the aim of changing lives, influencing attitudes, and marching truth out into its most practical expressions within the personalities of the hearers. We can drive for wrong goals, or for poor ones, and we can present our truths unclearly or in a disorder which works against their promotion of the ends sought. All this disunity can affect the depth of our communication.

Disunity Through Irrelevant Presentation

When a logical objective is sought, yet where the presentation is hazy, perception will be marred. Attention cannot be enlisted or maintained, nor can a climax be created unless material that does not contribute directly to the promotion of the ends sought is deleted. Many who preach include comment about Scripture or the topic under discussion which may be valid but is unrelated to the specific objectives sought in that particular sermon. Others, who desire to appear profound, insist on taking their hearers into what they assume are "deep waters" (because they lose their intellectual footing), when, in truth, they simply cannot "see the bottom" for the mud.

For too long we have preached with too little appreciation of the nature and function of the sermon. It should be viewed as an instrument, in the hands of God, to reach out to the individual and to motivate his actions more perfectly into line with the divine will. Hearers must become so involved that they are lifted to new levels of personal growth and ability to apply the truths propounded. *The form of the sermon will therefore follow its function.* A clear skeleton, which exhibits continuity of thought and has concrete illustration of its application, is the primary essential. Its organization must lead progressively toward the ends

---

11. Fosdick, p. 99.

sought. Such unity is seldom accidental, but is normally the result of very careful planning. Without careful arrangement the usual variety of ideas that cluster around a theme, when developed over twenty minutes, will simply be confusing. A clear path must reach from introduction to conclusion. It must be discernible, relating the parts to the whole and the whole to the objectives involved. Halford E. Luccock illustrates this point with the comment:

> Some preachers follow the plan of Joshua's capture of Jericho. They seem to have implicit faith that if they march around the outside of a subject seven times, making a loud noise, the walls will fall down! They rarely do![12]

COMMUNICATION AIDS

Interest in Personal Benefits

On the positive side there are distinct elements of interest that can be enlisted to work for attention and impact. Many of these develop in proportion to the personal relevance of the learning experience. Where a recognized practical gain is in view the listener-involvement level is always largest. The whole philosophy of the marketing of consumer goods in our society is based on the benefit-consciousness of the average personality. We are vitally interested in a product when we are aware of its values for us.

Consciously or unconsciously each listener is asking himself such questions as "What is in this for me?" "What problem will this solve for me?" "What dividend will I gain from the application of this in my own life?" The preacher must, therefore, give attention to the early appearance of listener benefits within his sermon. His introduction may develop a problem to be solved or a value to be sought, and will share the conviction that he proposes to provide answers to these questions and means to secure these benefits. Thus the utility of a sermon can be one of its best elements for positive communication. In the most effective preaching, applications will not be introduced at the conclusion, but merely clarified from those already formed through the sermon's progressive revelation.

---

12. Luccock, p. 132.

Interest in Pleasurable Experience

An intrinsic interest arises naturally when the process of learning is itself enjoyable. Logical clarity, warm enthusiasm, humor , and nonbelligerence in the speaker — all these are elements that contribute to pleasure for the listener.

Every salesman knows that product enthusiasm is his most indispensable possession. If he has a deep knowledge of the product and a personal conviction about its ability to meet the needs represented in his customer's interests, he will have an assurance that is contagious because it will be genuine. Such conviction brings the maturity of experience as witness to the ignorance of those who seek to learn, and it is a pleasurable bridge for communication.

In his classic text on education Gilbert Highet asserts that a wide and lively intellectual interest in the areas that border a teacher's main subject creates this enthusiasm. [13] When a teacher himself lives at the absolute level of "interestingness" in the enthusiasm for his subject demonstrated before his pupils, a pleasurable communications optimism is established. This can only arise from a depth and scope of personal knowledge of his subject far above normal levels needed for instruction.

Illustrations always carry a content of pleasure interest. They sustain attention by underscoring the personal relation of the truth presented. Jackson writes:

> The sense of communication must be continually renewed or revitalized. Long-distance cable communication is made possible by boosters every few miles to increase the signal. What is true of distance in electrical impulse is also true of the intensity of a direct communication. It must have a booster every few minutes to keep it vital and alive.
>
> . . . a class, . . . employee, . . . audience listening has serious lapses of attention every seven minutes. The expert public speaker jerks attention back by telling a story, making a demonstration, or doing something unusual about every five minutes. Interest, action, or noise, will renew attention. [14]

---

13. Gilbert Highet, *The Art of Teaching* (New York: Random House, Vintage ed., 1950), pp. 48-53.

14. Edgar N. Jackson, *A Psychology for Preaching* (Great Neck, N.Y.: Channel Press, 1961), p. 19.

Involvement Through Needs

Audience participation is at its height where audience needs are involved. A dull subject comes into intensive focus when the listener recognizes the vital connection between it and his needs. Persons must discover, clarify, and express their true needs; and part of the value of a good sermon is that it reveals areas of need to the listener, thus enlisting his attention.

The parable of the sower could be more aptly titled the parable of the soils. By inference Jesus taught that we ought to know our ground and don't waste effort or seed where it will be unproductive. One cannot scatter truth haphazardly and then blame God for a poor crop. The successful farmer is the one who has studied how God works in nature, and who intelligently cooperates with Him. In spiritual life and growth, God works with persons meeting their needs. People are never aware of all their needs, and part of the preacher's responsibility is to lead his hearers into such recognition. Good collections of need-slanted preaching are available for study.[15]

Involvement Through Dialogue

Preaching ought to be a two-way relationship in which the sense of partnership between preacher and listener in a joint discovery of truth can stimulate interest and communication. In a class situation the listener can verbalize his questions and intimately share in the discovery of the truths being presented. In the pulpit the teacher-preacher must so identify with his congregation that he is able to voice their needs, ask the questions in his discussion which are arising in their minds as he speaks, and in their behalf pose the problems with which they are wrestling. As the voice of the body of Christ he represents the individual, as well as the group, and his response to this task by a dialogical attitude will challenge involvement and stimulate attention.

---

15. The works of Charles F. Kemp, such as *Life-Situation Preaching* (St. Louis: Bethany Press, 1956) and *Pastoral Preaching* (St. Louis: Bethany Press, 1963), are prime examples which present collections of sermons from numerous contributors, plus analyses of their nature and value. Helmut Thielicke's *How the World Began* (Philadelphia: Muhlenberg Press, 1956) is also a collection of material illustrative of this approach.

Every listener must first be contacted via familiar concepts. As he then shares in mutual discovery he will enter into the same experience which has created the preacher's conviction. As thought development progresses, listeners should be encouraged to think back and feel back, when they cannot actually speak back. Then, as the preacher expresses his responses and reactions to truths presented, in their behalf, they can feel the gears of their own minds meshing with the pulpit wrestling that is enacted before them. Preaching that argues opposing perspectives creates involvement. Because listeners become aware of the preacher's openness and honesty, they can participate more freely at mental and emotional levels; and communication is nourished.

Etymologically, "homiletics" has this very meaning. The root ideas of this word have to do with conversation and discourse, and with the kind of informal discussion that provides for questions and answers. *Homilos* (ὅμιλος)"a crowd," and *homileo* (ὁμιλέω), "to be in company with," or "to commune with," appear regularly in the New Testament.[16] In essence the continual explanation of a Scripture passage in literal dialogue is inherent in the whole New Testament concept of preaching.[17]

A balanced sermon will demand open and honest evaluation of opposing points of view and will seek to structure a logical atmosphere for change. Care must be taken not to force a listener into an intellectual or emotional corner from which his obstinacy will not permit him to move. This will happen when cherished ideals are smashed by such rough tools as biting sarcasm and unwarranted invective. Mature decisions are based on response to more positive and constructive approaches. Where the listener is courteously recognized as an individual, assured that the discovery of truth is the major aim, and permitted room to retain personal dignity while changing his viewpoint, there is the optimum chance of adjustment.

The preacher ought to operate on the principle that he is not forcing the acceptance of authoritative answers, but journeying

---

16. See Luke 24:14, 15; Acts 20:11; I Cor. 15:33.

17. See the integration of Paul's teaching methods of discussion with his preaching approaches as presented in the previous chapter.

with his listeners down a pathway (which he may have traveled before) that will end in the joint discovery of truth. Authoritarianism enlists dependents; our job as preachers is to create partners. The superior experience, knowledge, or resources of the preacher will always mean that some essential information must pass in direct declaration; but it is the visible attitude of sharing that is conveyed in the preacher's manner which is here the communications dynamic.

Hearers thus form personal convictions through such discovery which are far deeper than the strongest formed by dogmatic force. For a man's responses to be real and lasting, his convictions and actions must arise from insight rather than by intellectual or psychological seduction. In a fair and open climate sermons often rise to fuller heights than even their creators anticipate. Jackson describes this situation: "Sermons do not happen. They grow. They root in life, branch in experience, and blossom in that creative interplay of minds that is the ideal preacher-listener relationship."[18]

Sensitivity is a good summary word for our understanding of communication helps. One authority considers this attitude the base of all the rest.[19]

Modern studies in psychology have contributed much to our greater understandings of pastoral care, and therefore of preaching. Insights into the nature and growth of personality set out in many studies will help every preacher to be more sensitive in these areas.[20]

Communication, although a vital phase of preaching, is only one aspect of the total problem of motivation. It is easy to see

_____

18. Jackson, p. 37.

19. Leslie J. Tizard, *Preaching: The Art of Communication* (New York: Oxford, 1959), pp. 39-43.

20. The following summarize the most valuable insights: C. W. Brister, *Pastoral Care in the Church* (New York: Harper, 1964); John W. Drakeford, *Psychology in Search of a Soul* (Nashville: Broadman, 1959); Seward Hiltner, *Self-Understanding, Through Psychology and Religion* (New York: Scribner's, 1951; also in Abingdon Apex paperback edition); Paul E. Jackson, *Psychology of Pastoral Care* (New York: Abingdon, 1953); Samuel Southard, *Pastoral Evangelism* (Nashville: Broadman, 1963); and Lewis Joseph Sherrill, *The Struggle of the Soul* (New York: Macmillan, 1951).

what ethical problems arise in this whole field as we realize that when motivation becomes *manipulation* we have attacked the freedom of the human personality. The demagogue may secure an unwarranted response from a gullible audience, or similar promotion may come through the more subtle techniques of less obvious persuaders. Our next chapter discusses these dangers, and how to avoid them.

6
Motivation

Poor salesmen force sales for quick profits. The best salesmen lead prospects to see their genuine need for the product, and use this insight to motivate their sales

Preachers are representatives rather than salesmen.[1] We represent Christ, standing in His place as ambassadors proclaiming reconciliation.[2] Persons need to become aware of their need to become Christ-like through their meeting with transformed pulpit personalities. They are not to be forced into a Christian commitment through cleverly presented promotion. The preacher who sells salvation, *manipulates*. The preacher who presents genuine values, and guides their exchange for the benefit of his hearer, merely *motivates*. Manipulation involves force; motivation bases on insight.

What are the ethics of a valid motivation? Some feel a reluctance to interfere in any way with the lives of others. Honest men respect human personality and seek to avoid any persuasion

---

1. II Cor. 5:14-20.

2. II Cor. 5:14-20. See Craig Skinner, "What's My Line," *Christianity Today*, 5 June 1964, pp. 3-4.

of others because they believe this implies some coercion of their wills. They point to hysteria in the crowd and to hypnosis in the individual as examples of the ease with which personalities may surrender their wills to others. What guidelines can be drawn for difficult decisions in this area?

EMOTION

Human nature can respond to truth, or be motivated, by emotional as well as rational factors. Sentiments, ideals, and moods influence our actions and convictions. Physical experiences, mental associations, and pressures—real or imagined—can induce states of feeling that lift us to levels of response above those prompted by logic or habit. Every audience has the capacity to respond to a preacher with joy, sorrow, love, hate, pride, shame, jealousy, anger, and in a multitude of other emotional ways. Human emotion in the preacher can call forth an audience sympathy that creates a like feeling and experience. The application of proclaimed truth can create a vivid identification so that the hearer will experience the actual emotions of the character whose experience is being described.

The emotional aspects of human personality relate to man's immaturity as he enters this world, and to the history of human growth and intelligence. Emotions can be classified as trigger mechanisms which create automatic and essential responses when a crisis situation does not allow for thorough rational action. Such factors raise the arms in self-defense when the body is struck, turn us into a protective position when falling, and snatch back the hand from a scalding stream of hot water. In some measure they all root back to basic fears as well as to body nerve reactions. As a man progresses in intellectual capacity he becomes less and less of an emotionally directed being, and more influenced by rational concepts.

It is obvious that such pressures, in the hands of a skilled and unethical manipulator, can be used to force undesirable action. The propaganda policies of the Nazi regime in Germany in the 1930s bear witness to this, as does the Communist brainwashing technique of today.

Edgar Jackson has investigated such concepts of group reaction that involve emotional motivation, and demonstrates that any blame for negative and dangerous dynamics rests squarely on the group leadership, particularly in the local church situation.[3] Such false pressures can be removed if the pastor is aware of his group leadership responsibilities, and exercises them. The preacher, above many others, ought to have a fine sense of his leadership responsibility, and exhibit a healthy respect for the individual freedom of volition.

Jackson believes that modern group process study reveals a definite therapeutic value for the individuals in congregational association. Spiritual fellowship is a dynamic that assists the individual to gain objective insights and personality wholeness—values that seldom arise from individual introspection.[4] Deeper understandings and higher levels of interest are naturally created through participation with others in a joint search for truth.[5]

The Bible endorses these ideas. Love for Christ is the major motivation for Christian service, and Paul clearly declares that this lifts persons to new dimensions of judgment, personal righteousness, and transformed relationships, and that it arises directly from Christian worship and fellowship.[6] The convictions of others do influence us for good in our Christian association, as does the Scriptural record of the convictions of believers in earlier ages.[7] The fellowship of the redeemed community builds strength, and its regular avoidance saps our courage.[8] When not in active Christian fellowship we miss the stimulation to deeper love and good works, as well as the knowledge of spiritual cleansing,[9] and the increase of faith.[10]

---

3. Edgar N. Jackson, *A Psychology for Preaching* (New York: Channel Press, 1961), pp. 95-111.

4. Jackson, pp. 113-35.

5. Jackson, pp. 177-80.

6. II Cor. 5:14-17; Phil. 1:9-11; I Cor. 13; Gal. 5:22-23.

7. II Tim. 3:10-17.

8. Heb. 10:25.

9. Heb. 10:22.

10. Heb. 10:23.

Such motivations are natural and normal by-products of the experiences of worship and teaching in the Christian assembly. There are also factors of value in music, liturgy, or environment; but there are dangers here. As H. H. Farmer says:

I suspect that in the church many a man has mistaken the oscillation of his diaphragm in harmony with a ten-foot organ pipe, or the quivering of his heart strings to the melting sweetness of a boy's voice, for a visitation of the Holy Spirit.[11]

EMOTIONAL ABUSE

In recent years U.S. producers demanded a new approach to merchandising. The fabulous output of consumer goods had crammed warehouses well beyond normal customer demand. Advertisers responded by reexamination of the major appeals which motivate buying, and turned to depth motivational research for psychological answers that would stimulate consumption. They believed that by so doing they would increase general living standards, and therefore ensure a rising economy.[12]

A sense of psychological obsolescence was thus created among the buying public, whereby many were manipulated into believing that the purchase of certain goods was desirable, and even essential, without waiting for those on hand to wear out. Studies show that vast staffs of social scientists were recruited as consultants for practices which were often most unethical. A nightmare world of promotion, based on market surveys, conditioned reflexes, and other psychological pressures has resulted. Prestige firms and topflight advertising agencies became involved in questionable practices as the art of image building replaced reality projection. Purchase desires were openly aroused through the tapping of subsurface drives of human nature and the instincts basic to every personality.[13]

---

11. H. H. Farmer, *The Servant of the Word* (New York: Scribner's, 1942; paper ed., 1964), p. 52.

12. Vance Packard, *The Hidden Persuaders* (New York: David Mackay Co., 1957).

13. Packard; also Edward L. Bernays, *The Engineering of Consent* (Norman: University of Oklahoma Press, 1955).

This field of motivational research spawned sales campaigns often carefully calculated to create illogical loyalties. Highly technical studies were instituted to guide producers in appealing to emotional factors for the placement of their goods. *One study indicated that seven out of ten purchases by the average housewife, in the supermarket, came by direct stimulation.* Visual images in packaging were planned to generate this impulse buying, and quality was regarded as quite secondary to appearance. As the greatest proportion of family income was under the direct control of the average housewife, there were, as predicted, great gains from this approach.[14]

The fields of politics, management, and labor relations were also affected.[15] Ethics have improved greatly since the movement began, but applications of motivational research now appear in the plans for the development of "executive personalities" from the staff of some of the larger corporations. Some now hold that "biocontrol"—the actual shaping of human personality into predetermined channels through experiences in controlled situations, and similar social engineering feats—are probable in the near future. Today most large organizations employ personnel who are involved in continual in-service employee training. Many of these build a company image into their students which is based, in part, on insights from motivational research.

Do we have the moral right to manipulate the human personality in this manner? Disrespect for the individual and his freedom must always lie behind any advantage which is secured through his weaknesses. When subconscious stimulations are hidden, and where persons are guided toward unrevealed ends, this amounts to outright dishonesty. *But people cannot be easily forced if they are aware of the processes to which they are being subjected and the goals to which they are being led.*

EMOTIONAL USE

We need not be afraid of the right use of emotion just because of its abuse by some persons. Most psychologists are

---

14. Packard, pp. 105-6.

15. Packard, pp. 105-6.

prepared to accept the fact that the freedom of the will is limited and conditioned. No act performed by the individual in the present ever stands in isolation. In a greater or lesser degree it always relates both to the past and to the future. Responses are always partly influenced by our human natures, capacities, environs, and experiences.

This does not imply a closed and mechanical fatalism, but rather a simple and rational freedom, consistent with our humanity. Each man is convinced about his own absolute freedom of choice. Yet each can readily discern what he feels are limits operating in the lives of others. As our knowledge of ourselves is limited, it is sensible to assume that our free volition is not necessarily interfered with by the right use of emotion, although it may well be under the pressures of emotional excess.

Great force, required for brainwashing techniques,[16] seems absent, for example, in the air of almost cold detachment obvious in a Graham evangelistic crusade invitation. When hundreds of inquirers step forward in ball parks and other contexts inconducive to forceful pressure, such moves must be basically rational, yet also carry emotional content.[17] Men are not simple machines who ever have the power for cold, mechanical judgments based on facts alone, and divorced from all emotion. No decision by a whole person can ever be with the intellect alone; the rest of us votes in everything we do.

Advertisers long ago proved that the rational bases for action have no effect until attention, interest, and even desire are aroused through balanced emotional communication. Each effort to reach persons must therefore involve emotion as truly as it does intellect. It will not be unethical if it has within it also the grounds for valid rational response.

We violate human freedom when the normal processes of rational decision are short cut by clever, one-sided propaganda techniques, or other false psychology. The pulpit is committed to the task of changing lives and must therefore bend all its energies

---

16. John W. Drakeford, *Psychology in Search of a Soul* (Nashville:Broadman, 1964), pp. 241-68.

17. Drakeford, pp. 241-68.

to *responsible* involvement of persons with its goals. As we study what conditions action, and seek to promote it, we are looking for legitimate means to secure a response. The volitional choice presented to our hearers must be between *live* alternates, and emotion is part of that which gives a potential response its life.

We do not seek an uncritical assent then, but a rational one. We do not wish to compel by suggestion, but to persuade by logic. Our desire is to engender action through an appeal to legitimate feelings, knowing that the rational mind is not the only factor involved in choices made by a total personality. But it must be noted that we *do* seek an assent, that we *do* seek to persuade, and that we *do* propose a response. This can never be done without the right use of emotion. Sweazey affirms:

> There will be no great religion without great emotions. Jesus did not argue philosophy with people—He won their love. The heart is the antenna, the brain does the tuning. . . . Emotions which are not rightly used will be perverted. It was the sophisticated youth of the European Universities whose emotions were exploited by fanatical leaders. The youth of America will be saved from the emotional appeal of false religions only by the emotional appeal which is the Church's birthright.[18]

Our problem, then, is not to manipulate, but to *persuade.* We can motivate change, not by outside dictation, but through insight. We are to help each person gain a new inner perspective so that this reality will motivate his true being in the most natural and acceptable manner. Paul was determined to do just this. He had renounced the hidden things of dishonesty [19] and all deceitful craftiness, in an attempt to commend himself to every man's conscience. It was from this, and similar convictions, he insists, that he sought to persuade men.[20]

Persuasion is the normal environment of decision. No man knows enough about motivation to play on the human personality so as to secure unrestricted responses, much as a master musician would play an organ console and create the melodies he wills.

---

18. George E. Sweazey, *Effective Evangelism* (New York:Harper, 1953), p. 172.

19. II Cor. 4:1-2.

20. II Cor. 5:11 (an extension of the thought above).

Human motivation appears to be the product of mental processes beyond any definable appeal. Some of these barriers seem never to be pierced, except by accident.[21]

There is an inherent communication in the authority of the Biblical message as a divine revelation. The preacher seeks to lead others into a self-discovery of truth, and, while so doing, adds his personal witness to its declaration. His testimony is a valid emotional factor which promotes the acceptance by others of the same truth. The great New York lawyer Louis Nizer expresses his conviction about the inner awareness of the authority of truth from a perspective almost ours, when he says:

> I like to think that the scales which the blindfold figure of justice holds in her hands are the symbol of the scales within each of us. We weigh right and wrong, not by erudite legal processes, but by simple moral processes. . . . Whatever their source these moral standards . . . are the target of the persuader. . . . There is no limit to the resourcefulness and agility of the human mind when it is tipped by these inner scales.[22]

FACTORS OF VALUE

Persuasive preaching must carry the elements of honesty and reality if it is to be ethically valid.

Clear Objectives

In a previous chapter it was mentioned that unclear objectives can ruin *communication.* Here we emphasize that when these are clear they promote *persuasion.* We must know that the goal we seek is worthy, and ensure that it is clear to us. We must also reveal it clearly to those who are listening, as hidden or confused aims cannot create responsible decisions. If the listener is made clearly aware of our objectives, and of the processes of transit involved, he is protected from any manipulative assault. The expositor Morgan says of such purposeful preaching:

> The intellect and the emotions are highways of approach, and both should be employed. The one thing of which we need to

---

21. See Robert T. Oliver, *The Psychology of Persuasive Speech* (New York: Longmans, Green, and Co., 1942), especially the preface.

22. Louis Nizer, *My Life in Court* (New York: Pyramid Publications, 1963), pp. 606-7.

be constantly reminding ourselves is that we have never accomplished the real end of preaching until we have reached the will, and constrained it towards the choices which are in harmony with the Truth which we declare. [23]
He insists that such constraint is not manipulation but the use of mind and heart to create self-movement.[24]

Our listeners should be made aware that we are seeking their voluntary assent to deliberate choices, and that we openly seek their cooperation in making such choices on rational and emotional bases in proportion. Farmer calls this balanced sense of summoning claim in preaching an element that gives to it " . . . the quality of a knock on the door."[25] He feels that a case for such directness is inherent in the "I-Thou" relationship concept, popularized by Buber,[26] and that the direct encounter of will with will is essential for effective preaching. [27]

Balanced Reasoning

We may view an audience as "souls for the kingdom," or as persons open for a relationship that does justice to their total nature. When the individual is instrumentalized, and looked on simply as a unit useful for the upbuilding of the church, his potential for self-discovery is limited. Our arguments to convince him will balance best when we include factors which enlist the self-esteem of the personality as a productive force for change. As Farmer phrases it: "How can your will condition mine, so that my will remains free? It can do so only by confronting me with an inescapable claim."[28] The dialogue of conflict, mentioned in a previous chapter, where we deal with questions which listeners ask within themselves as we proceed, is both a communications dynamic and an aid to rational evaluation.

---

23. G. Campbell Morgan, *The Ministry of the Word* (New York: Revell, 1919), p. 207.

24. Morgan, pp. 207-8.

25. Farmer, p. 44.

26. Farmer, pp. 21-36.

27. Farmer, pp. 38-44.

28. Farmer, p. 27.

There is still a final responsibility which we may not recognize. This is that *the preacher has the right and duty to preserve a climate conducive to the right kind of response—emotional as well as intellectual.*

Through his ignorance, or by design, a preacher may abdicate from the field of influence and leave his listeners at the mercy of the evil pressures that always surround them. A zeal for neutrality may actually create a situation that inhibits right actions. This is a violence to human freedom just as severe as any extreme of manipulation.

Legitimate Appeals

Listener benefits enlist response. To refuse to list these, and to use all other legitimate appeals for action, is like stacking the fireplace with logs and expecting a fire without ignition. If we avoid the responsibility to influence for the right we do our hearers a gross injustice. The will of man is twisted into such a sinful bent that we need never be concerned that wrong influences will not have a fair hearing. Men have never needed much encouragement to sin, to reject the truth, to turn away from God, or to refuse to assume their responsibilities. *The support needed to enlarge the freedom of the will must come from the other side—from the side of influence for the right.*

Volitional choice is an act of preference: the choosing of one stimulus and the rejection of another. This choice of will is in response to a judicial verdict which is returned on the basis of the evidence offered. Without the use of every legitimate and persuasive word, without each rational argument and right motivation, the powers of evil will always lead man to choose the wrong side.

We are expected to reason from balanced perspectives, but not to smooth the path for the devil's work. When we avoid legitimate appeals we do the human will the injustice of forcing it to wrestle unfairly against the forces of evil, without the reservoirs of good impulse to which it also is entitled. Thus a refusal to permit the most constructive influences to operate conditions a wrong motivation for our hearers.

Current standards of society are lower than the Christian ideal. Persons need guidance into the specifics of commitment as much as they need instruction in the truths that undergird decision. This is the preacher's task. The complex moral situations of everyday life baffle men, and every congregation has the right to look to the preacher for pulpit, as well as private, counsel. We talk far too much in the pulpit about *why* persons should do certain things, and far too little on *how* these should be done, and helping them to begin. Sweazey comments on this matter:

> The fear that giving an invitation in a public meeting may lead people to do something for which they are not ready must be balanced against the fear that not giving an invitation may keep people from doing something for which they are ready. The last may well do the greater psychic and spiritual damage. To stir people religiously without giving them anything they can do about it leaves them far worse off than they were before.[29]

---

29. Sweazey, p. 173.

PART IV
practice

7
Objectives

As the voice of the body of Christ, the minister is to function within a basic teaching role, geared to the development of each member into the full exercise of his part within the total ministry of the church. Insights into the nature of the teaching-learning process, and understandings built from the psychologies of communication and motivation, blend to give us some practical applications within his pulpit tasks. The first pertinent area to which these useful values can be related is that of preaching objectives. These may be grouped as *needs* and *aims.*

NEEDS

Christ Met Needs

Jesus used the vivid forms of parable and metaphor. He enabled His hearers to visualize life-situation experiences that allowed problems and their solutions to display themselves with clarity. Consequently, although confused and annoyed by the wooden methods and irrelevant content of the teachings of the scribes, "the common people heard him gladly."[1]

---

1. Mark 12:37.

Truth was directly and vividly related to personal needs through such stories as the sower and the seed, the fisherman and the net, and many others. Christ's picture of the Pharisee gulping down a camel, yet choking on a mosquito, illustrated as little else could the wholesale swallowing of legal formalities no matter how ungainly, and the protesting splutter at a good work because it was performed on the Sabbath. Thus the feelings of His hearers were focused and right responses motivated through analogies which took living forms before them.

Sometimes Jesus set out to meet the direct needs of His listeners, using their own specific vocalized wants as His teaching bases. His best-known prayer was given in response to a request to be taught to pray. The Good Samaritan parable came in answer to "who is my neighbor," and that of the unmerciful servant in response to Peter's inquiry in relation to this specific need. His teachings were delivered in answer to the questions of the theologians concerning His authority. He discussed the problems they raised about the nature of heaven, the relative value of the commandments, and many others.

At other times He taught from His own insight into the unfelt or nonverbalized needs of His listeners. Christ understood men, and His teaching was able to reach them. It was in contrast to the dry, traditional Hebrew teachers, because it carried the authority of insight. Consequently, when He taught, the people were "lifted out of themselves."[2] They reacted in excited involvement because the person-relatedness of His teaching was so evident. All of this is part of the relation of His teaching to their real needs.

Perhaps the greatest temptation Jesus ever faced, as a human teacher, was the desire to issue a crash course in theology as He was about to leave the disciple band. Knowing their weaknesses, and His imminent departure, He longed to say many things but refused to, declaring, "Ye cannot bear them now."[3] He realized that His curriculum had to be conditioned by their most urgent needs. They felt as orphans in the awareness of the isolation and

----

2. Matthew 7:29; Mark 1:22.

3. John 16:12.

loneliness that possessed Him at the sense of His going. So He turned to teach of the coming of the Holy Spirit, of His comforting presence and fellowshipping ministry. This pressing need was here placed above His own personal desire to share other, deeper truths. Teaching must always be an experience where the provisions of God march arm in arm with specific listener needs.

Discovering Needs

To discover human needs, the preacher must grasp something of both the mystery and mastery of life. He will capture special days and occasions—like Christmas, Easter, anniversaries, and dedications—to serve the purposes of his ministry and to meet relevant seasonal needs. The in-built interest that surrounds such occasions always provides factors of relevance and communication.

But needs may vary greatly. The rurally oriented congregation and the university related one will have different preaching demands. Their specific interests will vary widely from those who live, with their families, in the affluent suburbs. Varieties in environment, education, and experience in the congregation should always blend to shape the preaching program.

The first basic rule is to preach to ourselves. Let the preacher ask himself, "What are *my* individual and personal needs? What is there in faith, inspiration, knowledge, and conduct-response that will minister to *me?*" As a person the minister will find that in serving his own needs he usually is ministering to what is common to most men. The more he knows of himself, the more he will be aware of the needs of others.

We must also remember that *there are ages and stages of maturity.* Adults in the congregation will have different hungers and values than those of the children. Young people live in years of momentous decision, wrestling with their developing personalities and the mysteries that challenge the growing intellect. Young marrieds will be struggling with the family responsibilities, the building of their homes, and the development of their vocations. The approximately 10 percent within the average congregation who are retired or inactive will be facing economic and emotional tensions amid often cheerless days and empty years, which need a special quality of living to be worthwhile. The great bulk of the congregation, probably in the late twenties through the early fifties, will be enmeshed in the personal tensions, wild excitements, crushing disappointments, and other oscillations that come with contemporary living. In addition, they will often also be wrestling with marital adjustments and other personal relationship pressures. Often the best workers are the least served from the pulpit.

Therefore preaching about the afterlife, on maturity in spiritual growth, on difficult Bible passages, and concerning restful peace in situations which need acceptance when they cannot be changed, will have special relevance to older persons. Children will always discover truth easiest via a story, and they need especially to know what values can be found in Christian faith and witness in their junior world. Youth needs a dramatic challenge, some vital cause to espouse, and a graphic presentation of alternates and their consequences. Young people will respond to valid personal testimonies, as well as to sensible guidance in the areas of vocation and marriage. They need room to stretch their minds, assert their independence, and forge their own faith. Young adults are the most gregarious in fellowship and most responsive to conformity patterns among their peers. They are particularly concerned about the material and physical needs of themselves and of humanity.

The needs of persons can also be *grouped by association.* All homes have the need for daily worship, for prayer, and for family living for Christ. Persons need specific guidance and encouragement in such activities. Edgar Jackson claims that, at any one time, one-third of a congregation will be operating under a critical point of family strain.[4] Therefore the stresses, problems, pressures, and personal decisions of life will always have relevance. Each human being is subject to failure in emotional adjustments, to real or imagined feelings of guilt, to senses of inferiority or of pride and unwarranted confidence. All men search for assurance of forgiveness, for reinforcement to right actions, and for insight and understanding in complex situations.

Needs also have a direct relation to attitudes. Spiritual commitment may vary with the season, the weather, or the social

---

4. Edgar N. Jackson, *A Psychology for Preaching* (New York: Channel Press, 1961), p. 76.

pressures of congregational environment. Some will have deep demands forged by economic needs. Particularly the underprivileged and the overspoiled, materially, will have defensive attitudes toward each other and themselves which need Christian adjustment.

Many are indifferent neutrals in spiritual things. They choose what is seemingly advantageous, or personally appealing, in doctrine or experience, and feel little sense of duty or responsibility in the things of faith. They can be won by constant and sincere exposure to the truth, by attitudes of friendship, and by enlistment into some small decisions and service where they achieve success.

Others have plain hostility. This needs careful handling, as it may be hidden as well as open. When a fair and honest confrontation of opposing views is presented, with open acknowledgment of truth appearing on all sides, such persons can be reached.

In overcoming hostility it must be remembered that the average person, even the ordinary Christian, will become antagonistic if he is cornered, or deeply embarrassed. He will defend his reputation be it pseudo or real. Every person, even one's closest friend, has the potentiality of becoming ferocious, and of fighting his opponent to the bitter end. He may do so with sweetness, deceit, intrigue, lies, gossip, open attack, or in any other way which seems expedient to him at the time. Expediency is the first law of life for most of the people, most of the time.[5]

Pearson says the average congregation is characterized by attitudes of ignorance, hunger for spiritual truth, and by the restlessness of the age; and it suffers from the unrecognized results of sin. He affirms there is a great lack of doctrinal understanding and of conviction, and that this is compounded by the fragmentation and imbalance which must always be present among a large group of persons. Such attitudes always prevail in any congregation, in general, even alongside of the better ones in the lives of those who are steadfastly growing in Christ.[6]

---

5. John Edward Lantz, *Speaking in the Church* (New York: Macmillan, 1964), p. 108.

6. Roy H. Pearson, *The Ministry of Preaching* (New York: Harper, 1959), pp. 104-8.

Farmer sees this generation as one that is searching for meaning in existence, desiring a sense of God and an alignment with His purposes. Feelings of personal insignificance weigh on all men, along with basic senses of insecurity.[7] The force of evil is recognized and feared, and answers to its power are sought. Amid life's changing values every man yearns for some fixed absolutes. He will respond to the Christian answers of divine purpose in eternity, and to the reality of personal fellowship with God. Our task is to reveal the love of God as adequate and redemptive, and to share the peace brought through atonement and by abiding in fruitful discipleship.[8]

Insight into needs may come from many spheres of knowledge, but the revelation in Scripture must be a major source. The role of the preacher as prophet is declared by one authority as demanding that the minister have an insight into history so that he "knows enough of the past to interpret the present, and weigh the meanings of present action."[9] Such a sense arises naturally from a study of Scripture. The ministry must not focus on helping persons in personal adjustments alone. This may lead to a neglect of challenge to the established order, and even to the acceptance of wrong concepts and pressures.[10] The Bible, with its breadth of vision and revelation ranging over the whole history of man, the eternal world, and the kingdom of God, will deliver us from too narrow a concept of human needs. The sermon can be only a kind of glorified emotional and spiritual headache cure unless it deals with the eternal principles and issues which the Bible discusses—principles and issues that are often more truly the genuine needs of man than his felt symptoms are.

Harry Emerson Fosdick struggled desperately in learning how to preach, and was thrust toward his monumental ministry by the discovery of the needs and interests of his congregation. He was

---

7. H. H. Farmer, *The Servant of the Word* (New York:Scribner's, 1942; paperback ed., 1964), pp. 96-104.

8. Farmer, pp. 104-8.

9. Jackson, p. 207.

10. Jackson, pp. 216-22.

led to this discovery through his experiences in personal counseling, with the revelations of human nature found there.[11] He says:

> People come to church on Sunday with every kind of personal difficulty and problem flesh is heir to. A sermon was meant to meet such needs; it should be personal counseling on a group scale. If one had clairvoyance, one would know the sins and shames, the anxieties and doubts, the griefs and disillusionments, that filled the pews, and could by God's Grace bring the saving truths of the gospel to bear on them as creatively as though we were speaking to a single person. This was the place to start—with the real problems of the people.[12]

Fosdick's error was that he not only started with such genuine human needs, but he often *remained* with them. As detailed elsewhere in our study,[13] this life-situation preaching failed when it did not take into account the truths of divine revelation as fully as it should have. Consequently, it became, at the last, an almost humanistic philosophy—a little self-help psychology, with some Christian overtones.[14]

Paul summarizes it well when he says that those who have the spiritual oversight of a congregation should both know themselves and their flock, in order to be good providers for the people.[15] To this comment he added also the need to know *didache*, or the doctrine revealed in Scripture.[16] If we know ourselves, our people, and the revelation of God, we will minister effectively, because we will be setting true needs as primary objectives.

Pastoral care will discover needs. The knowledge of the "trinity" that Luccock phrases as that of "Tom, Dick, and Harry" can help us know needs. A pastor cannot know the true needs of

---

11. Harry Emerson Fosdick, *The Living of These Days* (New York: Harper, 1956), pp. 92-113.

12. Fosdick, p. 94.

13. See chap. 2.

14. Fosdick, p. 94.

15. Acts 20:28.

16. I Tim. 4:16.

persons only in the abstract; he must study human nature through his regular pastoral ministries. Sangster declares:

A preacher must know *people*. No amount of mastery of books can make up for not knowing people. One of the elements in powerful preaching is the skill some men possess to leave people feeling they have wandered through them with a lighted candle. "He showed me all my heart." Often it is done by an aside, a passing reference, an overtone. But all life seems open to such a preacher. The swelling passions of youth, the secret rationalisations of sin, the fingering of evil, the fear of the future, the fight against cynicism, the polluted springs of action—he knows it all. How? From his own nature no doubt, but also from his uncommon knowledge of people. Who received more confidences from men and women? To whom do people more completely reveal themselves? Whose eye is fixed most frequently on the microscope which magnifies our secret motives? The man who has walked through the hospital of souls.[17]

Kemp views the pulpit as almost entirely a precounseling relationship between pastor and people. It is, for him, unique in the opportunity given for regular and systematic discussion of the issues of life. He feels that persons who respond to pastoral counseling in life's crises do so because they have been ministered to in terms of their normal needs through regular pulpit service. They act or react toward their pastor as their previous association with him has conditioned them. The pulpit challenge and comfort is preventive medicine, as well as therapy.[18]

Hospital calling, home visitation, and other methods of pastoral care are not the only ways in which we discover needs through pastoral experience. The pastoral orbit is not, by itself, intimate enough to enable us to hear our people in depth, and share their joys and sorrows in the greatest reality. This requires *living* with them also.

It is the preacher's identity with the congreagational life that helps him to know needs. The teacher who will not desert his ivory tower, and will not work and play with his pupils, can never

---

17. W. E. Sangster, *The Approach to Preaching* (Philadelphia: Westminster, 1962), pp. 76-77.

18. Charles F. Kemp, *Pastoral Preaching* (St. Louis: Bethany Press, 1963), pp. 29-38.

reach them as he ought. The pastoral role requires a degree of separation in some areas of life, but a difference of life style that places us too far off from the normal patterns of congregational vitality cannot yield the insights which are essential for valid ministry. Natural illustrations will arise as the pastor walks beside his congregation in everyday situations. An inbuilt empathy and sincerity can arise naturally from such intimacy with our people.[19]

Highet's classic textbook on teaching lists the axioms of successful education as basing on the educator's knowledge, interest in his subject, and appreciation for the privilege of helping others know it.[20] Highet also considers that the depth of teacher involvement in the pupil's emotions and thought patterns governs good teaching. Social fraternity gives opportunity to listen so as to understand pupil motives and convictions, helping us also to discern needs. It can be asserted that all human beings can group into definable types of personality, and this knowledge, along with a familiarity with patterns of human relations psychology, can be a ready vehicle for our deepening understandings.[21]

Surveys help us to know needs. Questionnaires and other research procedures are always helpful. Vocational and leisure interests, relationships, environment, home background details, and hundreds of other characteristics can often be discovered in no other way. In the aggregate we are able to chart population facts and trends, neighborhood distinctives, and community aspects which shape and color the life of the congregation. Purposes can be selected and programs can be planned on these bases.

There are materials on file in local church records that can be used to chart progress (or its lack), and therefore to highlight needs. Intelligent programing is built by prognosis of the charted history of a church numerically, economically, and spiritually; and extensions of these present successes or failures into the future

---

19. Jackson, p. 202.

20. Gilbert H. Highet, *The Art of Teaching* (New York: Random House, 1950), pp. 8-33.

21. Highet, pp. 34-40.

reveal the depth of various needs. This is also so in preaching. If the need for sermon selection is partially channeled through congregational choices, they will interact and respond with interest.[22] Subjects, texts, and problems on which specific sermons are requested, can be placed on the agenda for preaching, as the church calendar, preacher's disposition, and divine guidance may indicate. Nothing has quite the impact or relevance for a local congregation, or preacher, than a series of request sermons. The preacher will prepare with a real sense of vital interest as he is assuredly preaching to meet defined needs.

God guides us to needs through prayerful concern. Besides our study of our people, and our life with them, we must pray for them. The nature of prayer is somewhat of a mystery, and the finest attempts of theology leave it still somewhat barren of complete explanation. We are taught in Scripture, however, that prayer is essential; and we note its significance in the ministry of all the great leaders of the Bible, including the great pastor, Christ, and the model pastor, Paul. Certainly prayer opens channels for the movement of the Holy Spirit; and, from the cyclic quality exhibited in the Lord's Prayer of Matthew 6, it would seem that prayer is a link we forge with the will of God, and with its fulfillment in and by us.[23] We recognize our relationship with the heavenly Father, line up our desires with His, and seek to make His kingdom come, by making His name holy. We pledge our partnership in these tasks, and what we pray for is often brought to pass through our own responses. Prayer, then, is the place where we fuse our wills with His and where He meets us in grace, molding us into instruments working with Him to achieve the ends desired. We dare not abandon prayer simply because we do not understand it fully, when we have direct command for its

---

22. Three such surveys, which I conducted in different pastorates, brought avid congregational interest. An intriguing sidelight was the bulk of requests for some sane exposition about Biblical teaching on the afterlife, heaven, hell, and general eschatology. This seems to indicate a deeper interest in, and need for, preaching in these areas than would normally be thought to exist. It is an area of concern to many mature Christians; but, unfortunately, little is usually available to them except the wild extremism of many of the false cults.

23. This, of course, is really the "disciples' prayer," our Lord's prayer being that in John 17.

continuity from Christ, and endorsed by His followers.[24] God will reveal needs as we wait on Him in prayer. He will often do this best as we pray back to Him the truths revealed us through our study of Scripture, and as we ask for the understanding of its relation to us and to those to whom we must preach.

AIMS

The needs of persons form targets for which the preacher may aim. The worship service should be designed for the transfer of relevant truth about God, as well as for the expression of love to Him. Liturgy, architecture, and music can all carry this dual significance, and so can the sermon. Unfortunately, however, a preacher may operate in the presentation of his sermon like a supermarket. From the moment he begins, listeners may be aware that he is not at all interested in home delivery. Facts and truths may ring up in multiplied confusion, and be bundled together as a heterogeneous load with which the hearers are expected to stagger away and sort out for themselves. *People will do this with groceries, but home delivery is essential for a sermon.* We consistently demand the careful and individual placement of each idea in its logical order on our own home shelves. Sermons must be delivered where people *live!*

Values of Aims

Many a preacher does not know what he is producing in his preaching until he has finished—and even then some are unsure! We must identify our purposes through clarity of aims. Every subject needs boundaries and limits so that unity and strength may be gathered to sweep hearers to new insight and experience within the confines of its exiguity. A congregation set afloat on a vast sea of thought, equipped with everything but a rudder and a sense of destination, will not only fail to complete the voyage but will also find the experience frustrating and enervating.

Failure in every department of life is linked, inextricably, with slovenly aims and unclear goals. Only as the preacher decides just what it is he desires the congregation to know, feel, be, or do,

---

24. Mark 11:24; Luke 18:1; I Thess. 5:17; I Tim. 2:8; etc.

can he lead them to achieve such ends. His sermon must be characterized by a balance and harmony in its component parts that will contribute to a logical and spiritual momentum, climaxing in a commitment to the goals presented.

An evident sense of purpose is also the best aid to all teaching and learning. Persons work most effectively when they are aware of that toward which they are headed. Without clear aims it is impossible to decide what is to be taught, how to teach it, or when learning has been achieved. Good aims thus stimulate teacher and pupil, and give meaning and clarity to every educational situation, including that of preaching.

General Aims

As the preacher aims to produce development in persons rather than mere sermons, his general purposes may relate to the activation of attitudes already present in the lives of his hearers but lacking in outward application. His drive may often be to focus hazy convictions by their reinforcement, until they reach a point of new significance. He will seek to increase levels of commitment to, and interest in, old truths. He will develop the understanding of what is new and until now undiscovered by his hearers.

But the goals that hearers have in mind as they listen may be quite different than those of the preacher. Motives for listening to sermons include habit, loyalty, desire for theoretical information, and respect for traditional authority. Simple needs for emotional experience, plus normal curiosity about what is unknown, will also regularly be present. All of these can be used as valid introductory approaches to meet the deeper and more primary needs.[25] The ministry of the Spirit is needed for the discernment of true personal needs by the hearer.[26]

Paul gives a clear description of the elements in his own

---

25. See Roy H. Pearson, *The Preacher: His Purpose and Practice* (Philadelphia: Westminster, 1962), pp. 89-107, for a good summary of some general purposes expressed under apposite Biblical quotations.

26. Such as conviction about personal sin, judgment, and needs, as indicated in John 16:7-13.

preaching related to general goals. I Corinthians 14:3 is particularly significant, as he here asserts that the preaching which arises from the desire to edify, encourage, or console is preferable to any ecstatic utterance in an "unknown tongue." The words used, *oikodomen* (ὀικοδομήν), "edification," *paraklesin* (παράκλησιν), "encouragement," and *paramuthian* (παραμυθίαν), "consolation," form a similar cluster in I Thessalonians 2:11-12, where he repeats the later two aims and adds *marturomenoi* (μαρτυρόμενοι), "witness" or "testimony," as a fourth. The context of this Thessalonian passage is that of a pattern of *didache* that enables Paul to fulfill a father's role, maturing his children into a manner of life worthy of the kingdom. [27]

We may, therefore, list the apostolic preaching as having the following four general goals: [28]

1. *To inform or enlighten. Marturomenoi* means "a sharing of information for the hearer's understanding." It suggests a witness's declaration of the truth. Every sermon carries this instructional and testimonial content. It is most evident in doctrinal sermons, Scriptural expositions, and other addresses which center on the interpretation of the Biblical revelation.[29]

2. *To inspire of comfort. Paraklesin* moves a step further, declaring this truth as "called alongside" human need. This is application, and is one step above enlightenment. It carries a devotional quality of comfort that uplifts the meaning of the truth declared into *specific* relevance for the hearer concerned. As the relation between the information and the personal need of the hearer is declared, there is a rise of faith and interest. Such

---

27. I Thess. 2:9, 11, 12.

28. See fig. 2, p. 137.

29. The object of Charles Dickens's *Tale of Two Cities* was for us to identify with the feeling of terror and tension created by the French Revolution, rather than of merely informing us about the facts of this historical event. So Shakespeare's *Macbeth* seeks to put the reader through emotional experiences engendered by the plot and its movement. Information or enlightenment in stories such as the above is but incidental to the author's goals. The inspiration or significance of meaning can, however, arise only when a knowledge of the facts which govern them is first shared. What is true in these secular illustrations is likewise true in spiritual ministry. There can be no inspiration without instruction, no significance without enlightenment.

preaching inspires and comforts by its specific application.

3. *To motivate or appeal. Paramuthian* carries the sense of a direct stimulus to action even further. The continuity of along-sidedness, arising from witness to the truth, and its specific significance to the hearer concerned is taken further with the assurance that this practical relevance can be real through a commitment to it. This life-changing persuasive element was clear in Paul's own preaching, and he declares that the Old Testament history and biography were given to us for these purposes.[30] Christ always emphasized that the words spoken by Him were not empty additions to the store of facts which life daily provides, but that they themselves were "life." They were given to live, to create understanding, to interpret experience, and to stimulate growth.[31] From beginning to end in Scripture, the truth of God is revealed, then related to need, and then used to structure the appeal to the will for moral action.

4. *To edify or develop. Oikodoman* is plain "upbuilding." As an edifice is brought to completion by a regular progression of constructed stages, so the individual disciple is to be built toward maturity. The character is to be shaped and fashioned more and more into the image of Christ. This is preaching's highest objective, and is mentioned in the Ephesians 4 passage, and again as the preacher's personal goal in the Philippians comment of 3:12-21.

The selection of attainable and measurable segments of growth to which persons may commit themselves will help build a Christian personality. Such specific and precise possibilities arise from general goals listed in figure 2 as *information, inspiration, motivation,* and *edification.* The process is outlined in the first three steps. The fourth step of specific commitment arises from the others. It lifts life to a new level and, as it becomes part of the regular cycle of growth, it promotes ultimate maturity. A full likeness to Christ awaits our conformity to His image in the life to come,[32] but edification ought to progress through a regular development under preaching which holds these goals.

---

30. I Cor. 10:11.
31. John 5:24; 8:12; 6:33; etc.
32. Rom. 8:28-30; I John 3:1-2.

Information foundations all progress, and each step increases in difficulty. A sermon planned to edify and mature the hearer must include knowledge, inspiration, motivation, and some specific challenge to a step of active commitment of the will into a new level of discipleship.

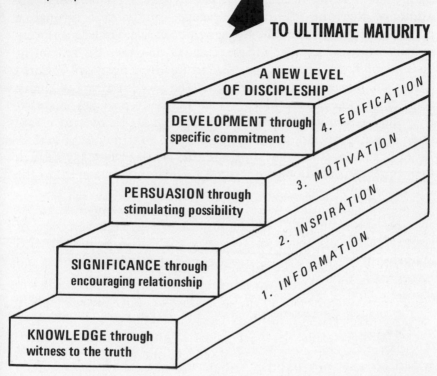

FIGURE 2: *Preaching steps that build increasing levels of spiritual life.*

Specific Goals

A specific aim is an accurate expression of our intended achievement within an individual sermon. It will avoid the experience of a twenty-minute period when only high ideals are discussed, and will bring relevance between preacher and hearer. Psychology affirms that most changes in patterns of human behavior occur in specific rather than in general areas. General changes are composite from sharp applications within many particular areas. A principle comes to new force and priority in a life as it arises inductively through a series of practical changes in attitudes, and in their results.

It is possible, therefore, to direct a sermon explicitly at the first general aim of information or enlightenment. Thus a sermon could be directed to "share Paul's understanding of love as shown in I Corinthians 13." The significance of this truth can be related by extension to an inspirational aim, such as "to show the value of the attributes of love in our own lives from I Corinthians 13." The second aim sets the plain truth of the first in deeper perspective as it encourages the hearer to perceive its personal relation.

The aim could be further strengthened by a persuasive element forming a direct stimulus to action through motivation. It could then be expressed as "to show how to apply the principle of love expounded in I Corinthians 13 in daily life."

The aim would be most specific where it focused onto a particular conduct response in a spelled out life situation. So it could be expressed as "to show the application of love, as expressed in I Corinthians 13, within family tensions." A concrete illustration of a family disagreement, with the bitter and unkind words and actions detailed, could be used as context in which to set the revealed attitudes of selfishness and hate. In this manner stage could be set for distinct and specific growth. This may need to include literal instruction, such as the need to pause to pray for power to speak and act in a Christian manner within this situation, and to claim the power of the Holy Spirit for its application.

Each aim for the individual sermon ought to be *brief* enough to remember, *clear* enough to be written down, *specific* enough to be measured so that its achievement may be recognized, and *related* enough to the total preaching program and everyday life of the listener to be of value. As Clarke has said, preaching aims to raise the dead and to make persons "alive at more points, alive at higher levels, alive in more interesting, worthy, and effective ways."[33]

Jesus did not die for ideas, for truth, or even for society, but for persons. The gospel then moves around the twin foci of both the needs of the kingdom and the needs of the individual. The promotion of particular and individual conduct response has its social implications as the shape and behavior of society is molded by the human unit. Personal growth is therefore a movement toward our collective, as well as individual, edification.

Specific aims always relate to personal commitment. It is within the sermonic conclusion that the threads of revealed application wind together, and a distinct delivery of persons over to the fulfillment of the goals promoted is possible.[34] The idea of a sermonic thesis, logical structure, and clear divisions, as detailed in chapter 9, seems to be one of the best methods for ensuring that specific aims are not sabotaged by vague and shallow reasoning or fuzzy presentation.

---

33. James W. Clarke, *Dynamic Preaching* (New York: Revell, 1960), p. 65.

34. See chap. 9.

8
Planning

The sermon is the final act in a process attempting to communicate spiritually, intellectually, and emotionally, the great bulk of which has been completed within the four walls of the preacher's study. The quality of this final segment always roots back to both the veracity and appeal of the original sermonic idea, and to the amount and character of the preparatory attention it has received.

APPROACHES

A major factor in all sermon planning is the preacher's basic approach to his pulpit situation. Each sermon will begin with an idea or subject, chosen from the Bible, from life, from literature, or from personal experience. Three traditional approaches have been customary since the 1500s.

Topical Sermons

These seek to bring many thoughts into a vital relationship with one single theme or idea. A subject, lifted from Scripture or elsewhere, is discussed in association with truth concerning it gleaned from a multitude of areas; and the whole is given some contemporary application in relation to personal needs. Topical preaching has the inherent tendency to be somewhat shallow and untrue to the total perspective of truth. There is also the temptation to express the preacher's personal views without a complete Biblical frame of reference. Nevertheless this approach has been used by some of the most effective preachers of history, and should form a part of every pulpit program.

Textual Sermons

These are very common. A text, phrase, or word is selected from Scripture which gives basis and authority for the message. A text is a good anchor for audience attention, and helps them to recall truths taught concerning it. A text likewise keeps the preacher on the track of his main purpose, helping him to avoid side issues. There is the danger of a temptation to make very mechanical divisions by breaking the text into segmented thoughts and portions which allow an ease of sequence in treatment. This can permit a lifeless type of discussion which concentrates too much on the diamond without its setting, and may miss real and vital meanings only discernible through a relation to its context.

Expository Sermons

These seek to expose the meaning of a text or passage within its context. They often take a theme or idea given in Scripture and interpret the truth there viewed in the light of the total Biblical revelation. No other method of sermonic approach is so demanding on the preacher, nor bases so firmly on detail exegesis. There is, however, great confusion as to what true expository preaching does involve.

Some feel that this is a *method* which can be applied in any sermon. Others feel that it has a definite relation to the size of the passage selected for discussion. One of the leading authorities, after listing the views of twenty others well known in the field, affirms that expository preaching is never a running commentary without an outlined unity. Such an informal and rambling style, however exegetical, can give only surface interpretation, and always lacks the persuasive drive that every sermon needs.[1]

---

1. Faris D. Whitesell, *Power in Expository Preaching* (Westwood, N. J.: Revell, 1963), pp. vii-viii.

Whitesell defines true exposition as involving the following:

1. It is based on a passage in the Bible, either short or long.

2. It seeks to learn the primary, basic meaning of that passage.

3. It relates that meaning to the context of the passage.

4. It digs down for the timeless, universal truths stemming out of the passage.

5. It organizes these truths tightly around one central theme.

6. It uses the rhetorical elements of explanation, argument, illustration, and application to bring the truth of the passage home to the learner.

7. It seeks to persuade the listener to obey the truth of the passage discussed.[2]

All three perspectives are valid, but the pastoral preacher will find exposition his most satisfying as well as most productive approach to the task of functioning in a teaching role within his pulpit task.

MATERIALS

The unbelievable productivity required from the faithful local minister has to be calculated to be understood. A twenty-five-minute sermon will use about three thousand words. This done three times a week will total some half million words per year. Where sermons are written or typed out several times, this figure increases in proportion. It is obvious that no average preacher can give every sermon the kind of attention deserved for a production twice the length of the average magazine article, although all will tackle certain addresses even more thoroughly at times. The pastoral preacher has many other duties that press on him for attention besides sermons; yet even the once-a-week preacher, if he prepares well, will tackle a responsibility above that which any average journalist would care to assume as an everyday full-time task in areas which require above average intellectual capacity.

The wise preacher, therefore, spends his time in the planting

---

2. Whitesell, p. xv.

of sermon seeds and in nourishing their growth. He reserves his hours of weekly sermon preparation to the harvesting of the fruit from his earlier and continuous labor. When can the farmer go each week and expect a crop? Only when he has sown week by week, and watered and cared for what he has planted, so that a rotation is assured for regular market delivery.

It is impossible to expect to plant, water, and harvest, all within the one week. Working at long range relieves pressures of urgency which can paralyze the mind. This creates a reservoir of familiarity with the subject which gives a fulness of power in presentation. The preacher who customarily faces the horror of a crossroad without direction signs late every Saturday evening can find relief only through a program of extended planning. We may in this manner spend time in studying a subject, rather than in searching for one, when the demands of production are on us. Jefferson observes:

> A pulpit discourse may be manufactured just as a piece of furniture. A man who makes a table picks out his pieces of wood, saws them, planes them, puts them together, and the article thus constructed is sandpapered, painted, and varnished. In the same mechanical manner it is possible to work in the study. A minister may bring out his materials, put in a piece of exegesis, add a piece of doctrine, tack on a piece of illustration, and then a piece of exhortation, and these having been nicely fitted together, he may sandpaper them, and varnish them, and the whole thing polished and labelled may be carried before a congregation and called a sermon, but a sermon in reality it is not. It is too wooden. It is dead, and a sermon is always alive. A sermon grows as an apple grows, and what it needs is sun and time. You may pick it green if you are in a hurry, and if you do it will set your people's teeth on edge. You may pick it half ripe and lose something of the flavor, or you may wait until it becomes mellow, rich, and juicy, and then the saints are glad.[3]

Maturity comes with an unhurried growth. Lack of power or evidence of shallowness in a sermon does not most often indicate an immature mind or spirit, but an immature cultivation of

---

3. Charles Edward Jefferson, *The Minister as Prophet* (New York: Crowell and Co., 1905), pp. 75-76.

material.[4]

In the natural world we can reap only after we sow, but it is true that we also reap *more* than we sow. One pound of seed will yield its own weight many times over in the harvest. In the world of ideas there is multiplication factor which develops under incubation in a like manner. The fruit of thought and reading over an extended period can be indexed and filed so that material on a given subject can be gathered at will. Material gathered for future needs, and stored wisely, will expand itself as it is gathered. A simple list of Biblical passages and sermonic ideas associated with those passages can be drafted for from five to six months ahead. As the coming preaching possibilities are regularly reviewed, the details will begin to sort themselves out. Current reading and filing is brought into relation, and the subconscious mind works on the ideas being considered.

I find that a loose-leaf notebook, with each sermon possibility entered on a separate page, and listing a future text, topic, or outline, with references to other filed materials is a most practical aid. This becomes a practical collation point at the start of each week, as a brief study of these sheets shows material shaping up for presentation, and the constant exposure to them sets the mind alive to new materials as they are discovered through the experiences of every day. The loose leaves are shuffled to keep a provisional schedule current for the first six to eight weeks immediately ahead, bearing in mind special occasions and seasonal requirements. Regular review of such a variety of materials brings out hidden meanings and unrecognized associations that would otherwise be undiscovered.

One who served the largest church of his denomination in a major city for forty-five years gives testimony to the value of a regular planting of material:

> I somewhat prize my library. It is not the greatest, nor is it the most valuable from the standpoint of volumes of the highest merit, but it has one feature that could scarcely be exceeded in all America; eighty-five scrapbooks, from one

---

4. Aspects of such sermonic growth are detailed in Andrew W. Blackwood, *The Fine Art of Preaching* (New York: Macmillan, 1945); *The Preparation of Sermons* (New York: Abingdon, 1948); and especially in *Planning a Year's Pulpit Work* (New York: Abingdon, 1942).

hundred to three hundred pages each, the depository of full sixty years of possible sermonic material; three-and-a-half shelves are needed to hold these volumes. To me, at least, they have more value than any dozen shelves found round about them. In fifty years never a sermon prepared and delivered without appeal to this reservoir, and in fifty years never a disappointment. In some instances after a quarter or half a century of waiting the time to arrive, the peculiar illustration or incident thus laid was needed, but what relief and joy when the hour arrived to find it waiting there![5]

The same testimony is given by almost every preacher of note. Brown records that during D. L. Moody's itinerant labors across the world, the great evangelist carried half a trunk full of such accumulated materials.[6]

Variety

Twentieth century man hates boredom. The contemporary world is complex and its inhabitants shrink from the mundane and the ordinary. Persons are so various, and their needs so full of change, that a many-faceted ministry is constantly needed. This was part of the secret of the great Spurgeon—his perennial freshness.

In the search for variety it is easy for the local preacher to share incohesive snippets of truth without order and balance within a total preaching program. The needed unity and continuity can be forged only by careful planning. Some feel this is best organized around the Christian year.[7] Blackwood suggests an autumn concentration on foundations for growth, a winter enlistment for service, a spring instruction for development, and a

---

5. W. B. Riley, *The Preacher and His Preaching* (Wheaton, Ill.: Sword of the Lord Publishers, 1948), p. 101. This pastor served the First Baptist Church of Minneapolis, authored seventy books, and was president of Northwestern Schools. He was called "the greatest Christian statesman in the American pulpit" by William Jennings Bryan.

6. Elijah P. Brown, *Point and Purpose in Preaching* (New York: Revell, 1917), p. 73.

7. See note 4; also Charles W. F. Smith, *Biblical Authority for Modern Preaching* (Philadelphia: Westminster, 1960), pp. 55-79; and B. S. Easton and H. C. Robins,*The Eternal Word in the Modern World* (New York: Scribner's, 1937), both of which give good attention to the Episcopalian applications of such preaching. Easton and Robins is the classic text in this area.

summer encouragement to practical spiritual living. Thus in one year the new Christian, or the potential disciple, can be taken from motivation to involvement in able service, and on to steady improvement.

Scripture

Jesus and the New Testament writers continually used Old Testament Scripture as basis for their teaching. This was not mere technique but the foundation for all authority and exhortation. True preaching cannot exist apart from the Word of God, because the Bible is not only content for revelation, but also its vehicle. As the history of redemption is focused in present experience, faith is generated.[8]

Scripture claims an inherent profit for teaching, reproof, correction, and instruction, and that it exists to furnish hearers with a growing spiritual maturity.[9] It is through the revelation given there that the sovereign Spirit elects to form His reproductions of Christ within human personalities. The Word is not a guaranteed instrument which by its exposure compels the mechanical cooperation of deity. There is no sacramental power within its form, or even within the truth which it contains. But there is an interpenetration of the free and sovereign Spirit's work and the heard Word.[10]

Preaching from the Bible makes use of the most relevant material possible. Expository preaching takes the truth revealed and sets it growing in contemporary soil. Because Scripture carries such a variety of content in the truth it reveals, this means that the variety and freshness of Biblical preaching is unlimited.

It is also worthy. Persons cannot grow spiritually on a string of illustrations, a clever diagnosis of social ills, or on relevant themes culled from altruistic newspaper editorials. *They need bread!*[11]

---

8. Rom. 10:17.

9. II Tim. 3:16-18.

10. See Rom. 10:17 as discussed in Pierre Ch. Marcel, *The Relevance of Preaching,* trans. Rob Roy McGregor (Grand Rapids: Baker Book House, 1963), pp. 25-27.

11. See W. E. Sangster, *Power in Preaching* (London: Epworth, 1958), pp. 29-43.

So many regard Christianity as either a benevolent and indolent attitude of gracious kindness or a rigid adherence to an old-fashioned code of ethics. They have little understanding of the great truths of redemption and justification that undergird the gospel message, and they therefore manifest little vital spiritual life. This was our Lord's own comment in the parable of the houses built on sand and rock, after He had taught concerning the kingdom. Without a meaningful relation to Christ and the foundational truths which alone have dynamic enough to create practical bases for Christian witness and service, discipleship will always be insecure and weak.

Sangster reminds us:

> Sermons without teaching in them run their course with vague reference to some body of belief which we all know (or do we?), sustained by sanctions we all accept (or don't we?), reared on a rock which cannot be moved (or can it?). The tragedy is that . . . in the end the faith for which the martyrs died vapourises into mild sentiment, and when you put out your hand to grasp it there is nothing there.[12]

Campbell Morgan considers that every minister must ask two questions concerning his preaching: What is the need I am addressing? and, What is the message I must deliver? He affirms that needs are discovered only by the speaker's complete identification with his fellows. He also insists that such need must be linked with Biblical material in which the objective sought allies with the need discovered. There is a kind of pastoral life that ought naturally to give rise to such understandings and clarify such needs. But the detail knowledge of Biblical content is essential if these are to be met. He says:

> Knowing the need he must then seek his message. Here again inclusively he is never at a loss. That by which a man lives, in the deepest of his life, is the Word of God. But the incidental application must be as varied as is the incidental expression; and he who would preach the Word prevailingly must live with the Word; he must know the Word of God as well as the human spirit. His business must be to know the remedy for the need he addresses.[13]

---

12. Sangster, pp. 37-38.

13. G. Campbell Morgan, *The Ministry of the Word,* The James Sprunt lectures delivered at Union Theological Seminary in Va. (New York: Revell, 1919), pp. 208-9.

That is why so much preaching fails to communicate: it has so little to say by way of provision for the needs which it is addressing. Far too much preaching is only a weak paraphrase of Christian truth, linked by some topical discussion and given a moral postscript which lacks specific relevance. The preacher who knows the Biblical revelation, and its authority, and has also an insight into the needs of persons, can set the eternal truth within a vital personal frame of reference.

The presence of God will stride through the sermons of the man who keeps these concepts in view. Nothing has the power of the incomparable teachings of Christ, the majestic themes of redemption expounded in the epistles, and the lessons of Biblical history and biography, as they are brought into mesh with the lives of our hearers.

Occasionally subjects worthy of pulpit discussion may not be found in full expository detail within the Bible, but every subject has some facet expounded in it. Germ-thoughts and ideas from the Bible can be used, not only as adequate bases for what is being taught but also as vital illustrations. General truths can be induced from historical narrative, and specific applications can be discovered in the detail exegesis of relevant passages. The free rendition of popular paraphrase translations is most helpful here.

Valid ways of preaching are as numerous as are preachers, but sermons whose basic ingredients do not build around Biblical content cannot expect to provide a situation that is truly an occasion of confrontation with God. Such preaching is as far from what preaching ought to be as was the proverbial bride's first baking from being a cake:

> She measured out the butter
> With a very solemn air,
> The milk and sugar also, and
> She took the greatest care
> To count the eggs correctly,
> And add a little bit
> Of baking powder, which you know
> Beginners oft omit.
> And she stirred it all together,
> And she baked it for an hour,

But she never quite forgave herself
for leaving out the *flour!*[14]

Biography

Human need and Scriptural revelation meet easiest, and
often, at the point of Bible biography. Above all else, persons are
interested in other persons, and in their lives. The appeal of all
spectator sports, of novels, movies, television, and other elements
of entertainment is built on the fascination we all have for drama
and biography.

Because the Bible is, in part, a history of humanity, it records
failures and successes, human progress and regress, weak fear and
triumphant faith.

We identify with Moses in his weakness and inability. We ally
ourselves with Samson in his temptations, with David in his sin
and introspection, and with Paul in his struggles to live for what he
knows is best. Biography in Scripture illustrates human actions,
attitudes, responses, and achievements. Faith is more real, and
more possible, because of Abraham's story. Courage to be what we
are called to be is not so difficult because of Peter's forgiveness,
and success. Life's big commitments are not so frightening when
we can see others who have faced them with faith and have
handled them with profit.

One of the best known of American Presbyterian preachers,
Clarence E. Macartney, secured ideas for a remarkable series of
sermons (later to appear in a number of collections) from a survey
of his own congregation. He asked his people for information
concerning Biblical stories, as preaching suggestions, and launched
into a series, centering on biography, which won him fame as a
preacher reaching human needs.[15] F. W. Robertson, T. DeWitt
Talmage, D. L. Moody, Alexander Whyte, Clovis G. Chappell, and
scores of others among the greatest pulpiteers of the ages have
found a similar power through biographical preaching. There are

---

14. Brown, p. 57.

15. Clarence E. Macartney, *Preaching Without Notes* (New York: Abingdon, 1946), pp.
    95-106.

several fine studies available in this field.[16] There are four hundred Bible characters of note, all worthy of at least one good sermon; and there are major figures whose history and experience are such that many, many series could be planned around them.

DYNAMICS

Attention is not a process which, once commenced, is guaranteed continuous throughout a sermon. It is rather a series of repeated interest levels that must be aroused continually right through the address. When attention is not *demanded* regularly, by various factors and devices, the congregational thought will always tend naturally to revert to those associations which are most pleasant or most pressing.

Could the preacher see the normal frames of reference for each mind among his audience, he would find the farmer, lawyer, businessman, schoolteacher, and housewife busy thinking about problems pertaining to their respective vocational locales. A teen-age girl may be romancing about marriage, a young man mentally renovating his favorite jalopy; grandfather, although in church, may be planning the new vegetable garden, and grandmother could well be involved in a rosy reverie of thanksgiving for her grandchildren. It is the preacher's task to demand attention for more important, and spiritual, issues during the period in which he is before them. To bring such issues to sufficient prominence, so that they will attain, and maintain, priority over the natural concerns, at least three elements must be enlisted as attention dynamics.

Vitality

The material that is vital as it is presented is attention compelling. The big subject has an inbuilt grabbing power. Great texts of Scripture, the strong sayings of Jesus, and the great themes of revelation have a life and vitality that demands interest. Just as the size of an advertisement has pulling potential, so also

---

16. E.g., Andrew W. Blackwood, *Biographical Preaching for Today* (New York: Abingdon, 1954); and Faris D. Whitesell, *Preaching on Bible Characters* (Grand Rapids: Baker Book House, 1955). See also Ilion T. Jones, *Principles and Practice of Preaching* (New York: Abingdon, 1957), pp. 226-27.

the expanse or significance of a subject gives it strength.

Vitality is as related to nature as it is to size. Antagonism is a great attraction in public address. In the evident clash and battle of conflicting ideas, the meeting of force with force, and the wrestling with opposing views there is an emotional factor which draws interest. This element of struggle gives vitality.

There is power in a moving mind. As a sermon carries a sense of challenge and an evidence of objectives, it will involve hearers in the invitation, motivating toward the goal. The preacher with flashing eye and soaring tongue has usually built to his enthusiasm dynamic by a deliberate opening up of truth, followed by a logic of progression that carries audience empathy and relevance. Such power can never be present when the preacher merely has a subject—instead of an object—in view. This vitality of sparkling onwardness in a sermon, with its definite points of departure and a clear destination, will avoid the sermon degenerating into a miscellaneous collection of information shared, but never truly communicated. It will also enlist desired attention.[17]

A sense of climax, then, often deliberately planned and discreetly created, is intrinsic to all good preaching; and the excitement it generates is valid as well as valuable.

While there can be no excuse for preaching dullness, pulpit drama can also be overdone. The worth of such a dynamic depends on the sincerity and honesty of the preacher, and the reality of his involvement, in depth, with the truth he is seeking to share. It is certain that, when such soul energy is evident, there is a dimension of liberty and vitality conveyed that is unobtainable in any other way. A cultured Black writer, discussing such expression, presses its reality in these words:

> If a man's soul is in a healthy condition and he is inspired by his message, his thought will inevitably reflect itself in his physical features. By subtle psychological law the whole nervous system responds to the emotions, and the will. Feeling and purpose in a strange and spontaneous fashion press for expression at every gateway of the personality—the eyes, the lips, the hands, and feet. The preacher's personality radiates and is lifted up in a great tide of energetic conviction

---

17. The chapter that follows gives structural detail for planning which ensures this quality of onwardness.

and emotional force. It seems to overflow its banks, and presses itself forth in the expression of his whole being.[18]

Our task is not the artificial creation of such emotional vitality. It is rather to be sure that an unwarranted embarrassment, or a withdrawal from personal involvement, does not unnecessarily restrain its natural exhibition.

Novelty

Closely allied with vitality is novelty, an attractive element in the sermon that impacts unexpectedly, and dramatically anchors truth to experience. Spurgeon likened these surprise elements in a sermon to the knots in a tailor's thread which ensure that it will not come out in the finished garment. He said that the simplest such factor—illustration—serves this double purpose.[19] It makes clear, and it fastens truth.

The predictable is always of minor interest. If a familiar subject or text is announced, there is a subconscious tendency to switch off attention. This continues as a speaker begins his address with traditional truth and says things that are normal and average. Yet the personality of each individual carries a unique potential. Because each preacher is an individual he is capable of expressing a personal perspective on any subject which can be his, and his alone.

Webb Garrison mentions a bus driver who called the cities of his route in *reverse* order, defending this practice by saying, "Since I started doing it this way, everybody sits up and takes notice before we get out onto the highway."[20]

Any mental withdrawal of attention is an indictment of both the speaker and the subject in view, as being unworthy of interest. This quality of freshness will ensure that interest is not lost because of the familiarity which breeds contempt.

----

18. John Malcus Ellison, *They Who Preach* (Nashville: Broadman, 1956), p. 105. Ellison was the first Negro president of Virginia Union University.

19. Charles Haddon Spurgeon, *The Soul-Winner*, reprint (Grand Rapids: Eerdmans, 1963), pp. 95-96.

20. Webb B. Garrison, *Creative Imagination in Preaching* (New York: Abingdon, 1960), p. 21.

Suspense

Emotion comes into association with attention, again, at the point of suspense. Story narration carries this power through its plot development. Specific and concrete details in a story highlight its realism, while vague generalities keep listeners at a distance.

A most effective preaching method is the simple discussion of a series of alternate solutions propounded, and developed, as possible answers to a problem. After thorough consideration and logical rejection, a solution that meets the need is finally propounded. The sustained attention value of such a treatment is intensive. Such crisis preaching is not for the every week experience; but it is legitimate as a regular factor in every preaching program, and is a most valuable one when volitional action is desired. If we are aware of the inherent dangers we may use such methods with confidence.[21] Emotional communication must be taken into account if we are to reach the full personality. One authority declares, "Preaching needs drama to save itself from walking off into a philosophical wilderness, a sort of Sahara Desert of abstraction."[22]

Relevance

Planned contact points in the sermon will build a genuine interest power through listener involvement. As the sermon obviously meshes with the lives of those who are listening, they will give attention. The simplest such device is the properly phrased rhetorical question, or other challenge to the hearer to examine where this truth collides with his personal life.

There are serious lapses in attention in the average audience, estimated to be as frequent as every seven minutes.[23] Interest must, therefore, be renewed every five to seven minutes during an address, and more frequently if possible. It can be demanded by an arresting phrase, an illustration, or the propounding of a problem to be solved or a question to be answered. These focal

---

21. See under motivation in chap. 6.

22. Halford E. Luccock, *Communicating the Gospel* (New York: Harper, 1953), p. 111.

23. Edgar N. Jackson, *A Psychology for Preaching* (New York: Channel, 1961), p. 19.

points of attention will aid both preacher and listener, giving the former *direction* for relevance, and the latter *indication* of it. Purposeful relevance is recognized when present, and so is its absence. As one teen-ager commented, concerning the sermons of her pastor: "When he preaches it is like dropping a custard pie. It shatters over everything, but doesn't hit anything very hard."[24]

Humor

The nature of humor remains an enigma to psychologists; yet all agree it is a dynamic means of welding rapport for any public speaker. Cynics reduce humor to a sense of superiority arising from the recognition of the absurd or the ridiculous in others, or from a sudden confrontation with incongruity. They say laughter is the result of an emotional release from the frustration of an anticipated conclusion or experience. We may laugh at poor logic; at the abnormal association of diverse objects, persons, or ideas; at the ignorance of a child; or the obesity of an adult (provided we ourselves are not fat). We laugh when verbally surprised, such as at an unexpected answer, or at a pun.

When true humor is shared by teacher and pupil there is the common enjoyment of a shared experience that is pleasurable. This builds a unity that is free and spontaneous. Real or imagined barriers between an authoritarian figure and a group of learners will then come down for a few moments while all relax in the luxury of being human.

Gilbert Highet comments, "The young think their elders are dull. The elders think the young are silly."[25] Humor builds a bridge of understanding that transcends all generation gaps, and, when conditions are right, breaks across a variety of cultures or inhibitions.

Humor, as the building up of emotion and its acceptable release, is a welcome experience for all. Other forms of wit, such as irony, sarcasm, or burlesque, have little place in regular pulpit

---

24. Jackson, p. 20.

25. Gilbert Highet, *The Art of Teaching* (New York: Random House, 1950; Vintage ed., 1954), p. 57.

use. Long ago Solomon said that "grievous words stir up anger,"[26] and the net result of such pulpit indiscretion is often simple antagonism.

Humor may bring the element of surprise to undergird a point, the element of relief to lessen pressure, or the element of affinity to smooth out a relationship and weld to a greater unity. Whenever it is wisely used it is always an attention dynamic and a plus factor within the general group climate.

Perhaps a wise comment would be that no preacher ought normally to go out of his way to *make* a joke—or to *avoid* one!

Illustration

The Latin *illustrare,* "to illuminate," suggests that an illustration is used to light up the meaning and significance of a truth, or to apply a practical end to a principle being expounded. Abstract ideas clarify as they shape into concrete situations, and their theory is thus shown as having a practical relevance. Life-situation illustrations carry the greatest impact, as their validity is open to verification from the commonsense experience of the congregation. The sense of reality present in an illustration, as contrasted with intellectual abstraction of pure reasoning in other parts of the sermon, rests an audience.

Jesus drew His illustrations from the home, the farm, the school, the society, and other everyday life. Paul used philosophy, poetry, and local customs and practices to great advantage. Biblical and secular biography is possibly the greatest source for illustration; but statistics, objects, literary quotations, personal experiences, and almost everything related to life's normal context can be used to advantage.

As law is taught by means of illustrative cases, and surgeons are trained through clinical experience, so spiritual life is soundly cultivated by the case method. The next best thing to actual personal involvement in a learning experience is a thorough identification with another in *his* experience. This is what is done when good illustrative material is used. Effectiveness reaches its high point with the ample use of names, dates, places, and other

26. Prov. 15:1.

facts which bring accuracy of detail to a story and thus aid its authenticity.

Imagination

The final dynamic element to be considered in all planning is imagination. The contemporary mind is accustomed to the rapidly moving sequence of images and pictures across the visual imagination. Magazines, newspapers, and the ever dominant television are all tailored for such an appeal. One researcher, after thorough investigation of the warrants for addressing and using the visual imagination in preaching, concludes that these are justified in the pulpit, both by Biblical precedent and by psychological demand.[27] He cites evidence to support the practice of imagination as an exercise which sharpens the preacher's awareness, develops his personality, and adds communication value.[28]

There is ample use of the imagination in both the literary forms and the figurative concepts of the Old Testament history and prophecy. If all metaphorical expression and figurative teaching was removed from the Bible, the gaps of revelation would be vast. The New Testament parables, the Pauline analogical insights, and the typological teachings deduced in the New Testament from Old Testament history are all illustrative of the imaginative content of traditional exposition.

Imagination is cultivated by psychological knowledge, by Biblical familiarity, and by bold experiment. Assuredly every preacher ought to read some of the great imaginative sermons of Beecher and Talmage. There is some current study available in this area,[29] but much remains to be developed there. While all will use something in this area, some will be wise to proceed gradually in its experiment. The vivid imagery and rich expression of the two masters mentioned above were the fruit of a long acquaintance

---

27. Samuel Laban Magbee, *Psychological and Biblical Bases of Visual Imagination in Preaching* (Richmond: Union Theological Seminary, unpublished Th.M. thesis, May 1961).

28. Magbee.

29. Garrison. Also see Halford E. Luccock, *In the Minister's Workshop* (New York: Abingdon, 1944), pp. 104 ff.

with art, poetry, music, and literature, plus a cultivation of personal relationships and involvement with human lives at their deepest levels. I find a common upsurge of preaching power in this area among ministers entering the middle years, whose understanding has been broadened and whose imaginations developed through several decades of such application. Of course, for every one like this there are another ten who do nothing but traverse the first ten years of ministry again and again, and whose preaching horizons are bounded by an unnecessary pastoral busyness. Unquestionably the scope and depth of a preacher's reading is the surest limitation, or expansion, of his growth in this area of enlargement.

A philosophical imagination can be exercised to great profit. An American theological professor had his students analyze the basic concepts undergirding news reporting and advertising in two of the nation's top journals, and in a leading daily newspaper. He comments:

> Their studies in recent months yielded the following complete list of axioms:
>
> 1. It's the surroundings that give life its meaning.
> 2. Religion's all right in its place, but that isn't in politics.
> 3. Immortality is just your influence going on in the world.
> 4. These days you have to become a martyr to make the Christian religion real—and I don't have a martyr complex.
> 5. We must do what's right—to keep other people on our side.
> 6. You deserve the best; you owe yourself easy-chair comfort. Forget the discomforts of others and live it up. Take care of number one.
> 7. Is it right? We'll take a vote and see.
> 8. Certainly we need it; they have one next door.
> 9. What's new must be good; what's old can't be.
> 10. Who is God, that we are mindful of him?[30]

---

30. Merrill R. Abbey, *Preaching to the Contemporary Mind* (New York: Abingdon, 1963), p. 75.

He also lists ten other axioms, expressive of similar attitudes of contemporary society, which are the result of some ecumenical studies in this area.[31]

The church is certainly called to challenge the sub-Christian concepts in society. We need to exercise our imagination in the formulation of base philosophies like these, and thus meet the modern mind at a point of justifiable collision. Merrill R. Abbey makes some constructive suggestions in this matter.[32]

Thus in all our planning we must first choose a basic philosophy for preaching, and suitable methods of approach. Expository preaching will serve us best; and its material content will involve variety, plus the ample use of Scripture, particularly biographies of Bible characters. Good dynamics of attention will include vitality, novelty, suspense, humor, illustration, and imagination. McCracken's comment seems a suitable summation and a worthy plea for rational planning:

> It is invariably the case that powerful preaching represents an achievement behind which there lies an infinite capacity for taking pains. The biographies of all the great personalities of the pulpit all tell the same story, a story of dedication and discipline, of men who toiled unremittingly at their task, never taking their skills for granted, but endeavoring year after year to raise the standard and quality of their work. Aren't the ablest preachers you know men whose application and industry are limitless? I find them jealous of their study hours, keen on their intellectual interests, making an attempt to be wide in their reading, taking endless pains over their sermons, and ceaselessly on the lookout for anything that will make them more effective.[33]

---

31. Abbey, pp. 71-72.

32. Abbey, pp. 66-81, 159-87.

33. Robert J. McCracken, *The Making of the Sermon* (New York: Harper, 1956), pp. 68-69.

9
Structure

The greatest aid to homiletic power is the clarity of the preacher's grasp of his subject and his object. Impact, attention, and response are promoted by good sermon structure because this enlists the involvement of both preacher and hearers at the highest levels possible. A strong and logical framework will carry truth firmly home and compensate for other weaknesses.

The traditional description of the structure of a sermon has been that of an outline. This all too vague symbol suggests an exterior line figure with no detail or strength. Far too often this has been exactly our conception of preaching form: an outline of somewhat related thoughts has been collated and put together surrounding a subject, and a search begun for material that will fill out the picture and give it some substance.

True sermonic structure is better symbolized in terms of a figure that foundations and stabilizes the entire address. There must be a planned, organized, and developed strength and unity supporting all the parts and making them a viable whole. Structure for the sermon is as the *skeleton* is to the body, as the *timber framework* is to the house, or as the *steel ribs* are to the skyscraper.

A physician prescribes for his patient in awareness of the

basic body anatomy, yet he seldom discusses it. The painter needs a familiarity with the techniques of handling his brush, he must study the textures of canvas and paint, he must know the laws of color and perspective; yet all the viewer sees in his finished picture is an emotion-stirring scene. An architect takes his soaring edifice into exciting and novel shapes and contours; yet each section must carry an unseen structural framework, based on simple forms and elementary geometrical figures, which will bear the loads he plans to erect.

The musician cannot build his inspiring arrangements and compositions without a detailed knowledge of the mathematical bases that structure harmony and counterpoint. He must master scales, chords, and arpeggios to use these rigid bases for the creation of his fluid productions.

But it is easy to confuse the art of the doctor, painter, architect, and musician with their science. Because the basic knowledge that undergirds their successful activity does not readily appear on the surface, we wrongly assume its insignificance. In discussing preaching, as related to teaching, we must affirm that the art is always most effective as it bases most clearly on the science. *Homiletic power bears direct relation to the clarity of the sermonic skeleton, or frame.* Where inadequate attention is given to this, power will fail.

A clear sermon framework helps logical progression. It is to be erected logically, proceeding from foundation to climactic apex. The movement is from common ground to new territory in a systematic order, focusing truth, and with a clear sense of direction and purpose. When the preacher himself has absolute confidence that he is going somewhere, and can get there, he can communicate best and lead others most effectively.

THESIS

The major need for every sermon is for a single, strong, clear *thesis.* Often referred to as the *proposition,* this is the central idea of the sermon which is supported by the points presented, and is treated from various perspectives or divisions. This central idea will be clarified, or its validity enforced, by every element included in the address. Many years ago Jowett summarized this concept in terms of personal testimony:

I have the conviction that no sermon is ready for preaching, not ready for writing out, until we can express its theme in a short, pregnant sentence as clear as crystal. I find the getting of that sentence is the hardest, the most exacting, and the most fruitful labor in my study. To compel oneself to fashion that sentence, to dismiss every word that is vague, ragged, ambiguous, to think oneself through to a form of words which defines the theme with scrupulous exactness—this is surely one of the most vital and essential factors in the making of a sermon: and I do not think any sermon ought to be preached, or even written, until that sentence has emerged, clear and lucid as a cloudless moon. Do not confuse obscurity with profundity, and do not imagine that lucidity is necessarily shallow. Let the preacher bind himself to the pursuit of clear conceptions, and let him pursue his purpose by demanding that every sermon he preaches shall express its theme and purpose in a sentence as lucid as his powers can command. All this will mean that the preparation of Sunday's sermons cannot begin on Saturday morning, and finish on Saturday night.[1]

Every word in the above is deserving of the closest scrutiny. Unless the preacher can reduce his major thought to such concise verbal expression, his understanding of his sermon, and its objectives, is *not* clear; for human thought is such that the only way it can be shaped for understanding and communication is through language. Concepts cannot be captured for the human intellect in any other way than in words. Clarity comes as we frame ideas into the words and sentences that express them best. Consequently, words are our means of communication with ourselves, as well as with others.

A sermonic thesis, then, is a propositional statement that defines an aspect of a subject under discussion. It may be described as "the conclusion in reverse," as it represents the central idea, which becomes foundation and core around which the sermonic framework is erected. The thesis condenses the sermon into a single sentence, stating or implying its purpose. It may be an affirmation, an exhortation, or even a question; but it is always selected, in expository preaching, directly from the truths revealed in a given passage, and as the supremely important value

---

1. J. H. Jowett, *The Preacher: His Life and Work* (New York: Harper, 1912), pp. 133-34.

to be shared from it, for that particular occasion.

Every preacher ought to aim to deliver such a timeless truth into the lives of his people. This proposition states the truth chosen, then relates it to the revelation of God and the needs of the congregation. The preacher has only to believe that his thesis is vital, reasonable, and desirable, to be able to commit himself to the preaching task with enthusiasm.

In the choice and framing of a thesis we will seek to show what the sermon sets out to prove, illustrate, or apply. Steps for its creation are as follows:

1. *Know the need which the sermon sets out to meet.* This may be felt by the listener, or unrecognized by him.

2. *Know the Biblical revelation well enough to select a passage where this need is met.* Study the passage thoroughly, with the normal aids of exegesis and good commentaries. Analyze the passage into paragraphs.

3. *List the principal idea or thought movement in each paragraph,* stating the truth presented as simply as possible.

4. *Determine which one of the truths thus discovered in the passage is the main, central idea to select as a sermon core;* or decide which common principle or truth is supported by them, illustrated from them, or applied by them.

5. *Refine this central idea into a concise and simple sentence,* with only one subject which states the truth involved in a relevant manner. This is the thesis.

Examples of theses:

a) *The life of Christ proves His deity.*

b) *Christians should pray without ceasing.*

c) *Your responsibility is to witness.*

d) *Holiness is valuable.*

e) *Salvation is a process.*

f) *Christ died for our sins.*

g) *Temptation can be resisted.*

KEYWORDS

One of the most practical homiletic devices for unlocking the divisions most suitable for discussion in a particular sermon, and for building a strong framework, is that of the *keyword.* Each keyword is always a plural noun which arises naturally from the posing of an interrogative over against the thesis. It tells us the *nature* of the divisions best considered, and directs us back to the passage in view to group the other truths presented there under these divisions.

One of the seven normal interrogative pronouns or adverbs is selected. These are *how, when, where, why, who, which,* or *what.* Several may be tried to see which suits a particular need best, but only one must finally be chosen. Applying this to the above we have the following:

a) The life of Christ proves His deity. *How?* In the following *ways.*

b) Christians should pray without ceasing. *Why?* For the following *reasons.*

c) Your responsibility is to witness. *Where?* In the following *situations.*

d) Holiness is valuable. *When?* At the following *times.*

e) Salvation is a process. *Who, which,* or *what* (process)? Of the following *steps.*

f) Christ died for our sins. *Why?* Because of the following *evidences.*

g) Temptation can be resisted. *How?* By using the following *resources.*

In each case the words *ways, reasons, situations, times, steps, evidences,* and *resources* are keywords, which will suggest the main points around which material can be grouped and organized. Divisions of the thesis are created and areas of thought collated around these aspects which support, illustrate, or apply the proposition. Each *way, reason, situation, time, step, evidence,* or *resource* evident in the passage becomes a major division in the sermonic framework in the above examples.

Only one interrogative and only one keyword is used for each separate sermon. The keyword tickets each division as being within a particular category, and assists unity and balance.

Figure 3, on pages 166 and 167, is a table of suggested keywords, capable of infinite expansion.

FIGURE 3: *Table of suggested keywords*

abuses	compulsions	exchanges
accusations	conceptions	exclamations
acts	concessions	exhortations
actualities	conclusions	expectations
admonitions	conditions	experiences
advantages	consequences	expressions
affairs	contrasts	
affirmations	corrections	facets
agreements	credentials	factors
aims	criteria	facts
alternatives	criticisms	failures
angles	customs	faults
answers		favors
applications	dangers	fears
approaches	decisions	features
areas	declarations	finalities
arguments	defenses	forces
aspects	deficiencies	functions
aspirations	definitions	fundamentals
assertions	degrees	
assumptions	demands	gains
assurances	denials	generalizations
attainments	destinies	gifts
attitudes	details	graces
attributes	devices	groups
	differences	
barriers	directions	habits
beginnings	directives	handicaps
beliefs	disciplines	hopes
benefits	disclosures	hungers
blessings	discoveries	
	distinctions	ideas
calls	doctrines	imperatives
causes	duties	implications
certainties		impressions
challenges		improvements
changes	elements	impulses
charges	encouragements	incentives
claims	essentials	incidents
clues	estimates	indictments
commitments	events	inferences
comparisons	evidences	injunctions
compensations	evils	insights
compromises	examples	inspirations

instances
instructions
instruments
intimations
invitations
items

joys
judgments
justifications

kinds

lessons
levels
liabilities
losses
loyalties

manifestations
marks
methods
mistakes
moments
motives
movements
mysteries

needs
notions

objections
observations
obstacles
offers
omissions
opinions
opportunities

particulars
peculiarities
penalties
perils

phases
phrases
pledges
points
possibilities
practices
premises
prerogatives
principles
priorities
probabilities
problems
processes
promises
promptings
pronouncements
proofs
prophecies
propositions
provisions

qualifications
qualities
questions

realities
realizations
reasons
reflections
refusals
remarks
remedies
reminders
requirements
reservations
resources
responses
restraints
results
revelations
rewards

risks
rules

safeguards
satisfactions
secrets
sins
sources
specifications
statements
steps
stipulations
successes
suggestions
superlatives
suppositions
surprises
symptoms

tendencies
testimonies
tests
thoughts
threats
topics
totalities
truths

urges
uses

values
views
violations
virtues
voices

warnings
ways
weaknesses
words

*A keyword is always a plural abstract noun. This list can be infinitely expanded by using a good thesaurus or a dictionary of synonyms.

DIVISIONS

Unless there is a narrative element such as in a biography, or parable, with great plot interest continuity, it will never be sufficient just to talk about a subject, or even a thesis, for twenty minutes, without some *divisions.* Divisions help understanding by viewing the truth from a variety of perspectives, and they gather relevant material into natural groupings at a particular aspect of the thesis.

Divisions, a firmer word than the simple *points,* are the main concepts presented within the sermon. The best psychology is to announce these as they develop, and not to lose the element of surprise en route. There are certain factors of major importance in their creation.

Divisions must be as *mutually exclusive* as possible. Each section should be clear and distinct, save for what is normal for transition. If they are *parallel in form and structure,* both clarity and memory will be aided. So if one division is a question, normally all ought to be questions. If one is an imperative declaration, a single phrase, or merely one word, its fellows ought to have the same characteristics. There must be *a continuity relationship* between them which builds a logical sequence resulting in a climax just prior to the conclusion. There is also need for *balance.* Subpoints will be of similar weight, and material of similar length, under each heading, and the whole proportioned so that no one section is unwieldy in size or impact.

Divisions organize and classify materials. They create an invisible framework by which the team effort of all the content is marshaled to reach one required purpose.

Figure 4, page 170, shows the complete charting of expository sermon structure on these principles, whereby thesis, interrogative, and keyword are combined to produce strong divisions for the sermon frame. Knowing the *need* to be met, we define an *aim*, choose a *subject,* select a *passage* which treats that subject, define the *aspect* of the subject within that passage which we will use, and frame this into a *thesis.* To this thesis we apply one of the seven *interrogatives,* which yields for us a *keyword,* which in turn unlocks the subject into natural *divisions* under which we can group the exposition, enabling us to develop our thesis and reach an adequate *conclusion.* The keyword may actually appear in the statement of each division, but more often it is implied as the division is itself phrased in words which indicate it is a *way, reason, situation, time, step, evidence, resource,* and so forth, each of which is an element supporting the main thesis.

A number of writers have developed lists and applications of the thesis-interrogative-keyword concept.[2] The list of conceivable keywords is limitless, any plural noun being available for consideration.[3] The procedure can be mechanical, but it never has to be. A mastery of the technique can lend itself to as much "art" in preaching as any other method, and more than most.[4]

Sometimes a transitional verb should be used to associate the passage concerned with its thesis and the divisions. Thus "this passage *teaches* us that the life of Christ proves His deity in the following ways," or "we note here that Jesus *illustrates* that Christians should pray without ceasing for the following reasons," or "the experience of the Philippian jailor here *shows* us that salvation is a process of the following steps," will be ways in which transition from thesis to divisions may be naturally taken.

---

2. See Perry and Whitesell, and Koller in bibliography.

3. The list of figure 3 is from Koller.

4. I have examined many hundreds of volumes, including many in the general preaching and secular speech fields, for this study and found nothing of any quality in terms of valid sermon structure other than this thesis-interrogative-keyword approach. This perspecitve is the finest developed for expository preaching and is in full accord with the best ideas in contemporary speech theory and educational psychology.

It can be an approach full of variety and interest, as evidenced by the work of Perry and Whitesell (see bibliography). A proposition need not be stated to the congregation initially. Its revelation may well be delayed until it reaches such significance in the sermon that it becomes the conclusion. The "art" of preaching will show in the preacher's skillful handling of a thesis like this so that it is discovered by the hearers with as much impact as if they had found it for themselves. Divisions, too, need not follow rigid lines, but can be gathered up also at the end. This approach to preaching can be abused, just as any other method can; or it can become the most valued approach of all through its effective use.

We cannot insist that every effective sermon must fit this mold; but we may well insist that any sermon without a thesis, expressed or implied, cannot be a sermon, as it advocates no basic truth. We can also insist that most good sermons, on analysis, will be found to have affinity with the structure outlined in this chapter, although this may be unrecognized at surface level.

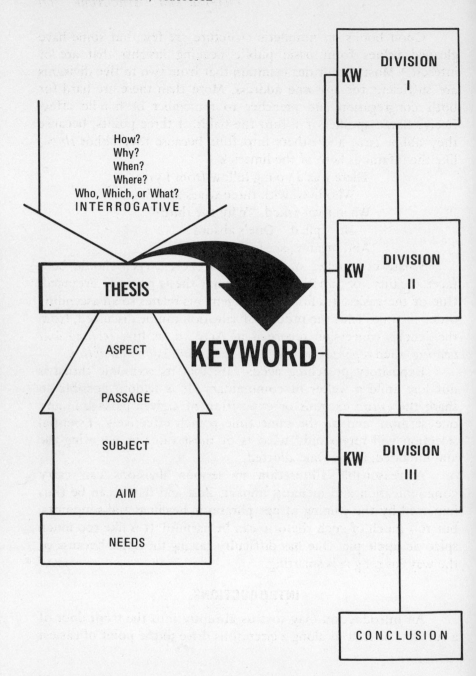

FIGURE 4: *Chart of expository preaching structure.*

Good books on homiletic structure are few, but some have gleaned values from basic public-speaking insights that are of interest.[5] Most authorities maintain that from two to five divisions are sufficient for any one address. More than these are hard for both congregation and preacher to remember or handle effectively. Some speakers fall into the habit of three points, because they abhor *two*, and others into four because they abhor *three*, like the infamous hero of the limerick —

> There was a young fellow from Lyme,
> Who lived with three wives at a time;
> When they asked, "Why the third?"
> He replied, "One's absurd;
> And bigamy, sir, is a crime!"

Whatever number of divisions is chosen, each should be a facet, quality, or function of the major thesis properly arranged. One of the easiest traditional arrangements relates to an ascending order in time. Thus the process of salvation can be discussed, from the jailor's conversion recorded in Acts 16, as first *seeking and hearing*, then *repentance and faith*, then *confession and action*.

Expository preaching needs care that its sermonic thrust is not lost amid a welter of commentary. It is seldom possible to share the *entire* exegesis or exposition of a given passage in any one sermon, and at the same time preach effectively. Essential selection will retain only what is of most value in achieving the aim intended, in the time allotted.

A reasonable alliteration in sermon divisions can carry communication and memory impact. Zest and flavor can be thus imparted by the coining of apt phrases in headings and subpoints, but too much of such rhetoric can be harmful. It is like too much spice on apple pie. One has difficulty tasting the apple because of the way his tongue is smarting.

INTRODUCTIONS

An introduction may toss us abruptly into the front door of a subject, or lead us along a circuitous drive to the point of easiest

---

5. See books by Harold A. Brack and Kenneth G. Hance, by G. Ray Jordan, and by Ilion T. Jones, as listed in the bibliography. Andrew W. Blackwood's books are also full of such insights.

entrance. Neither approach has the effectiveness of a motivation of personal interest in the subject, created in the congregation by the preacher. This can make the transition from the familiar to what is new almost an imperceptible movement. As the basic purpose of every introduction is to secure attention that will prepare the way for the introduction of the thesis or proposition, it should aim at the creation of an acceptable frame of mind and interest toward the speaker, and seek to underscore the relevance of the matters under discussion with the listener and his needs.

Thus word-origins, quotations, illustrations, unusual statements, or challenging facts and startling statistics can carry a kind of surprise power that meshes as a forceful impact with the modern mind. Any experience that reveals the reality with which the speaker faces life, or his humanity, will build an interest affinity. All apologies, banalities, and most irrelevant humor ought to be avoided.

The preacher who invites his hearers to "turn with me this morning to the eleventh chapter of Hebrews for our edification," throws a mental switch, by such an introduction, which isolates a large proportion of his congregation. He gives little sense of arising from among his peers to lead them into the discovery of a fresh perspective on matters of vital significance, but rather trumpets his conviction abroad that all are about to consider something which is almost two thousand years removed from today, and therefore almost certainly out of harmony with present needs. The subject must first be related to the listener and his needs before attention can be legitimately demanded. This is not merely good technique. It is also simple courtesy.

The basic requirement, then, is for life-situation *beginnings.* The problem should be stated, and our unmistakable involvement with it declared, before we may turn to the Bible for a solution. The first need is for some listener identification with the matters in hand. As we wrestle with a challenging question, ponder an absorbing fact, or face and feel a poignant problem at personal levels, we are then willing to turn to the Scriptural revelation for answers.

Contextual introductions are always helpful; but the more Biblically literate a particular congregation is, the less it will need of these. Today's hard-core realism does not allow for the interest once engendered by the grand historical and imaginative introductions that were so popular among preachers of several generations back. Yet, where these carry narrative or descriptive content in unusual depth, they can also cause listeners to become involved in the unfolding drama of Biblical biography or history, and lead to its application.

At an informal evangelistic service recently a preacher entered the pulpit holding a large newspaper. He proceeded to display it to the congregation page by page, indicating, as he did so, the content of the major news stories, reading their headlines aloud. As the paper was displayed it was revealed that he had scored through almost every item with large heavy strokes of black crayon. He explained that he had bought that day's newspaper, published in that city, and experimented with the idea of crossing out every story which was directly related to crime, failure, or sin. He ended with less than ten percent of the news columns intact, and these were of very nominal interest, being related to insignificant subjects such as the weather, or to general feature articles. This attention-getting material was used to introduce the text, "All we like sheep have gone astray, we have turned every one to his own way . . . ," as an indictment of modern society and an illustration of universal depravity. There was rapt attention, and the transition to the Biblical exposition was achieved almost imperceptibly.[6]

CONCLUSIONS

Every preacher has had firsthand experience of Phillips Brooks's immortal description of denominational conferences where "speakers tow all great subjects out to sea and then escape in small boats through the fog."[7] But all preachers have the same tendency in their regular pulpit ministry. It is not *diagnosis* that is difficult: it is *therapy* that is hard. Symptoms are easier to discuss than remedies. Unless we make genuine effort to bend our

---

6. This sermon was an experiment I conducted to confirm convictions relative to this study.

7. Raymond W. Albright, *Focus on Infinity: A Life of Bishop Phillips Brooks* (New York: Macmillan, 1961), p. 316.

sermons to practical ends, they will always bore. The sermon conclusion is the last and best chance to relate the great truths of theory, brought out in our preaching, to the practical realities of life.

Each member of the congregation has the right to ask the preacher, as he concludes his exposition of a timeless truth, "So what?" "What am I to do about this?" "Why did you share it with me?" "How does it all relate to me in the here and now?" "What specific attitude or action ought I to develop from this, and how can I achieve it?" The conclusion, then, will focus truth—into both the present tense and the second person. The challenge of commitment to a specific task will call for some decisive action, focusing the force of the sermon to convert the hearer into an actor.

Because the conclusion is so strategic, many consider it essential to write out, and perhaps commit to memory, the closing sentences. Certainly in preaching final impressions are lasting ones, and the hearer is more likely to take away with him what he has heard at the closing as the most significant theme. A closing weakness, such as, "Let us, therefore, meditate on these things," may well destroy all the previous sermonic force and power. Such a statement is like addressing a letter in care of general delivery, without specific instruction as to the individual who should receive it. Instead, the main divisions can be repeated, and the whole bundle of truth tied neatly with an apt illustration or specific application which will draw its power from all the previous exposition.

The great Jesuit teaching manuals of the sixteenth and seventeenth centuries, which detailed the educational principles that had such impact on the emerging age of discovery, made much of repetition. Review shows where we are headed, how far we have traveled, raises questions that whet the appetite for progress, and deepens the total impact of the lessons learned. Brief, simple, energetic words can list the benefits and results from practical applications of the truths expounded. R. W. Dale thinks that Charles G. Finney was successful as a preacher because he learned the value of repetition by his turning and re-turning over of the same points of evidence before a jury when he was a barrister. Dale comments: "We should all preach more effectively if, instead of tasking our intellectual resources to say a great many things in the same sermon, we tried to say a very few things in a great many ways."[8]

Thus the conclusion should gather the strength of all our hammer blows into one last stroke and hit hard. The concreteness with which we complete our exposition will determine much of its reality for those listening.

INVITATIONS

The spirit of invitation is evident throughout Scripture.[9] It is legitimate to appeal to our listeners for specific commitment to faith, for an open acknowledgment of the salvation experience, for enlistment into church membership, for baptism, for the response to the will of God in obedience for special service, and for many other needs. Such an appeal, at the end of a sermon, must be *clear* and without confusion, stressing one individual response.

It must also be *honest*. There can be no hint of the preacher's using such response for other ends, and there must be total respect for the freedom of the individual. Such entreaties should, therefore, always be *courteous*, and without undue emotional pressures. Faith and expectation in the preacher should lead him to express such appeals with *confidence* and *earnestness*. No call for spiritual response ought ever to be issued in a trifling or offhand manner, but with sincerity and a genuine concern for the well-being of those who respond.

Basic drives of human personality have been revealed in studies by social psychologists as relating to our needs for personal happiness, status and security, guilt-freedom, and for new experiences. Persons desire to find and know God, to discover resources for successful living, to respond to valid challenges, and to contribute the best of which they are able, in life. In other years some preachers resorted to unwise pressures arising from fears of judgment as motivation for Christian response. Where guilt

---

8. R. W. Dale, *Nine Lectures on Preaching* (New York: Geo. H. Doran, n.d.; lectures delivered at Yale in 1878), p. 150.

9. See Exod. 32:46; Josh. 24:15. Christ constantly spoke of those who were not with Him openly as being absolutely against Him.

is real it ought to be applied, but the more positive approach of release available from a right relationship with God is just as effective, and less unstable emotionally. The judgments of God declared on guilty men must be expounded, but these deserve attention mainly as the bases on which the grace of God becomes operative. The dividends received from salvation, from Christian fellowship, and from worthy service for Christ are benefits which, when given emphasis, will motivate action more readily than the exclusive discussion of penalties incurred by refusal.

Whitesell has summarized persuasion as an outgrowth of the exposition of Scriptural truth, and as relevant to the character of the preacher, as much as an element within the appeal itself. He emphasizes the need for meeting objections within the listener's mind as we proceed.[10]

C. W. Koller lists seven areas of approach. The appeal to *altruism*—a benevolent regard for the interests of others; the appeal to *aspiration*—a universal hunger for spiritual happiness and a sense of completeness; the appeal to *curiosity*—an interest in what is novel; the appeal to *duty*—the urge to do what is right, and to avoid the wrong; the appeal to *fear;* the appeal to *love;* and the appeal to *reason.*[11]

Sweazey identifies twenty appeals considered legitimate for evangelism, and warns against the abuse of fear, social pressure, worldly values, and superstition.[12] Lantz lists fourteen appeals under three groupings that are legitimate for Christian motivation. Appeals that furnish confidence and security he classifies as doing the will of God, exhibiting loyalty to Christ and the church, union with God through Christ, salvation from sin, and service for others. Under appeals that result in personal achievement he lists living an abundant life, obtaining assurance of heaven, the possession of peace, and power in service. Under social and ethical

10. Faris D. Whitesell, *Power in Expository Preaching* (Westwood, N.J.: Revell, 1963), pp. 63-73.

11.   C. W. Koller, *Expository Preaching Without Notes* (Grand Rapids: Baker Book House, 1962), pp. 109-12.

12. George E. Sweazey, *Effective Evangelism* (New York: Harper, 1953), pp. 58-71.

appeals he groups such motivations as equality, fairness, fellowship, and leadership.[13]

Responsive action to a sermon should be viewed as a most natural and normal expression of inner conviction. The solid intellectual *why* will undergird the emotional and volitional *when* of such response best where the conclusion is created with an exact explanation of what is both involved and required. This will be at its highest where the conclusion is not so much an added unit to the sermon but rather a natural termination of it.

Sermon application should be intrinsic to the entire address. The conclusion will therefore be, at its best, a collation of such elements into a final form created from the application points as they have developed throughout the sermon. Phelps says that such application continuity arises as the preacher is consciously aware of its need through the planning and preparatory stages, as well as in presentation. He states:

> Therefore preach very little in the general, and much in the detail. Preach little on truth, and much on truths. Preach rarely on religion, but constantly on the facts, the doctrines, the duties, the precepts, the privileges of religion. Divide, discriminate, define, sharpen, clarify, doctrine by doctrine, duty by duty, fact by fact, till the whole map of the Christian faith is outlined and clear. You thus gain the power of pointed preaching.[14]

---

13. John Edward Lantz, *Speaking in the Church* (New York: Macmillan, 1954), pp. 143-48.

14. Austin Phelps, *Theory of Preaching*, rev. ed. F. D. Whitesell (Grand Rapids: Eerdmans, 1947), p. 58.

10
Presentation

We have seen that objectives, planning, and structure are all practical elements of sermon preparation which give it power. Presentation is the final practical factor which determines the sermon value. Its success involves the use of various methods, the presence of empathy, a sense of dialogue, image validity, the right oral style, and good delivery.

GENERAL METHOD

Most students are familiar with three basic teaching methods. *Lecture* involves the flow of information through a continuous delivery of factual material by the teacher. Those listening note important facts and ideas, or are given these in written form. Apart from an occasional question there is little intercommunication between student and teacher.

In contrast with this, the *tutorial* method, used by Socrates and others in early days, is now very popular as it discourages transmissive learning and encourages the student to a self-discovery of truth. This method is at its best where the teacher can concentrate on one or two pupils alone. It involves independent work by students, as well as effort by the teacher.

Classroom *recitation,* a combination of both of these methods, is the normal in most teaching situations, particularly at advanced levels. Here some preliminary materials are well studied by all, and the class period is spent in filling in the gaps, making applications, and in interpretation and explanation of the materials studied. Where a problem emerges the leader will often resort to some lecturing for a portion of the class period.

This was Jesus' basic method. Jesus sought to emphasize principles, in contrast to the scribes who taught history and its accepted interpretation in a transmissive manner. He tried to lead His hearers away from the concept that all virtue was in the good act itself, and applied the insight of His omniscience to relevant illustration and application.

He did not develop a church with formal organization, but rather provided twelve trained and experienced leaders. He taught no dogmatic creed, but sought to lead His disciples to see the essence of true religion as love to God and man, based on the fact of personal forgiveness through the atonement. His teaching, although God-centered, was also person-related, in contrast to the Jewish tradition which was content-centered and action-related.

Christ used the Old Testament as His point of interest and contact, using allegory, objects, and everyday experience to illustrate His thought and to involve His hearers. He gave full play to His unique personality, using the tactics of surprise and humor, plus His superior resources of knowledge, as avenues of approach.

Gilbert Highet analyzes four methods in the teaching of Jesus. He says that He taught in memorable forms of wise statement, rich with a depth of suggestion, and meant to be reflected on (such as the Beatitudes). He taught through stories and parables. He taught in His own actions—such as His approval of marriage by His presence in Cana, or driving out the money changers from the temple. But He mainly taught through a multiplication of His message and work through the disciples, giving them assigned responsibilities, working with them and counseling in these.[1]

In His training for discipleship Jesus used the nurture of the group, formal instruction, and practical apprenticeship. His pupils learned by solving problems. They were involved in firsthand experiences which practically applied the truths the Master was teaching. He showed them humility via His taking of the servant's place and its practical assiduity by the actual washing of their feet. When the disciples drove away the children He had them cooperate in bringing them back, taking them into His arms as a visual and physical reinforcement of the lesson that none should be turned away.

To follow good general teaching method, the modern preacher will need to visualize himself accurately, and continuously, in the role of a member of his congregation. If he can place himself within the particular, or average, hearer's frame of reference he will achieve a major step toward good presentation. This leads us to the question as to how we can achieve such a relationship.

Empathy

A sympathetic understanding is not enough. Sympathy is an emotional identification in which the sympathizer's experience allies with another's as fellow feelings are projected. But to have empathy is to possess an additional quality of detachment and objectivity, in such an association, so that we may see the other person and his feelings in full perspective, but *apart* from our own. Overidentification with another can mean that our own fellow feelings are victimized, and we may lose the insight gained from a balanced view through our overinvolvement. A disciplined detachment allows us to be conscious of the need, yet also aware of personal resources so that we may help.

A collective audience makes more demands on us than does the individual pastoral counseling situation. Preaching requires concentration on representative individuals in the congregation, and presentation empathy may be best cultivated by a role-

---

1. Gilbert Highet, *The Art of Teaching*, Vintage ed. (New York: Random House, 1954), pp. 166-76.

rehearsal which comes in the preparation period.

If the preacher is to speak about family tensions he will practice placing himself in the position of the father, the mother, and the child in a given situation, and think things through from these several angles. He will project his own knowledge and resources into a given experience, and try to look out at the issues from there. Such role-play, necessarily an intellectual exercise performed in the study, will help frame a pulpit presentation that gives fresh perspectives to those he seeks to minister to.

Jeremiah looked for such illustrations for his sermons, searching for apt metaphors that would involve them in revised understandings. Incidentally, he complained that this was difficult work.[2] Solomon likewise searched for ideas and for words in which to express them, knowing that wise choices in this area hammered truth home to its most effective position. He too found this a "weariness."[3] Empathy is not easy but it is essential.

Dialogue

We have seen that persons respond best when they learn through some active participation in the working out of solutions to relevant problems. Learning is best where it is the personal discovery of truth. *Teaching is the art of guidance, exercised by a wise leader, which brings the student to the self-discovery of truth.* The process of education is at its highest point when it becomes a team enterprise in which all work together to achieve ends that are relative to their needs. The preacher as a teacher, then, is not a dominant mind guiding passive minds, but rather an active person who possesses the art of meshing with the activity-potential of other persons in a common search for truth.

Discussion, an ideal teaching method, can sometimes be operative within church situations; but this is seldom possible during the actual sermon presentation. By tradition the preached sermon has a monological quality. Many churches have found

2. Lam. 2:13.

3. Eccles. 12:9-12.

after-sermon discussion groups to have value in improving the impact and understanding of the pulpit message.

After surveying 244 Congregational and Christian churches in eastern Massachusetts, in which he found under 10 percent were involved in some type of ongoing sermon discussion group, C. H. Reid discovered that only a small minority of the membership cared to be related to these. He was able, however, to document a high proportion, among those who did associate themselves with such groups, who evidenced a spiritual growth, a deepening appreciation of Christian fellowship, and a greater faith and understanding from them.[4]

Reid postulates the possibility of a future church which is thoroughly group centered, with its preaching channelled accordingly. He suggests that such an experiential church could be organized around subgroups, and feels that this would accelerate the whole growth process of spiritual life.[5]

While such organization is possible, it would seem to be improbable, as the normal preaching function is so much a traditional part of church life and worship that it would seem impractical to delete it. Southern Baptist churches, and others, have applied the subgroup principle in the full-scale formation of adult classes in strong Christian education programs. These are vital elements in the framework of local church organization, and they involve participants in weekday study of the Bible, and in other outreach and growth programs. This appears to be a more valid application of group-process values than would be the breakup of the standard preaching relationship. The inherent teaching content of good preaching is the Biblical vehicle for the growth of faith.[6]

How then is it possible to gather the values inherent in discussion, and other group-process dynamics, into the average preaching situation, with its built-in monological quality? The

---

4. Clyde Henderson Reid, *Two-Way Communication Through Small Groups in Relation to Preaching* (Boston: Boston University School of Theology, unpublished Ph.D. thesis, 1960).

5. Reid.

6. Rom. 10:13-17; I Cor. 1:21. See chap. 4.

only answer is for the preacher so to think himself continually into the listeners' minds that he can openly discuss the thoughts raised through his sermon, *as they would wish them discussed,* during his presentation. He must meet objections which he feels they are mentally raising. He must start where they are, and, reaching forward in logical steps, move from the familiar to the unknown, basing his approach on their interests. He must stimulate. He must challenge. He must query. He must react. He must refuse to dodge problems or to gloss over difficulties. Thus he will be *in mental dialogue* with them, where literal and oral discussion is not possible.

The sermons that have meaning for the listeners are those in which they respond to an awakening insight, self-discovered, under wise guidance. They are those in which they feel a sense of fellowship and participation with the preacher. As he exhibits a capacity to sit where they sit, and to think aloud alongside of them while he is preaching, they cannot but be involved. A problem may be posed, unsatisfying answers dismissed, and perplexities and difficulties interpreted. Then, when a logical consideration of a possible solution is developed, they find themselves discovering a conclusion with him. Such a preacher is truly the *voice of the body,* representatively reflecting listeners' needs and reactions, as he guides them into new truth.

A sensitivity to persons and their needs can grow from many areas. Insight into the psychology of personality, and the techniques of counseling that have grown from it, will help greatly. The preacher must view his sermon as an occasion to confront the individual with the will of God within his context in the church. His sermon ought not to be a series of detached segments handed to the congregation for approval or rejection, but its unity should be matched by a bond of partnership between preacher and congregation. Reuel Howe, a helpful writer in this area, has said:

> The ministry of the ordained member has the ministry of the layman as its context. Pathetic is the condition of the minister who does not realise the need for that context. He is like an arm that is severed from the body; he is vainly trying to do a part of the work of the body without dependence upon the body. Some ministers preach, for example, as if they could, and should, do it all alone, as if

the sermon which they prepare and deliver is all-sufficient. How tragic that they do not realise that they need the meanings, thoughts, questions, understandings, interests, and encouragements of their congregation in order to prepare and preach their sermons; and that their sermons, far from being the great production of the occasion, are only a preliminary contribution to the sermons which are formed in each hearer as he responds out of his meanings to the meanings of the preacher. The Church's sermon is one born in the hearer, and this is the only one taken, and delivered in the world. The clergyman's ministry is only auxiliary to the ministry of the whole Church.[7]

Howe lists four changes produced by a genuine dialogue-form approach to preaching. He urges a literal sharing of the pulpit with members from the congregation in oral dialogue.

Howe and others have issued other studies in dialogue preaching since he first developed the approach in 1963,[8] the study by Thompson and Bennet being especially helpful, as it includes eight examples of such shared sermons.[9] However, all this literature continues to enunciate a skeptical view of the current value and significance of preaching because of its poor communication *alone,* and pays little attention to content and message.

Unquestionably preaching today is being justly criticized because of its archaic language, general dullness, irrelevance, and weak communication. Preaching is often nonauthoritative, and lacks the courage to tackle sensitive issues. It often fails in power and results, is seldom change provoking, and is given a status above its significance. The addition of dialogue through preaching plus discussion, ongoing study groups, or provision for other congregational feedback, does answer questions, explore doubts, and clarify information; but this remains mere *method*

7. Reuel L. Howe, *The Miracle of Dialogue* (Greenwich, Conn.: Seabury Press, 1963), p. 145.

8. Reuel L. Howe, *Partners in Preaching* (Greenwich, Conn.: Seabury Press, 1967); Clyde Reid, *The Empty Pulpit* (New York: Harper, 1967); William D. Thompson and Gordon C. Bennet, *Dialogue Preaching: The Shared Sermon* (Valley Forge, Pa.: Judson Press, 1969).

9. Howe, *Partners in Preaching;* Reid, *The Empty Pulpit;* and Thompson and Bennet.

as distinct from much vital change in the reality of preaching itself.

Dialogue preaching, as proposed by Thompson, Howe, and others, has great value in helping toward an understanding of both the preacher and listener as persons in the preaching relationship. It emphasizes the experience as a true partnership and clarifies the responsibilities of both persons involved.

Much of its weakness arises from little analysis of other factors which combine to make contemporary preaching ineffective. Many current sermons pay little attention to human needs, lack clear aims, have their materials organized poorly, and do not relate the Biblical revelation to the contemporary scene. The best application of its insights is found in the intellectual dialogue of the preacher with himself and, in imagination, with others. All the values of dialogue preaching can be applied within the standard preaching format to upgrade its communication and significance, without the destruction of the traditional pulpit-to-pew relationship which is so intrinsic to Christian worship that most persons react with deep concern when it is radically changed.

Image Validity

Not only must the preacher be authentic, spiritually real, open, honest, able to listen, and willing to change, he must also have a real maturity of intellect and practice. More important still, he must *convey* these attributes to those who listen. The congregation needs to *feel* that the preacher is an open person, in order to accept him as such. The emotional discipline which creates temperament stability needs therefore to be cultivated. The preacher who reacts with shock in face of the unusual will create a fear within his audience. The extremes of surprise, disgust, or disappointment will all promote adverse reactions which hinder communication.

One classic study of public speaking suggests several factors which contribute to the speaker's image validity and which therefore promote acceptance. These are *assurance*—an emotional climate that transfers confidence from speaker to listener; *preparation*—which creates confidence in the truth of the shared facts by rationality of argument and clarity of thought; *intensity—*

which supports the significance of the material presented; *sincerity*—which assures the honesty and fairness of the subject handling; *directness*—a technique of delivery which communicates reality and urgency; and *self-involvement*—which illustrates and associates practical applications of the truth within the personality of the one presenting the message.[10]

The preacher speaks by his character, his bearing, by what he chooses to speak about and avoid speaking about, and by what he faces and chooses not to face. Crocker insists that interesting speakers cannot be made from uninteresting people.[11] The self-centered, the immature, and the self-satisfied exhibit these idiosyncrasies in wearying speech.

Crocker also lists three areas that must be under constant development. *Intelligence,* reflected in quick and accurate judgments, and in tact, taste, and breadth of interest, is paramount. The practical person who exhibits discernment, control of temperament, and an approach to life that seeks constant growth and refinement, ready to learn from as many fields of study and experience as possible, is he who can best bend his personality to public speaking. Next comes *virtue.* If motives are questionable, or if insincerity is suggested, communication is always retarded. Kindness, humility, sympathy, and optimism blend to bring a genuineness which dispels indifference and antagonism in an audience.

The final element in Crocker's triad is *goodwill,* by which he means a personality adjusted with respect to others, and which makes one easy to live with or to converse with, and which carries the same agreeable quality into public speech. Appearance, dress, good health, and aspects of deportment have distinct values in creating visual impressions which convey a state of mental well-being to the audience, and to the speaker.[12]

---

10. James H. McBurney, James M. O'Neill, and Glen E. Mills, *Argumentation and Debate: Techniques of a Free Society* (New York: Macmillan, 1951; a revision of *The Working Principles of Argument,* first issued in 1932), pp. 210-14.

11. Lionel Crocker, *Public Speaking for College Students* (New York: American Book Co., 1941), p. 25.

12. Crocker, pp. 25-26.

ORAL STYLE

At best, language is an oral code used to communicate mental images. Nida suggests that information material has impact in relation to its unpredictability, as well as in relation to the nature of the material involved.[13] Because the ideas are themselves somewhat shaped by the words selected to express them, there must be careful attention to language style in presentation so that listeners are kept in attention to the ideas desired. The boring speaker usually bores because he is treating the familiar in a predictable, normal manner.

The formal arrangement and selection of words to be used in delivery—usually referred to as the "style" of the sermon—reaches its best development as it blends perfectly into the task of being an invisible vehicle for the ideas being shared. There are few rules, for this is where the *art* of public speech is at its highest. Style is always a reflection of the individual personality, and often reflects also the environmental and educational background of the speaker.

Certain figures of speech carry extra impact. Well-controlled alliteration can bring balance and harmony. Onomatopoeia[14] arouses the visual imagination through auditory channels. Metaphor and simile, allegory and hyperbole, irony and parable—all these have value, but there are no static rules for their application. Each must feel his own need to use them at the appropriate juncture. Dramatic events, vividly portrayed, are advantageous, but only in the hands of an experienced and mature speaker.[15]

---

13. Eugene A. Nida, *Message and Mission: The Communication of the Christian Faith* (New York: Harper, 1960), pp. 72-75.

14. I.e., "sound-echoing sense" in word selection—such as "trembling at the edge of temptation," "the subtle hiss of the serpent," etc.

15. An experienced preacher could draw a picture, in words, of the sinner at the bar of God's judgment, and imagine a variety of personified entities, such as the world, the flesh, the devil, Scripture, his conscience, etc., bearing witness against him and his sins. An effective finale would be the appearance of the Advocate (I John 2:2) presenting His intercession and claiming the atonement of Calvary as the sinner's way of escape. Such drama must be used sparingly, but occasionally it can underline truth in a manner that enlists certain attention.

For good style all sermonic material must be reduced to written form. Only the pencil or typewriter can pin down actual words in permanent association in a manner which will best carry the weight of our ideas. The writing out of material tends to write it also into the memory, and to shape it into the most logical order so that the whole sermon can be viewed as a graphic unit. The extraneous may be deleted, and the four basic rules of style, *force, economy, subtlety,* and *clarity* can be practiced.[16]

Force

Force, or energy, is the first major need. Dynamic, energetic, and picturesque speech has power. Short sentences will be sparks to explode ideas. Suspended sentences, with no early verb, can create strong contrast. Energetic flow is the basic characteristic of all good style.

Economy

Economy is also demanded. We live in a tabloid generation that delights in concentrates and condensations. The simple, lively, short approach to truth is the most valid of contemporary techniques. We must relinquish all trivia and side issues, to drive straight for our preaching objectives. The Gettysburg Address, the wartime speeches of Churchill, and the twenty-third psalm are all fine examples of word power through economy. Precise and concise description creates sentence structures which hit, and fit.

Subtlety

A third valuable essential is *subtlety.* Overdrawn conclusions lose weight. If a point being made is borne into the hearers' minds via an explosive insight formed from a new grasp of facts and their significance, response will be truly motivated.

This is just what Jesus did when He talked about the kingdom of God being discovered by accident, by some (as a

---

16. See Sue Nichols, *Words on Target—For Better Communication* (Richmond, Va.: John Knox Press, 1963).

treasure hid in a field), or by search, with others (as the pearl of great price), yet each discovery involving the absolute surrender of all else to possess it. He answered the question "Who is my neighbor?" in a similar vein. He marched the great ideas He wished to present to His hearers through life-situation illustrations that were so real that truths were revealed as insights already discovered by His hearers.

Clarity

Clarity is style's final necessity. A kiss may be accurately described as "the anatomical juxtaposition of two orbicular muscles in a state of contraction." This is technically correct but emotionally uncommunicative. In His preaching about God, Jesus did not refer to a first great cause, an eternal reality, an architect of the universe, but simply and clearly to one who is "our Father." He did not talk about abstract humanity, but called us "brethren." The wise preacher will always seek to simplify and clarify, and to illumine the abstract via the concrete, real-life illustration of his ideas.[17]

A modern German theologian has become so enamored of the "wordly" style of a nineteenth century English evangelical pastor that he has been constrained to edit a new production of his works, and has written a magnificent introductory essay lauding the value of his style for today.[18]

Thielicke, in a clear enunciation of the elements that make up this manner of presentation used by Spurgeon, indicates the clarity of his explicit application as being a major factor in its power. In picturing the difference between implicit and explicit application of truth he gives a vivid illustration of two men attending a Nazi rally in the days of the infamous German Third Reich. One shouts "Christ is the Messiah," and is regarded with simple amazement; another, who declares the same truth, but applies it to the situation by decrying the dictatorial powers

---

17. These four elements of good style are developed in Miss Nichols's excellent little study.

18. Helmut Thielicke, *Encounter with Spurgeon*, trans. John W. Doberstein (Philadelphia: Fortress Press, 1963); see especially his introductory essay, pp. 1-45.

assumed by Adolf Hitler, is, as a result, made the subject of violence for his statement.[19] Today's preacher needs just such an explicit style or his utterances have no contemporary relevance.

Jefferson summarizes rules for style by saying:

Be natural. This is the sum of the whole matter. Do not push the voice into clerical cadences but let it flow out of an open throat, breaking into syllables which tell truly what you think and feel. Do not push the language into inflated and bombastic forms, but let it flow as naturally as a brook through one of God's own green meadows. Do not shove the thought into artificial altitudes, but let it move along the level on which you do your ordinary thinking. If you are altogether natural, you will become invisible. Style is perfect when it cannot be seen.[20]

GOOD DELIVERY

When method, dialogue, image, and style are in balance the sermon may yet lack presentation quality through its poor delivery. The greatest value in effective delivery is naturalness.

A reservoir of vocal power builds from exercise and experience. The wise speaker will practice his delivery using only the exhaled breath. The chest should be held as full as possible, with a reserve supply of air constantly replenished by central breathing from the diaphragm.[21] The most general faults in delivery include mumbling of words and giving a falling inflection to words incorrectly at the end of a sentence. Some strangle words, others bellow them. Most treat enunciation with normal respect; but many forget to project at a volume and to articulate at a sufficient level necessary for public address—which ought to be at least twice that of normal conversation. The voice can be improved as it is consciously projected toward the hard palate behind the front upper teeth, and it will fall from it with the most natural resonance and force. This will add clarity, fulness, and flexibility, and avoid a strained throat.

---

19. Thielicke, p. 34.

20. Charles Edward Jefferson, *The Minister as Prophet* (New York: Thomas H. Crowell and Co., 1905), pp. 143-44.

21. Most general books on public speaking, or preaching, carry a chapter or two on the better techniques for good delivery.

The force and distinctiveness of pronunciation will always need some enlargement in addressing an assembly. Some variation in pitch, inflection, volume, and emphasis will add color and strength to any address, and can all be improved with diligent practice. Again, however, naturalness is preferable to artificiality. An evident professionalism in delivery is barrier rather than asset in communication. If the preacher rehearses thoroughly, and consciously projects a sense of dignity and controlled ease while preaching, this in itself will aid in natural competence.

Jefferson comments:
Remember that the congregation is nothing but a man. It is not a colossus to be attacked by rhetorical bludgeons, or a baby to be tickled by vocal pyrotechnics, or a monster to be tricked and trapped by oratorical stratagems and devices. To speak to a man you must be one yourself. Never endeavour to be eloquent. It may be that God will let you be eloquent a half a dozen times in your life, but I am sure you cannot be eloquent if you try to be. And never declaim. Declamation makes a noise and interests the children, but grown-up people care nothing for it. . . . Scatter God's truths through your congregation, and rest assured that someone will carry one of them home![22]

Regular eye contact with the congregation is an essential. A sense of directness is thereby established, and a point made under such encounter will register. Like gesture, this contact must again be normal and natural. It will relate to the form of delivery chosen, and to the place that manuscript, or notes, will have within that delivery form.

Delivery may be done in one particular form, or in any combination of four common forms. A sermon can be presented from memory, from manuscript, or in impromptu, or extemporaneous manner. None of these alone is always satisfactory in terms of teaching method and listener involvement; but the fourth, when based on the second, seems to be the most generally acceptable.

Memory

The first method, preaching from *memory*, is possible, but

---

22. Jefferson, pp. 141-42.

most difficult. A well-experienced preacher, an unusual occasion, and a vital message may combine to demand such a method; but this is always subject to failure. The attempt at total recall tends to withdraw the speaker from the situation, and thus decrease his communication. The method can impose severe limits on liberty, utterance, and enthusiasm; and these restrictions will be felt by the hearers. If memory fails there is no recourse from the embarrassment that is always possible. It is better to memorize short passages, sentences, or illustrations, and then place these within an extemporaneous sermon.

Manuscript

Preaching from a *manuscript* is an alternate method, and one that is very popular. Nevertheless, it always brings with it the temptation to read rather than to preach, however well done this may be. Paper ruins the attention which a speaker can pay to an audience, and consequently that with which they can respond to him. The great value of a manuscript is that what has been prepared will of necessity be shared. In any other method of presentation there is always the danger of omitting something that is of real value. It is only where the pulpit utterance is tied closely to the hours of preparation and study via a manuscript, that accurate phrasing, logical continuity, and spiritual inspiration can be at its best. There is also the added advantage of having the material ready for filing, for later use, or for publication.

The problem is that it must not only be worth reading when it is written, but, when being delivered from a manuscript, the sermon must also be read well. Occasionally a preacher has the ability to read a manuscript without a congregation's being unduly aware of his reading, but it is a rare art. If hearers realize that he has a manuscript its possession suggests a psychological communications barrier, whether it is actually so, or not! They tend to feel that no subject can be of significance to them if it cannot master the speaker sufficiently to allow him to speak about it in a direct manner. The sly sliding of pages, combined with the reading of small print—usually held at three times the normal reading distance—places an obligation on the average preacher that must restrict his power.

Impromptu

Impromptu preaching is a third method. It is the delivery of a totally unpremeditated address. Unforeseen and unplanned-for occasions do sometimes arise when the preacher is called on to speak without preparation. At such times he will be wise to fall back on old, or familiar, material, or to take a previous remark, or an aspect of the current situation as a basis for discussion. As he repeats or rephrases these, his mind will begin to move. Every preacher ought to have at least the bare bones of a reserve sermon, plus a suitable story or two, in his pocket or in his mind at all times.

Extemporaneous

Extemporaneous preaching is the best, and it includes values gleaned from the other three methods above. It is that evolved from normal preparation, but leaves the actual outward form of presentation to the moment of delivery. This makes it most adaptable to a variety of situations. The fire of inspiration can burn on the thoroughness of preparation, and the most apposite contemporary remark or illustration can be introduced on the spot, if required. Condensation, or enlargement, can be balanced in relation to the actual occasion.

The danger in some extemporaneous preaching is the tendency to depend too much on the inspiration of the moment, thus allowing the sermon to become impromptu. If a thorough preparation is made, as normally, including the writing of the finished sermon in manuscript form, then a page or two of brief notes can be culled from it for the pulpit; and this will combine the best of all the methods. The preacher has already written the detail of how the sermon could be delivered; and, although he may not follow this absolutely, he is able, from this previous experience, to create an on-the-spot presentation with some previous knowledge of how to go about it most effectively. Extemporaneous preachers who continually avoid detail manuscript preparation fall into the trap of repeating boring cliches and using predictable phraseology, and they are usually the last to realize how dry their sermons have become.

The following should be noted:

1. *Extemporaneous preaching is not work saving.* It is more strenuous than any other in its preparation, and more taxing in its delivery.

2. *Thoughts are never clear until they are expressed in words.* Vocabulary and communication can grow only as the preacher sees and studies his sermons in their written form.

3. *Before the actual delivery the mind ought to be stimulated by a brief rereading of the manuscript, and by earnest prayer.*

4., *The preaching framework of thesis, keyword, and divisions is most suited to good extemporaneous delivery.* [23]

Notes should include the sermonic framework, key thoughts and sentences, and illustrations. The parish pastor who prepares a number of addresses each week ought to strive to handle at least one sermon in this thorough manner, despite its demanding preparation, if he desires to grow in preaching skill. The opening and closing sentences of introduction and conclusion will also be best used when included in the pulpit notes.

I have found that two facing pages (about 9" x 6" each) in a small loose-leaf binder which can open out flat, can be placed on a pulpit beside a Bible. Ample notes can be written on them, large enough to be read from a distance. Open facing pages avoid any necessity for the turning of leaves. Scripture readings, hymns, and details of the place where the sermon is preached can be recorded on the reverse side of the left page, and any other details which it is desired to memorize, such as quotations, illustrations, and so forth, recorded on the reverse side of the right-hand page. Main divisions can be underlined or outlined in contrasting colors; and signs, such as an asterisk, can be used to denote the place of an illustration or some other feature. Every man must determine the details of his own method; but regular use of a system such as this, illustrated in the appendix to this study,[24] will aid freedom in delivery.

---

23. See chap. 9.

24. See app. C.

Conclusion

The Divine Dynamic

The preceding pages have led us in a study of the science of teaching within preaching. The historical, theological, and psychological perspectives yield the theory which we have sought to apply in the objectives, planning, structure, and presentation of the Word of God.

All these are mechanics of technique. They involve the intellectual, emotional, and volitional elements of the sermon which aid its power. The plea has been for a greater understanding of the function of the parish preacher as a minister to help the total ministry of every member of his congregation be more effective. As the *voice of the body* his function always embraces the teaching task, and he has direct responsibility to be as knowledgeable, and competent, in this role, as it is possible for him to be.

Yet all these elements, which we have discussed, may be present in adequate strength and proportion without true preaching being in evidence.

We may have a genuine message of truth to deliver, and be eloquent in it, for real eloquence moves under the impact of great ideas and relevant truths; yet what we deliver may be but the presentation of a lecture, not the preaching of a sermon. We may be enriched by insights into the nature and needs of persons; aware of the attitudes and responses necessary in the learning process; and expert in the order, selection, and arrangement of words to communicate truth; yet we can still fail *spiritually,* for preaching is a spiritual function.

The temptation in any responsible scientific examination of a subject is to remove God from it. *But the Holy Spirit is the divine dynamic. He is the essential element that transforms teaching into preaching.* His ministry alone can bring life to what otherwise has only form.

Some preachers exhibit a dynamic in preaching that has

indescribable reality and depth. To them comes a liberty in delivery, an evidence of practical results, an acceptable passion and intensity, and a communications quality which wrestles with the hearts of men in dimensions otherwise unknown. For the preacher who has ministered in this manner—and most have at least occasional experiences of this nature—there is a soaring motivation and an aura of relaxed naturalness and satisfaction in such service which is beyond all verbal description. This is the work of the Holy Spirit.

Christ's preaching power can be explained only in such terms.[1] Spiritual power was also a basic characteristic of the apostolic ministry,[2] and Paul himself took pains to emphasize this to his hearers: "And my speech and my preaching were not with enticing words of man's wisdom, but in demonstration of the Spirit and of power: that your faith should not stand in the wisdom of men, but in the power of God."[3] It was his conviction that it was impossible to preach, in the sense of expressing a true revelation from God, without the ministry of the Spirit; for the Biblical revelation was not *of* men but something manifested *through* men.[4] Writing to the Thessalonians he also indicated that an inbuilt authority accompanied his message, an authority related to a confidence in the genuine work of God through his preaching, and an energy directly associated with the Spirit's ministry within this proclamation.[5]

W. E. Sangster uses the phrase "the Plus of the Spirit" to indicate power in preaching. By this he signifies this divine dynamic, the mystical and inspirational element in preaching, which is always felt when present but which eludes definition. It is related, he feels, to the preacher's life, devotion, personality, gifts, and training. It is spiritually expensive to obtain; but without it, while a man may teach, he will not truly preach.

---

1. Isa. 11:2; Luke 4:18.

2. Acts 4:8, 31; 5:32; 6:10; 7:55; 13:9, 52.

3. I Cor. 2:4-5.

4. I Cor. 2:4-5, 10-14.

5. I Thess. 1:5.

SUPERNATURAL REALITY

This element can be identified in relation to its nature, as an employment of personality under the direct sovereignty of God. The primary outreach of God to men, in our age, is through His Spirit, and in accordance with His sovereign will. In this sense the inherent power in all preaching is somewhat unrelated to personal achievement, and often those most used are somewhat unaware of its presence. The reality, however, is always recognized by those listening.

The supernatural nature of such liberty cannot be too strongly emphasized. In these days of emphasis on Rogerian counseling theories, many believe that human nature is positive, constructive, forward moving, and trustworthy. This humanistic technique is premised on the philosophy that the individual has power to grow and to meet his own needs consequent on a true insight of them. It is the view of such proponents that man can discover the capacity to change for the better within himself, and that the counselor's task is merely to provide situations that meet the essential conditions for such self-discovery.[6]

Nothing is more at variance with the Biblical view of man at several points of major importance. The Bible reveals the absolute and universal depravity of man in his natural state, and gives no encouragement for his improvement by natural means. The shunting of a variety of possibilities through the human mind for choice needs the endorsement and clarification of a divine revelation to be in line with eternal truth. Such insight as may come can never guarantee a concomitant power to change for the better. We cannot build new lives on a human nature which both Scripture and history have long ago proved to be untrustworthy and with a twisted bias to be bad. This humanistic philosophy carries some truth; but, in the main, it does violence to the freedom of the human personality by demanding from it a natural improvement which it cannot produce. A Christian may respond to such therapy with the added insight and power of supernatural light and strength. On the purely human plane such changes as occur—and there are many—must be basically "of the flesh."

---

6. Carl Rogers, *Client-Centred Therapy* (Boston: Houghton-Mifflin Co., 1951).

If then, by preaching, we aim to change lives for God, and for good, we dare not depend solely on natural means and natural truth. There must be both a supernatural revelation and a supernatural power if God is to work in the hearts of men.

In His work God does not ignore the nature and needs of persons. The Spirit's communication can reach men without the regular avenues to which this study has given previous attention, for His work is essentially spiritual and supernatural. Other things being equal, however, just as the becalmed ship with its sails up will travel farthest and fastest when the sudden wind blows, so the prepared person will be better used than the unprepared. The winds of the Spirit seem to move more obviously on those who have planned for them and are ready when a sovereign Providence sends them.

Paul also said that preaching is only possible because of the supernaturalness of our possessions in Christ.[7] Andrew Bonar once listened to a probationary minister's sermon on the text "Come unto me," which he bore with patience. Then, when asked by the student pastor to say a word at the close of the service, Dr. Bonar commented with deep feeling: "We have all heard a great deal tonight about the coming; a great deal about the coming! But it's not the coming that makes the difference. It's not the coming! It's the *Me!* It's the *Me!*"[8]

Scripture teaches us that *the Holy Spirit works through the exaltation of Christ.* John 16:7-14 says that the Spirit's ministry in the world is wholly concerned with God's Son. He promotes a conviction of sin, a stirring of the conscience, an awareness of judgment, and a concern for change, to the end that the things of Christ may be revealed and received.[9] The preacher must therefore prepare consciously to exalt the Savior. Ribs of doctrine must always structure the bridges of appeal; and, in particular, the central doctrine of atonement through the mediatorial work of Christ is central to all effective preaching.

---

7. See I Cor. 2, especially vv. 12-16.

8. T.S. Cairncross, *The Steps of the Pulpit* (London: Hodder and Stoughton, 1910), p. 61.

9. See John 14:16; 15:26.

The Spirit works also through the personal communion which the preacher has with God. Our surrendered lives are vehicles for His ministry. He illumines the memory, and witnesses to others, through our genuine holiness. Spurgeon, declaring that the Holy Spirit was given to teach us and interpret to us, says the human tongue is thus freed from its natural limitations, an emotional elevation is promoted, communication is enhanced, and spiritual life is generated in our hearers. The Spirit intercedes for us above our abilities. Genuine piety and discernment are always the attributes that evidence His presence.[10]

Shoemaker defines this ministry as a felt presence, associated Scripturally—and therefore practically—with a unity in fellowship, with power, cleansing, judgment, and also with inner renewal and guidance.[11] Factors that work against His ministry include spiritual disobedience, mediocre commitment, pride, indolence, and lack of prayer continuity.[12]

James W. Clarke describes "a sense of the Infinite which gives to preaching massiveness, tenderness, proportion, sincerity, and directness."[13] He names the besetting sins of preachers as being spiritual laziness, selfishness, and smugness; and he warns: "Now, so many are no longer preachers and pastors, but mechanics, ever busy around the ecclesiastical machine, oiling gears, tightening nuts, screwing bolts, and pulling levers."[14]

Sangster characterizes the possession of such spiritual power as being grown from the preparation of life, the day, and the moment. It involves prayer for people and for power, and an unreserved offering of oneself for God's use at the actual moment of preaching opportunity. We need to examine ourselves faithfully, in dialogue with the Spirit Himself, through meditation, and

---

10. Charles Haddon Spurgeon, *The Soul-Winner* (Grand Rapids: Wm. B. Eerdmans, 1963), pp. 63-75.

11. Samuel Shoemaker, *With the Holy Spirit and with Fire* (New York: Harper, 1960), pp. 27-35.

12. Spurgeon, pp. 74-76.

13. James W. Clarke, *Dynamic Preaching* (New York: Revell, 1960), p. 126.

14. Clarke, p. 108.

turn from prayer to study and service, seeking to carry this atmosphere with us as we go.

Prayer brings a passion to preaching that cultivates this "sense of startled awe" that is felt throughout the New Testament alongside of its preaching. The English word "enthusiasm" is simple transliteration from *enthus,* which is the contracted form of *en theos* (ἐν θεὸs): "having the God in oneself," or "inspired." Etymologically, then, enthusiasm is simply divine inspiration. The power and demonstration of the Spirit is not the faked feeling of unbalanced emotional excess, but the simple fulness of God in possession of a yielded instrument bent on exalting Christ.

TESTIMONIAL AUTHORITY

True zeal and passion in preaching, kindled by love for Christ and fanned into steady flame by a life of genuine devotion, can be yielded to God for such supernatural ends. Preaching enthusiasm becomes a spiritual value as it exhibits the authority of a firsthand experience that is positive, and glows with sincere reality. Abbey defines preaching as "a divine-human act in which men in their lostness are summoned to a saving encounter with God's Word through the spoken words of a convinced witness."[15]

Preaching is not professional spiritual promotion. It is *testimony.* The dogmatism of the New Testament was a testimonial authority, not a forced and artificial enthusiasm. Every man born can tell the difference. It is required of a witness that he be authoritative. If he lacks positive assurance he has no right to offer his testimony. A genuine assurance that he does carry a revelation from God, born from a personal involvement, will make the preacher an effective instrument for the work of God.

It was where such personal spiritual experience created a deep spiritual authority that new life came to the church in both the evangelical revival under Whitefield and Wesley, and in the second worldwide spiritual awakening one hundred years later.[16]

---

15. Merrill R. Abbey, *Preaching to the Contemporary Mind* (New York: Abingdon, 1963), p. 49.

16. See J. Edwin Orr, *The Second Evangelical Awakening* (London: Marshall, Morgan, and Scott, 1955); and James Burns, *Revivals: Their Laws and Leaders.* reprint ed. (Grand Rapids: Baker Book House, 1960).

In each case the spiritual upsurge was in vital relation to an evangelical dogmatism born out of the depth involvement of the leaders of these movements in a deep commitment and meaningful relation with God.

Hearers must know and feel that the preacher is not a passive spectator, but an active participant, in the sermon. Such a person, truly remade in Christ, conscious of his own unworthiness and of the free gift of forgiveness, ought to exhibit a natural enthusiasm born from deep personal thanksgiving. A proper sense of awe and wonder at the magnificence of redemption, and a deep and growing understanding of the doctrines of grace will add an authority in delivery which will be natural and real. The preacher is no advocate assisting in the presentation of a plea. He is a person involved as a witness in the truths being shared.

D. Martyn Lloyd-Jones has an excellent study of the place of this authority in the preacher's life. Speaking of the Holy Spirit and the relation of His ministry to our practical plans, he says:

> Let us go on with our practical efforts, and let us go on with our study, but God forbid that we should rely upon them. Let us equip ourselves as best we can. We shall never be as able and as learned as the Apostle Paul, St. Augustine, Luther, or Calvin. These were men of great learning, and giant intellects. That is the kind of man God seems to use when He does His greatest things in the history of the church. Let us go on, however, and seek to equip ourselves as perfectly as possible. But, in the name of God, let us not stop at that. Let us realise that even that, without the authority and the power of the Spirit, is of no value at all. . . . It does not matter who I am or what I may do: it will get me nowhere. It is the authority of the Spirit that alone avails.[17]

The words we speak share life and death. The spiritual element that summons men into encounter with God through our preaching is our participating witness. This "plus of the Spirit" is the one essential dynamic that lies within the realm of divine sovereignty, and which alone can transform good teaching into real preaching. To this supernatural possibility we must make definite commitment of ourselves. Within the preaching occasion we must ensure that we will be as valuable an instrument in His

---

17. D. Martyn Lloyd-Jones, *Authority* (Chicago: Inter-Varsity Press, 1958), p. 49.

hands as it is possible for us to be, by the thoroughness of our preparation and the depth of our personal and experiential involvement with the truth being shared.

Ultimately the preacher's function is simply to make himself available for God's use. Our prayer should be for an identification and involvement at the level of the great apostle, as expressed by one many years ago in words as if uttered by Paul himself:

> Oft when the Word is on me to deliver,
>   Lifts the illusion and the truth lies bare;
> Desert or throng, the city or the river
>   Melts in a lucid paradise of air.
>
> Only like souls I see the folk thereunder,
>   Bound who should conquer, slaves who should be kings;
> Hearing their one hope with an empty wonder
>   Sadly contented in a show of things.
>
> Then with a rush the intolerable craving
>   Shivers through me like a trumpet call;
> Oh, to save these, to perish for their saving,
>   Die for their life, be offered for them all.[18]

---

18. Frederick W. H. Myers, *St. Paul* (London: Samuel Bagster and Sons, n.d.).

APPENDIXES

APPENDIX A
Some Elements of Verification

An attempt to marshal proof from pulpit masters of historical and contemporary importance to support the basic principles and practices expounded in the foregoing study would be a limitless task. It would also be somewhat redundant in light of the liberal footnotes and references that have been included.

Several aspects of verification are, however, worthy of some note.

The Yale Lectures and Others

A summary of this well-known preaching series, compiled after examination of the content of sixty-six of the published volumes in the series, endorses concepts listed in the foregoing study, with an emphasis on aims and purposes related to the needs of the congregation, the attitudes of the preacher, and his partnership with his people in a joint search for truth.[1] A recurrent theme is the breadth of reading and knowledge of human nature exhibited by the great preachers of history. A deep homiletical interest in both the method and biography of other preachers is also shown to be a characteristic of leading pulpiteers of every age.

Collated books of sermons, in which a number of preachers express their preparation and presentation methods and give sample addresses, show similar support. Great emphasis is again given to ideas of planned preparation relative to aims and goals, and the clarity of a central thesis or proposition around which the whole sermon is structured appears continually as a major essential.[2]

Great Evangelical Preachers

Sidelights on the methods of well-known evangelicals enunciated by a recent writer show great affinity with similar elements.[3] A recent revision of Spurgeon's lectures, edited by a leading German theologian, clearly demonstrates his evaluation of Spurgeon's approach as being in line with much of

---

1. B. B. Baxter, *The Heart of the Yale Lectures* (New York: Macmillan, 1947), pp. 288 ff.

2. See books in bibliography by H. C. Brown and C. S. Roddy.

3. James McGraw, *Great Evangelical Preachers of Yesterday* (New York: Abingdon, 1961). See particularly chapters on Wycliffe, Huss, Luther, Zwingli, Melanchthon, Knox, Calvin, Wesley, and Whitefield.

the thrust of this study.

Thielicke's emphasis in the fifteen-thousand-word essay with which he introduces the material is laudatory of the preacher's great faith, common-sense communication (which he calls "worldliness"), and confrontation with persons in practical application of Biblical truth. He regards the Spurgeonic ministry as an existential encounter in its best sense, and links it with the evident evangelical and conservative theological position having pragmatic application to salvation, openly evident in the preacher's own experience.[4]

Karl Barth and Modern Theologians

In one of the best summaries of Karl Barth and his concepts, it is emphasized that the whole Barthian theology arose from homiletical demand. Thrust away from a liberal theology by the facing of congregational need, Barth took the Biblical revelation as the valid means of ministry to meet them in that need. The author quotes personal conversation and discussions with the theologian (after an intimate association with him over a considerable length of time) and includes the following as his comment on preaching (i.e., Barth's own view):

> For myself, I seem to come to a sermon from one of three starting points. A text grips me and I want to preach it. Or a deep need of man cries out to be met and I seek the answer from God in Jesus Christ. Or a luminous truth about life dawns in my mind and I wish to proclaim it in a way that is rooted in God's Word, and that is relevant for my fellow men.[5]

Another compilation of studies by leading teachers (Tillich, Hoffman, Niebuhr, etc.) endorses the need for the training of preachers in the dialogical approach to the ministerial function, and advocates the demand for a right sharing of the total ministry of all members of the congregation, developed by the preacher.[6] This concept of a total ministry by the laity is coming increasingly to the fore in all theological discussion.[7]

---

4. Helmut Thielicke, *Encounter with Spurgeon*, trans. John W. Doberstein (Philadelphia: Fortress Press, 1963), pp. 1-45.

5. Arnold B. Come, *An Introduction to Barth's Dogmatics for Preachers* (Philadelphia: Westminster Press, 1963), p. 166.

6. Hans Hoffman, ed., *Making the Ministry Relevant* (New York: Scribner's, 1960). See especially pp. 143 ff.

7. Howard Grimes, *The Church Redemptive* (New York: Abingdon, 1958), and *The Rebirth of the Laity* (New York: Abingdon, 1962); Hendrik Kraemer, *A Theology of the Laity* (Philadelphia: Westminster Press, 1962); etc.

Norman Vincent Peale

Another study, worthy of note, comes from an unusual quarter, in that it covers a detail study of one of America's most popular preachers. In analysis of Dr. Peale's ministry, Broadhurst endorses the popular concept that Peale's preaching includes themes of "positive thinking" and other psychological truth as motivation factors for vital Christian living. He also, however, after a thorough evaluation of Dr. Peale's preaching ministry, gathered from fourteen years of filed sermons and researched with the aid of electronic computation, makes this enlightening comment:

> His sermons are nearly 100% problem-solving sermons. . . . A subject is important only if it has direct, immediate, and practical usage for the members of his congregation.[8]

In this light it is probable that Peale's great attraction does not lie in the "self-help" idea, as some have suggested, but rather in the simple fact that he deals with Christian truth at a level where his congregation is helped. The self-help theme may be more a means of communication: a means, and not an end. Dr. Broadhurst proves, by incontrovertible statistical analysis, that this is dramatically so. Referring to "positive thinking" as a "thought theme," he says:

> In his sermons the Thought Theme is never presented in isolation, but is consistently embedded in what can only be described as a primarily conservative Protestant theology.[9]

He also indicates Peale's support of the idea of a central proposition, and to psychological and sociological aspects of communication. The simplicity and directness of his preaching he views as explanation of his power, and as arising from his exposition of the Christian revelation geared to human needs.

---

8. Allan R. Broadhurst, *He speaks the Word of God: A Study of the Sermons of Norman Vincent Peale* (Englewood Cliffs, N.J.: Prentice-Hall, 1963), p. 86.

9. Broadhurst, p. 91.

APPENDIX B
Southern Baptist Materials

Southern Baptist Materials

From the *Church Program Guidebook* (Nashville:
Sunday School Board of the Southern Baptist
Convention, 1965), appendix on the
"Theological Foundations of the Curriculum."

The material in the following pages details the basic theological foundations and objectives of Christian teaching and training for the educational ministry of the church, as prepared by leaders in the Southern Baptist Convention, U.S.A.

These seem to be among the best adaptations of the pragmatic educational philosophy, set within a Biblical framework, that are in operation within any major denomination.

The preacher who would understand his hearers, and his task, would be well repaid by a detail study of this material, particularly part II.

FOUNDATIONS OF THE CURRICULUM

PART I

If we accept the idea that the educational task is both central and comprehensive in the life and work of a church, we are then confronted by important questions: What is the philosophy which is to guide in the ministry of teaching and training? What are the concepts of divine purpose, human need, religious experience, and personality development which are to determine the educational program? What are the theological assumptions on which the curriculum rests? What are the objectives to be sought? The answers to these questions point to the foundation of the curriculum.

The purpose of this appendix is not to answer in detail the questions stated above. It is rather to set forth a viewpoint that underlies the curriculum designed for use in Southern Baptist churches. We begin with God and his revelation. We consider persons and their potential in the purpose of God. We recognize the church as the divine instrument for Christian teaching and training. We assume the unity of the church's educational mission.

In curriculum building, as in all other areas, the foundation is important. Solid content and sound principles must constitute the foundation if the educational structure is to be strong and enduring and if it is to provide for the learning needs of persons of all ages rightly related to God, to themselves, and to society. The foundation of the curriculum must have values which do not vary from age to age or church to church or situation to situation; but the curricular structure must have qualities which are dynamic and creative, adjustable to the church situation and adaptable to the needs of individuals.

The Nature and Message of the Bible

The curriculum rests, first of all, on the nature and message of the Bible. We declare that the Bible is our authority for faith and practice. We look to the Bible for our message, our polity, and our pattern. We turn to the Bible to learn the way of salvation and the standards of Christian living. We search the Bible to find God's plan of the ages and his will for mankind. It is fitting, therefore, that we accept the Bible as the authority and guide for our teaching ministry and as the subject matter for Christian faith and character and for Christian learning and development.

Though the Bible is the basis of the church educational program, one is not to conclude that the curriculum is chiefly content centered. That is both true and false. The content and meaning of the Bible revelation are the subject matter for instruction, but the experiences and needs of persons are the factors to which subject matter must be related and the determinants of teaching method and objective. Hence, a curriculum based on the Bible is also life centered. In this way the wisdom of God is brought to bear on the problems of human experience.

There is both necessity and logic in building the curriculum on the revelation of truth found in the Bible. It is God's message to men. It alone speaks with finality about redemption and righteousness. It is the criterion of moral values and human responsibility.

In recognition of this fact, we present in this appendix a statement of basic theological assumptions. This is in no sense a definitive statement of theological thought. Neither is it meant to be a confession of faith. Instead its purpose is to set forth in summary form the biblical ideas which constitute the foundation for curriculum materials and objectives. These concepts are of utmost importance. They constitute, either directly or by implication, something of the scope of Christian understanding and learning. They provide the basis for Christian faith and duty.

It is believed that the educational leaders in a church will find a study of these assumptions fruitful in sensing the biblical perspective of the curriculum and in sensing the necessity for a solid biblical content in the materials for Christian teaching.

Basic Theological Assumptions

I. *The Bible.*—The Bible is the inspired record of God's revelation of himself and of his way and will for mankind. It is the word of God, revealed to chosen men through the illumination of the Holy Spirit. It speaks with final authority about all matters of spiritual faith and moral duty. It has meaning for all age groups with capacity for conscious spiritual responses. Its message of redemption through Christ is the hope of mankind. Its principles of conduct are God's pattern for human living. Its truth is the interpretation of existence and the clue to the meaning of history. Therefore, its content is to be the object of purposeful study, and its promises and precepts are to be proclaimed and taught to all men everywhere.

II. *God.*—God is. He is the Creator, the Sovereign, and the Sustainer of the universe. God is a person—infinite in knowledge, power, righteousness, and mercy. God is active, purposeful, and redemptive. God is spirit. God is love. God is light. God is one; but he reveals himself to men as Father, Son, and Holy Spirit. As the Heavenly Father, he loves all persons with an everlasting love. He is gracious and merciful toward the evil and the good. He searches for lost men with reconciling grace. He justifies all who come to him through Christ. He disciplines his children through chastening and loving providences. He deals righteously with all who reject his mercy. God is to be worshiped and accorded reverential respect; he is to be loved and trusted, to be obeyed and served.

III. *Jesus Christ.*—Jesus Christ is the eternal Son of God—one with the Father—and the Saviour of the world. He was born of a virgin and became in the likeness of men. As the Son of man he was God incarnate in the flesh, the Messiah promised to Israel, the Redeemer sent to save men from sin. He was and is the full and final revelation of God's nature and purpose. In the days of his flesh he was tempted in all ways common to man, but without sin. Thus he became the example of perfect righteousness. His life is the standard of goodness. His teachings are the criterion for personal character and social responsibility. His voluntary sacrifice on the cross is the atonement for the sin of the world. His resurrection is the assurance of life after death and the ground of his universal lordship. His ascension marked the beginning of his mediatorial ministry as our great High Priest. It is an assurance of his eternal sovereignty and his coming again in triumph and judgment. He is the one way to God; he is the living Lord, the all-sufficient Saviour.

IV. *The Holy Spirit.*—The Holy Spirit is the third person of the Godhead, one with the Father and the Son. The Spirit is a person. He is the spirit of truth, of holiness, of power, and of life. He is the agent of the Godhead in regeneration, in preservation, and in sanctification. He abides in the hearts of Christians. He is the helper in prayer, the guide in spiritual decision, the interpreter of truth, the power for Christian witnessing and Christlike living, the ever-present Comforter. The Christian life is new life in the Spirit.

V. *Man.*—Man is a person, created in the image of God, with moral competence and moral responsibility. He is a thinking, feeling, willing being. Man's nature is both body and soul: the physical is made sacred by the spiritual. Every man is of infinite worth and possesses the dignity of personality. Man is free: his will cannot be coerced; he is competent under God to deal with God for himself; spiritual faith and moral choice must be personal and voluntary. Man is a sinner, corrupted in his moral nature by evil and inclined toward sin. Therefore, man is helpless to save himself and is utterly dependent on the grace of God. But at heart man hungers for God and seeks for inner peace, security, and self-realization. He possesses capacity for faith and for infinite transformation through the redemption of Christ.

VI. *Sin.*—Sin is a fact in human experience. It is not a subjective creation of the imagination; neither is it merely an error of mind or an expression of human weakness. It is an act of will or an attitude of mind on the part of responsible persons in relation to God. The essence of sin is self-love and self-will. Sin entered human experience through the fall of man. All men have sinned as a result

of their natural bent toward evil and as a result of Satan's assaults upon the soul. Sin is against God. It finds expression in countless forms, such as disobedience, indifference, unbelief, ingratitude, irreverence, deceit, infidelity, impurity, malice, pride, and covetousness. Sin separates one from God, corrupts the mind and heart, enslaves the will, and brings upon a person the just condemnation of God. The wages of sin is death. The only way of deliverance from sin is the forgiveness of God through faith in Christ. The one way of victory over sin is the power of the indwelling Spirit.

VII. *The cross.*—The death of Jesus Christ is the central fact in God's redemptive activity. The cross was the divinely devised means for redeeming sinful man and for overcoming evil in the world. It was God's response to man's disobedience and man's plight in sin. It is the expression of God's judgment on sin and the revelation of God's love for sinners. It is the demonstration of his power of redemptive love in a world of evil. The message of the cross of Christ is the heart of the gospel. The principle of the cross is the heart of Christian discipleship. The cross declares that self-sacrifice is the way of self-realization. It enables us to understand suffering in a world of evil and to relate suffering to the providential purpose of God.

VIII. *Salvation.*—Salvation from sin is man's most urgent need. It is made possible for any man because of God's grace, because of Christ's atonement for sin, and because of the Spirit's convicting and regenerating power. Salvation, in the initial sense, is a new birth, wrought by the Spirit, conditioned upon personal faith in Christ as Saviour and Lord. Such faith is a voluntary committal to Christ accompanied by repentance or turning in godly sorrow from sin. God forgives one's sins, imparts to him eternal life through Christ, and receives him into the kingdom of heaven. Therefore, salvation is by grace through faith. It is a real experience, at a point in time, and is the result of a redeeming act of God in response to the voluntary faith of man. In a continuing sense, salvation is union with Christ, life in the Spirit, sonship to the Father, membership in the body of Christ—in a relationship of love and trust expected to issue in holiness and service. The end of salvation is life everlasting, the reception of an eternal inheritance in heaven.

IX. *Christian growth.*—The new birth anticipates growth. The new life in Christ is not static but dynamic. Christian experience is both a state and a process: the Christian has been justified; he is becoming sanctified. The Christian life, therefore, should be a continuous experience of growth—in spiritual knowledge and understanding, in Christian attitudes and appreciations and loyalties, in the capacities and skills and habits of Christlike living and serving. Growth is not automatic. It requires nurture and training. It calls for self-discipline, dedication, and perseverance. It involves conflict and the chastening of God. It is subject to the laws of personality development. Since personality has unlimited capacity for change, the goal of Christian personality development is likeness to Jesus Christ. The goal of Christian experience is Christian maturity—in intellectual discernment, in moral strength, in social vision, in Christian virtues, and in personal dedication to the will of God.

X. *The church.*—The church is composed of the people of God, the redeemed family. It is the body of Christ, of which he himself is the head. It is thus a divine creation with a divine mission to represent Christ on earth. The church is imperishable and eternal: the gates of Hades shall not envelop it or overcome it. The church finds its truest expression in churches, which—according to New Testament pattern—are composed of regenerated persons who have confessed their faith in Christ through baptism and who have voluntarily associated themselves together for worship, fellowship, mutual reinforcement, and service in the name of Christ. A church is a fellowship of believers bound together in Christian love. A church is autonomous, answerable only to Christ the Lord. But churches are interrelated, bound together by a common faith and the common purpose of their Lord. They are under obligation to co-operate for their mutual welfare and their mutual effectiveness in serving the cause of Christ. To churches Christ has committed the gospel and the cause of world redemption. Loyalty to one's church is of supreme importance, and service through one's church is the foremost means of serving the objectives of the kingdom of God.

XI. *Evangelism.*—The gospel is good news—the good news of salvation through Jesus Christ. The Christian, therefore, is to be a herald of the gospel: he is to be a witness for Christ, striving to persuade lost persons to repent of sin and believe the gospel. Evangelism is the response of Christians individually, and collectively through churches, to the plight of persons in sin, to the compulsion of the cross, to the commission of the risen Lord, and to the supremacy of salvation as life's greatest need and man's greatest blessing.

XII. *Missions.*—Missions is the concept and program of world evangelization. It is the sharing of the whole gospel for the whole of life with the whole of mankind. It is the program under the power and direction of the Holy Spirit whereby God's purpose in history, revealed in and achieved through Christ, is to be realized in the redemption of men. Missions, therefore, represents God's plan of the ages and is the expression of God's redemptive concern for every human being. It challenges Christians individually and churches corporately to their utmost concern in terms of intercession, dedication of life, and material support. Hence, missions is the inescapable obligation of every Christian in recognition of the command of Jesus Christ as Lord.

XIII. *The kingdom of God.*—The kingdom of God, or the kingdom of heaven, is the reign of God: in fact, the reign of Christ, to whom has been given all authority in heaven and on earth. Specifically, it is the rule of Christ in the hearts of all who have acknowledged him as Saviour and Lord. The kingdom of God is a present fact. It

has come through the redemptive activity of Christ. It is here in the power of the living Lord. It is coming through the sovereignty of Christ, the power of the gospel, and the work of the churches. It will come in consummation in the return of the Lord, the judgment upon evil, and the fulfilment of God's redemptive purpose in history. The kingdom of God, therefore, stands for the will of Christ for mankind. Its principles are the eternal standards of right living: moral purity and integrity, Christian love, unselfish service, and reverential worship. The kingdom of God calls for the complete allegiance of Christians. It challenges an evil world with the supreme values of redemption and goodness. The coming of the kingdom is the assurance of righteousness, joy, and peace in all the earth.

XIV. *The world order.*—The fall of man led to a race in rebellion against God—hence, a world order under the dominion of Satan, marked by moral perversion and corruption, under the judgment of God. But God's grace has wrought redemption and called out a people for his own possession—an elect race, a holy nation, a royal priesthood—zealous for good works. Christians, therefore, are in the world but not of the world. They are members of society and responsible citizens of the state. They share with all men the aspirations and afflictions of their common humanity. They live in a material universe and are subject to the laws of nature. But they are in conflict with the world rulers of darkness and the spiritual hosts of wickedness. Christians are set in the midst of the world order to be salt and light, to be evangels of salvation. They may not expect freedom from trial or deliverance from suffering. But they can know that nothing can separate them from the love of Christ and that Christ must reign until all enemies are put under his feet.

XV. *Last things.*—The Christian view of history is not mechanistic and materialistic but purposeful and redemptive. Human history had its beginning in the creation of man. It will come to an end in the return of the Lord Jesus Christ and the consummation of his redemptive activity on earth. He will come in glory and judgment. Related to his coming will be the resurrection of the dead, the final victory of the kingdom of God, the final judgment upon evil, and the final award for the righteous. The final word for the lost person is separation from God, certain torment, eternal death—hell. The final word for the Christian is certain triumph, hopes realized, eternal life—heaven.

The Nature and Needs of Persons

In the second place, the foundation of the curriculum is the nature and needs of persons.

This is a corollary of a biblical basis for the curriculum. The Bible is meant for persons. It speaks to the human race. The Bible is never to be thought of as pure subject matter for intellectual investigation, theoretical evaluation, and cultural stimulation. It is addressed to the issues of life. It has to do with the realities of human experience. The teaching and the study of the Bible are the means of discovering the will of God for life and coming to grips with the problems of personality development. In the truest sense, a curriculum based on biblical teaching is life centered in emphasis and purpose and potential.

Emphasis should therefore be placed on the fact that the curriculum for the educational task of the church must reflect a true concept of persons. (Note the paragraph on "Man" in the statement of theological assumptions.) How are we to think of the persons to be taught and trained through the educational ministry of the church? They were created in the image of God. They were endowed with freedom. They are morally competent and morally responsible. By virtue of man's fall into sin, all persons are by nature corrupted by evil. They thus need redemption from sin. They are the objects of God's redeeming love. They can, at the age of personal accountability, respond to God's grace and become true children of God by faith in Jesus Christ. When redeemed from sin and made partakers of the divine nature, they possess immeasurable possibilities for growth toward the full stature of Christian maturity. Such persons are indwelt by the Spirit of God and are the disciples of the kingdom of God.

Persons are born as infants. They have inherent capacity for physical, intellectual, emotional, and moral development. As they grow toward adulthood, they hunger for knowledge, for an interpretation of the meaning of life, for adjustment to the world around them, for personal security, for recognition, and for power. They hunger for God; they feel morally responsible; they yearn for assurance as to life after death. Persons are members of families. They have capacity and needs which can be fulfilled only in the family relationship and in the experience of community. Persons are citizens of the state and are involved in the problems of human society. Persons must live in an evil world and are subject to the onslaughts of Satan. They have almost unmeasured possibilities for good or evil.

It is thus obvious that persons have desperate needs. Life calls for adjustment, reinforcement, and development. Persons need love, truth, guidance, inspiration, fellowship, and salvation. They need instruction and discipline. They need comfort and hope, as well as a feeling of acceptance, both on the part of God and their fellow man.

The educational task of the church is a ministry to persons. It is aimed at definite changes in their understandings and attitudes and actions. It is designed to modify conduct and character. It seeks to help persons experience the abundant life in Christ and become the true servants of his kingdom.

We can now see that the curriculum for Christian teaching and training must be vitally related to human experience. It must aim at definite and worthy objectives in terms of the nature and needs of persons of all ages.

It is on this basis that the curriculum committee of the Sunday School Board has formulated a comprehensive statement, "The Objectives of Christian Teaching and Training." Careful consideration was given to two questions: (1) What are the objectives set forth in the Bible growing out of God's purpose for living persons? (2) What are the needs of living persons which can be met by a ministry of Christian teaching and training?

The answers to these two questions led to the statement of objectives in seven areas: (1) Christian conversion; (2) church membership; (3) Christian worship; (4) Christian knowledge and conviction; (5) Christian attitudes and appreciations; (6) Christian living; (7) Christian service. In the light of the needs and experiences of persons on all age levels, the objectives in these seven areas were expanded into a statement of specific objectives by age groups, with sequence and progression from one age group to another. The form of the statement is not from the standpoint of church organizations or functions but from the standpoint of personal experience and learning development. Clear emphasis is given to the nature of the teaching function, namely, guidance and assistance in the learning experience.

We present here this comprehensive statement of objectives, which is developed for application to the various age groups.*

PART II

THE OBJECTIVES OF CHRISTIAN TEACHING AND TRAINING

The overarching objective is to help persons become aware of God as revealed in Jesus Christ, respond to him in a personal commitment of faith, strive to follow him in the full meaning of Christian discipleship, live in conscious recognition of the guidance and power of the Holy Spirit, and grow toward the goal of Christian maturity.

Summary

1. *Christian conversion.*—To lead each person to a

genuine experience of the forgiving and saving grace of God through Jesus Christ.

2. *Church membership.*—To guide each Christian into intelligent, active, and devoted membership in a New Testament church.

3. *Christian worship.*—To help each person to make Christian worship a vital and constant part of his expanding experience.

4. *Christian knowledge and conviction.*—To help each person to grow toward mature Christian knowledge, understanding, and conviction.

5. *Christian attitudes and appreciations.*—To assist each person in developing such Christian attitudes and appreciations that he will have a Christian approach to all of life.

6. *Christian living.*—To guide each person in developing habits and skills which promote spiritual growth and in applying Christian standards of conduct in every area of life.

7. *Christian service.*—To lead each person to invest his talents and skills in Christian service.

Nursery

I. *Christian conversion.*—Our aim is to begin to lay, through the child's earliest experiences, basic foundations for Christian conversion which may be realized after he reaches the age of accountability. This means helping each child:

(1) to begin to associate God and Jesus with feelings of love and happiness; (2) to think of the Bible as a special book that tells about God and Jesus; (3) to feel that the church is a place where he can go to learn more about God and Jesus.

II. *Church membership.*—Our aim is to begin to lay foundations for church membership. This means helping each child:

(1) to have happy experiences with friendly people at church; (2) to feel that the church is a special place where all members of the family may go to learn more about God and Jesus.

III. *Christian worship.*—Our aim is to help each child to experience moments of worship. This means helping each one:

(1) to feel that he can talk to God at any time; (2) to want to say thank you to God; (3) to grow in his enjoyment of beauty, music, and meaningful Bible stories.

IV. *Christian knowledge and conviction.*—Our aim is to help each child to begin to develop basic elements of Christian knowledge and conviction. This means helping each one:

1. With respect to the Bible—(1) to grow in awareness that what the Bible says is more important than

what other books say; (2) to gain some acquaintance with Bible stories and verses which are meaningful to him.

2. With respect to the great realities of the Christian faith—(1) to begin to think of God as the one who made him; (2) to begin to think of God as the one who helps him to have good things; (3) to begin to think of God as one who cares for him; (4) to begin to think of Jesus as one who loves him.

3. With respect to his church—(1) to begin to think of his church as a place where people love Jesus and help others; (2) to begin to be aware that there are many churches.

V. *Christian attitudes and appreciations.*—Our aim is to help each child begin to develop good attitudes and appreciations. This means helping each one:

1 and 2. Regarding God and the meaning of existence—(1) to begin to associate feelings of happiness with God; (2) to want to thank God for good things; (3) to begin to be aware of the difference between fantasy and reality.

3. Regarding self—(1) to begin to realize that he is a person; (2) to feel loved and wanted; (3) to begin to realize that there are certain things he can and cannot do.

4. Regarding others—(1) to begin to be aware of the feelings of others; (2) to begin to adjust to the needs and interests of others; (3) to experience some feelings of wanting to help others; (4) to begin to be aware of what others do to help him.

5. Regarding the Bible and divine institutions—(1) to enjoy the Bible as a special book; (2) to enjoy church as a special place; (3) to enjoy Sunday as an especially happy day; (4) to begin to feel that God wants families to be happy.

6. Regarding the present world—(1) to begin to feel that the world God made is good; (2) to begin to be aware of life and death processes of plants and animals.

VI. *Christian living.*—Our aim is to help each child to have happy experiences. This means helping each one:

(1) to begin to associate some simple Bible truths with his daily living; (2) to begin to recognize the rights and feelings of others.

VII. *Christian service.*—Our aim is to help each child to want to help others. This means guiding each one:

(1) to begin to help at home and at church; (2) to begin to learn to play happily with others.

Beginner

I. *Christian conversion.*—Our aim is to lay early foundations through the child's continuing experiences which will lead him toward the time when he will be capable of accepting Jesus as his personal Saviour. This means helping each child:

(1) to feel that God loves him at all times; (2) to realize that there are some things that please God; to love God and want to please him; (3) to learn that the Bible is a special book that helps us know how to please God; (4) to think of Jesus as his friend and helper.

II. *Church membership.*—Our aim is to begin to lay foundations for an understanding of what it means to be a member of a church. This means helping each child:

(1) to think of his church as a place where he has happy experiences; (2) to grow in his ability to participate in church worship services with his family; (3) to feel that he is a part of the church life.

III. *Christian worship.*—Our aim is to help each child to have moments of satisfying worship experiences and to grow in his ability to participate in group worship. This means helping each one:

(1) to know that he can talk to God at any time and anywhere; (2) to have satisfying experiences in talking to God; (3) to grow in his ability to participate in worship with children of his own age; (4) to develop a growing appreciation of beautiful surroundings, music, Bible passages that are read aloud, prayer, the offering, and the preacher's message.

IV. *Christian knowledge and conviction.*—Our aim is to help each child to know that the Bible is a special book which tells about God and Jesus and that the people of his church help others to know about God and Jesus. This means helping each one:

1. With respect to the Bible—(1) to begin to understand that God helped men know what to write in the Bible; (2) to become familiar with some of the surroundings and customs of the people the Bible tells about; (3) to enjoy hearing Bible stories and verses; (4) to grow in his understanding of Bible truths and learn to relate them to his own experiences; (5) to grow in his realization that the Bible is God's way of telling us how to live happily with others; (6) to know that the Bible was meant for all people.

2. With respect to the great realities of the Christian faith—(1) to know that God made the world and everything in it; (2) to know that Jesus can do things that no one else can do because he is God's Son.

3 and 4. With respect to his church, denomination, and the larger Christian movement—(1) to know that there have been churches for a long time; (2) to know that his church is one of many churches all over the world; (3) to know ways his church and other churches help people to know about Jesus; (4) to know that the money brought to church is used to help others know about Jesus.

V. *Christian attitudes and appreciations.*—Our aim is to guide each child in the development of his attitudes and appreciations that will encourage him in his personal growth. This means helping each one:

1 and 2. Regarding God and the meaning of existence—(1) to experience a deepening reverence for God's power and greatness; to accept the fact that God made the world; to have a growing appreciation of ways God cares for the things in it; (2) to love God and to want to do the things that please him; (3) to trust God as the one who loves and cares for all people; to feel that God is near and that one can talk to God any time, anywhere; to want to talk to God; (4) to feel thankful for the many ways God helps him; (5) to grow in awareness of the difference between fantasy and reality.

3. Regarding self—(1) to feel secure in God's world, because he is an important part of God's plan; (2) to begin to realize that God made him and gave him the ability to think; to make choices and decisions, and to be creative; to begin to realize that people are more important than any other thing God made; (3) to realize that God wants him to have a strong, healthy body and to use it in ways pleasing to God; (4) to realize that God can help him in ways that no one else can; (5) to want to do things in ways pleasing to Jesus and to want to grow in the ways in which Jesus grew.

4. Regarding others—(1) to realize that it is a part of God's plan for people to be friendly and to help one another; (2) to grow in his appreciation of others and what they do for him; (3) to develop in his ability to share, to work, and to play happily with others; (4) to accept the fact that God made and loves all people and to have kind attitudes toward them; (5) to want others to know about Jesus.

5. Regarding the Bible and divine institutions—(1) to develop a growing love for the Bible and a growing appreciation for ways it can help him in everyday life; (2) to grow in his understanding of the importance of his church; (3) to think of Sunday as a special day of worship and activities pleasing to God; (4) to think of happy homes as a part of God's plan; (5) to grow in his appreciation of people in authority and in his willingness to co-operate with them.

6. Regarding the present world—(1) to feel that the world God made is good and that nature, work, and the ability to do many things are gifts of God; (2) to want to help others in making his (the child's) world a better place.

VI. *Christian living.*—Our aim is to help each child to develop habits and to have experiences which encourage his spiritual growth. This means helping each one:

(1) to begin to accept the Bible as a guide for his conduct in everyday life; (2) to grow in his understanding of prayer and in his ability to pray; (3) to want to do things in ways pleasing to Jesus; (4) to grow in his ability to make right choices; (5) to develop in his ability to help make his home happy; (6) to have an increasing love for all people everywhere which he will

express in friendliness and in co-operation.

VII. *Christian service.*—Our aim is to help each child to grow in his desire and ability to help others. This means helping each one:

(1) to tell others about Jesus; (2) to be a helper in his home and church; (3) to be happy as he gives his money to help others know about Jesus; (4) to do helpful things for others; (5) to begin to accept his limited abilities and to help as best he can; (6) to receive satisfaction from doing things with others; (7) to participate in group activities that make others happy.

Primary

I. *Christian conversion.*—Our aim is to lay foundations for a genuine conversion experience on the part of each child when he is ready for it. This means helping each one:

(1) To feel love and reverence for God and to know that God loves him; (2) to have a real desire to do things that please God and to grow in his understanding of ways he can please God; (3) to learn to love and trust Jesus as his friend and to have a growing awareness that Jesus is God's Son; (4) to grow in his understanding of what it means to forgive and to know that God wants to forgive him when he does wrong; (5) to develop a consciousness of his personal need for God's help in doing right things; (6) to feel free to approach Christian adults for understanding guidance.

II. *Church membership.*—Our aim is to lay foundations for an understanding of what it means to be a church member. This means helping each one:

(1) to like to attend church and to participate in the worship services with his family; (2) to grow in his understanding of the fact that members of the church are a special group of Jesus' friends who have had the experiences of conversion and baptism; (3) to begin to understand that joining the church is a serious matter, always to be preceded by conversion, and that it involves responsibilities as well as privileges.

III. *Christian worship.*—Our aim is to help each child to develop ability to participate actively and intelligently in worship and to find satisfaction in worship experiences. This means helping each one:

(1) to feel and demonstrate loving respect for God; (2) to talk to God spontaneously and naturally at any time he feels a sense of wonder, worship, or need; (3) to have meaningful experiences in private worship and in worship with members of his own age group; (4) to participate regularly in public worship and to find satisfaction in doing so.

IV. *Christian knowledge and conviction.*—Our aim is to help each child to gain such knowledge of the Bible and Christian faith as can be related to his daily experiences. This means helping each one:

1. With respect to the Bible—(1) to develop love and appreciation for the Bible as a unique book and to feel that it is true and deserves respect and obedience; (2) to develop an elementary understanding of its structure, how it came to be written, and how it has been preserved; (3) to become acquainted with customs, geography, and other facts concerning Bible backgrounds; (4) to enjoy hearing, reading, and learning Bible stories and truths; (5) to grow in his understanding of ways the Bible can help him in everyday life; (6) to commit to memory many Bible verses.

2. With respect to the great realities of the Christian faith—(1) to have a growing understanding of what the Bible teaches about God, about Jesus, and about right and wrong; (2) to realize that the friends of Jesus should believe and do what the Bible teaches.

3. With respect to the Christian movement—(1) to realize that the church he attends is one of many such groups of Jesus' friends in many parts of the world; (2) to recognize that people of other Christian groups also help in Jesus' work.

4. With respect to his church and denomination—(1) to know why we have churches and some of the things churches do; (2) to find answers to his questions about church ordinances and church membership.

V. *Christian attitudes and appreciations.*—Our aim is to guide each child in the continuing development of attitudes and appreciations that will encourage personal growth. This means helping each one:

1 and 2. Regarding God and the meaning of existence —(1) to experience deepening reverence and respect for God and his work in the world; (2) to trust God as the one who created, loves, and makes provision for the needs of all people and all other creatures; (3) to feel assured that God listens when people pray to him and answers in the way that is best; (4) to feel sorry when he disappoints God but to know that God loves him and wants to forgive him; (5) to feel a sense of gratitude to God for all of his good gifts; (6) to feel that Jesus loves and helps him, to love and trust Jesus as his friend, and to please him.

3. Regarding self—(1) to develop wholesome appreciation of his own value as an individual whom God loves and who can make important contributions to the group at home, at school, at church, and at play; (2) to think of his body as something good and something to be cared for and used in ways pleasing to God; (3) to grow in ability to evaluate himself and to recognize his responsibilities; (4) to grow in understanding of the values of co-operative work and in ability to be a good member of the group; (5) to recognize all his talents and abilities as gifts from God and to want to develop and use them in worthwhile ways.

4. Regarding others—(1) to feel kindly toward all people everywhere regardless of their difference; (2)

to respect the feelings, the rights, and the property of others; (3) to grow in his willingness to share his work, play, and possessions with others; (4) to recognize that others make real contributions to his life and to want to make some friendly return; (5) to want to help others to know about Jesus.

5. Regarding the Bible and divine institutions—(1) to grow in his love for the Bible and his desire to use it in his everyday living; (2) to love and show respect for the church building as a special place of worship; (3) to begin to appreciate the elements of public worship; (4) to think of Sunday as a special day to be spent in worship and other activities which honor God; (5) to recognize the home as part of God's loving plan for people and to develop an attitude of love, respect, and consideration for all in his home; (6) to continue to grow in his appreciation for authority and in his willingness to co-operate with persons in authority.

6. Regarding the present world—(1) to feel secure in the knowledge that God's plan for the world provides for each person's needs; (2) to begin to realize that although he sees others doing wrong and is often tempted himself, Jesus can help him to choose the right way; (3) to realize that work is part of God's plan for everyone and to want to do what he can to help.

VI. *Christian living.*—Our aim is to guide each child develop and use in everyday life habits and skills which ll help him grow spiritually. This means helping each e:

(1) to grow in ability to relate Bible truths to daily problems and needs; (2) to continue growing in his understanding of prayer and in his ability to pray; (3) to make sincere efforts to be more like Jesus; (4) to develop growing skill in self-control, self-direction, worthy self-expression, and ability to make right choices; (5) to develop habits of friendliness, helpfulness, co-operation, kindness, and courtesy toward all with whom he comes in contact, in work and in play.

VII. *Christian service.*—Our aim is to guide each child use his talents and skills in ways that will help others. is means helping each one:

(1) to tell others about Jesus; (2) to participate and co-operate in all the church activities in which he may have a part; (3) to enjoy giving his offerings of money and of other possessions which he can share; (4) to begin to discover his talents and to have opportunities to develop and use them in worthy self-expression; (5) to accept his limitations and to use his abilities to achieve; (6) to participate in group activities that make others happy.

nior

I. *Christian conversion.*—Our aim is to prepare each boy and girl for a genuine conversion experience when he or she is competent to receive Christ as Saviour and to lead each one who is ready for it to such an experience. This means helping each one:

(1) to understand that all people do wrong and that all wrongdoing is displeasing to God; (2) to face the fact that the wrong things which he does are sins against God; (3) to realize that Christ's death for our sins makes possible forgiveness and new life for every person who repents of sin and trusts Jesus Christ; (4) to understand that a person becomes a Christian by trusting Jesus as Saviour—not by being baptized and joining the church or simply trying to be good; (5) to realize that he needs God's forgiveness for his own sins; (6) to turn from sin to simple trust in Christ as his personal Saviour and Lord when the Holy Spirit has made him ready for such response and commitment.

II. *Church membership.*—Our aim is to help boys and girls to understand what it means to be a church member and to lead each Christian boy and girls into intelligent, active, and devoted membership in a New Testament church. This means helping each one:

(1) to form the habit of regular church attendance and of participating with understanding and joy in church services and activities; (2) to understand that a New Testament church is composed of persons who have already become Christians and who have been baptized in obedience to Christ; (3) to understand that a person joins the church only after he has trusted Jesus as his Saviour; (4) to want to unite with the church as soon as he has trusted Jesus as his Saviour, with a conviction that he is a Christian and should be baptized in obedience to Christ.

III. *Christian worship.*—Our aim is to help each boy and girl to participate actively and intelligently in worship and to find increasing satisfaction in worship experiences. This means helping each one:

(1) to understand that worship is an experience of reverent communion with God and that a person may engage in worship alone, with his family, with his friends, and with groups at church; (2) to cultivate the practice of regular private worship, including daily Bible reading and prayer; (3) to do his part to maintain and to participate in family worship; (4) to attend regularly the worship services of his church and to participate meaningfully and reverently in praying, singing, Bible reading, and listening.

IV. *Christian knowledge and conviction.*—Our aim is to help each boy and girl grow in Christian knowledge and conviction. This means helping each one:

1. With respect to the Bible—(1) to recognize that the Bible is an inspired message from God and that its teachings are to be accepted and followed in all that we believe and do; (2) to develop an increasing understanding of the origin, structure, and transmission of the Bible; (3) to learn about the customs and geography of Bible lands in order to understand better many of the

teachings of the Bible; (4) to develop a growing knowledge of basic Bible stories and truths; (5) to gain from individual and group Bible study increasing guidance and motivation for daily living; (6) to grow in skill in the use of the Bible; (7) to memorize appropriate Bible passages.

2. With respect to the great realities of the Christian faith—(1) to recognize increasingly that God is real and that a vital relationship with him through faith includes many doctrines which are important for one's belief and conduct; (3) to gain increasing knowledge of basic Christian doctrines.

3. With respect to the Christian movement—(1) to grow familiar with the lives and work of some of the early leaders in the growth of the Christian movement; (2) to become acquainted with the names and work of some of the great Baptist leaders; (3) to gain some acquaintance with the history and beliefs of other Christian groups; (4) to learn some ways in which our beliefs are like those of other groups and some ways in which they are different.

4. With respect to his church and denomination— (1) to grow in understanding and appreciation of Baptist beliefs and practices; (2) to grow in knowledge of Southern Baptist life and work and to develop increasing loyalty to his denomination.

V. *Christian attitudes and appreciations.*—Our aim is to help each boy and girl to develop Christian attitudes and appreciations in every area of his experience. This means helping each one:

1. Regarding God—(1) to reverence God and to want to know and to obey his commandments; (2) to love and trust God as the all-wise and all-good Heavenly Father, who loved us and gave his Son to be the Saviour of the world; (3) to feel secure in God's care and grateful for his goodness.

2. Regarding the meaning of existence—(1) to think of the beauties and wonders of the world and of science as expressions of God's greatness and goodness; (2) to feel secure in the world because God made it and controls it and cares what happens to people; (3) to believe that God has a purpose for his life and to want to use his life for God's glory and for the good of others.

3. Regarding self—(1) to realize that because God made him, his mind, his body, and his life are important; (2) to realize that he needs God's forgiveness, love, and help; (3) to understand that his mind and body are gifts from God to be cared for and developed; (4) to want to use his mind and body in Jesus' service.

4. Regarding others—(1) to begin to appreciate the worth of all people regardless of their race or other differences; (2) to feel responsible for the way he treats people of all groups, races, and nationalities; (3) to grow in his ability to love other people and to treat others as Jesus would have him treat them; (4) to feel responsible for telling others about Jesus.

5. Regarding the Bible and divine institution—(1) to develop a growing love for the Bible and a deeper desire to govern his everyday actions by its teachings; (2) to grow in love for and loyalty to the church; (3) to develop increasing respect and appreciation for baptism and the Lord's Supper; (4) to respect Sunday as the Lord's Day and to enjoy doing on Sunday things that honor Jesus; (5) to appreciate his home as part of God's plan of caring for him and to desire to do his part to make his home happy; (6) to feel that rules and laws are a necessary part of God's plan for living and to want to obey the laws of his home, his school, and his community.

6. Regarding the present world—(1) to feel secure in the knowledge that God made and cares for the world and gave men the ability to discover and use the secrets of nature; (2) to feel that though there is sin and wrongdoing in the world, he can have the strength through Christ to choose the right way; (3) to want to do his part to make his home, his school, and his neighborhood better.

VI. *Christian living.*—Our aim is to guide each boy and girl in learning skills and in developing habits which promote spiritual growth and Christlike conduct. This means leading each one:

(1) to depend on Jesus each day to help him choose the right way; (2) to learn how to use his own Bible and to gain from it direction for daily living; (3) to make progress in developing Christian character which will express itself in all areas of his experience; (4) to gain strength for Christian living through private and group prayer; (5) to try to grow as Jesus grew—in his mind, in his body, and in his relationships with God and with other people; (6) to do his part to make his home happy by obeying his parents and accepting cheerfully his share in the work at home.

VII. *Christian service.*—Our aim is to lead each boy and girl to develop and use his or her abilities in worthy ways that will help others. This means leading each one:

(1) to show his love for Jesus by telling his family and friends about him and inviting them to church; (2) to serve in his church through the organizations, through attendance at regular church services, and through giving his money for the work of the church; (3) to try day by day at home, at school, and wherever he goes to treat others with kindness and fairness as Jesus would; (4) to begin to develop a sense of citizenship responsibility by participating in group and community service projects which contribute to fair play, justice, law enforcement, general health, relief of distress, and other worthy causes.

Intermediate

I. *Christian conversion.*—Our aim is to lead each unsaved Intermediate to experience the forgiving and saving grace of God through Jesus Christ. This means helping each one:

(1) to recognize his failure and his inability to live up to God's standard of righteousness and his consequent need of a Saviour; (2) to turn from sin and to commit himself to Jesus Christ, trusting him to give complete and continuous salvation; (3) to gain, after conversion, a growing sense of assurance as to the reality of that experience and its implications in terms of the lordship of Jesus.

II. *Church membership.*—Our aim is to help each Christian Intermediate to grow as an intelligent, active, and devoted member of a New Testament church. This means helping each one:

(1) to unite with a church by baptism upon public profession of faith in Christ as Saviour and Lord (if he has not already done so); (2) to grow in understanding and appreciation of the nature, mission, practices, and leadership of his church; (3) to grow in loyalty to his church and to endeavor to render faithful service to Christ and fellow men through the church; (4) to develop the habit of attending services regularly and of participating in the fellowship and program of the church with understanding and appreciation; (5) to give regularly and proportionately for the support of his church and its worldwide program; (6) to transfer his church membership promptly when he changes his place of residence.

III. *Christian worship.*—Our aim is to help each Intermediate to make Christian worship a vital and constant part of his expanding experience. This means helping each one:

(1) to understand further the meaning of worship and to desire to engage in worship; (2) to grow in appreciation of all elements that make worship meaningful, both in worship services and in personal devotions; (3) to grow in ability to participate meaningfully in worship experiences with members of his own age group and with the church congregation; (4) to practice daily individual worship, including devotional reading of the Bible and prayer for self and others; (5) to encourage and participate in family worship experiences.

IV. *Christian knowledge and conviction.*—Our aim is to help each Intermediate grow in Christian knowledge and conviction. This means helping each one:

1. With respect to the Bible—(1) to accept the Bible as a way by which God speaks to him and as the final authority in all matters of faith and conduct; (2) to understand something of the origin of the Bible and of God's use of man in writing, preserving, and translating it; (3) to grow in understanding of the contents of the Bible and of the customs, geography, and history

out of which the Bible came; (4) to acquire a growing comprehension of how Bible truths apply to personal daily living and to community and world problems; (5) to commit choice passages to memory.

2. With respect to the great realities of the Christian faith—(1) to grow in his concept of the reality and nature of God as a personal, loving Father; (2) to grow in his understanding of God and man, sin and salvation, and the Christian's life and work; (3) to develop a growing conviction about the truth and finality of the Christian faith.

3. With respect to the Christian movement—(1) to learn some of the outstanding facts of Christian history; (2) to become acquainted with some of the outstanding facts about other Christian groups and our common heritage with them; (3) to become aware of present-day trends and issues in the Christian movement and to realize that they hold meaning for his own life as well as for the cause of Christ.

4. With respect to his church and denomination—(1) to grow in understanding distinctive features of Baptist doctrine and polity and to develop growing convictions as to their soundness; (2) to add to his knowledge of the history, organization, program, problems, and needs of Southern Baptists and to develop an increasing sense of responsibility for the work of his denomination.

V. *Christian attitudes and appreciations.*—Our aim is to help each Intermediate develop Christian attitudes and appreciations in every area of his experience. This means helping each one:

1. Regarding God—(1) to love and trust the Heavenly Father, Jesus Christ as Lord and Saviour, and the Holy Spirit as ever-present counselor and source of power; (2) to reverence God, respect his commands, and seek to know and do his will; (3) to develop a sense of gratitude to God for all his goodness.

2. Regarding the meaning of existence—(1) to regard all existence as the expression of God's creative power, wisdom, and goodness; (2) to feel secure in the knowledge that this is God's world and that God's purposes are being worked out in it; (3) to realize that a person created in the image of God is of infinite worth, has marvelous possibilities, and possesses spiritual needs which only God can supply.

3. Regarding self—(1) to recognize his body, mind, and total personality as gifts from God to be cared for, developed, and used for God's glory and the good of others; (2) to have as his personal ideal the attainment of a mature Christian personality; (3) to evaluate his talents as he considers his future vocation; (4) to realize that he stands in constant need of God's forgiveness and help.

4. Regarding others—(1) to acquire a sense of kinship with every other person in the world and to cultivate an attitude of unselfish devotion to the welfare of people of all cultures, races, and social levels; (2) to

cultivate the desire to apply Christian principles in relationships within the family, at church, at school, and in the community; (3) to feel a concern for the salvation of others and to accept the obligation to help give the gospel to the world; (4) to develop wholesome attitudes toward persons of the opposite sex in his peer group.

5. Regarding the Bible and divine institutions—(1) to develop a growing love for the Bible and an appreciation of its teachings as guides for daily living; (2) to develop a growing appreciation of the purpose for which Christ founded the church and an increasing concern for its life and work; (3) to develop an increasing love and appreciation for his home and feel a growing obligation to contribute to the happiness and well-being of his family; (4) to develop increasing loyalty to the ideal of personal purity, looking toward marriage and family life; (5) to regard Sunday as the Lord's Day to be used to honor the risen Christ; (6) to respect the ordinances of baptism and the Lord's Supper as means of honoring Christ; (7) to respect civil government and to feel the obligations of good citizenship as set forth in principle in the New Testament.

6. Regarding the present world—(1) to feel that the world as God made it is good and that all the resources of nature and the necessity to work are gifts of God designed for the enrichment of life; (2) to recognize the many manifestations of evil in the world and to resolve to live a life dedicated to God, to resist the appeal of evil in one's life, and to be a positive force for morality and justice; (3) to feel a deepening sense of responsibility for the improvement of moral and social conditions in his community.

VI. *Christian living.*—Our aim is to guide each Intermediate in learning skills and in developing habits which promote spiritual growth and Christian conduct. This means helping each one:

(1) to grow in consciousness of the living Christ as the Lord of his life; (2) to accept with confidence the Bible and the Holy Spirit as guides in making the best use of his life; (3) to grow in understanding of why to pray and how to pray; (4) to seek to pattern all personal conduct in accordance with the teachings, spirit, and example of Jesus; (5) to strive to be Christlike in attitudes toward and relationships with his parents and other members of his family; (6) to continue to make progress in developing Christian character which will express itself in all his relationships.

VII. *Christian service.*—Our aim is to lead each Intermediate to seek to make his maximum contribution to the cause of Christ. This means helping each one:

(1) to dedicate his talents to God and to develop skills in Christian service; (2) to seek God's will for his life and to begin to prepare for a vocation in keeping with that will; (3) to witness faithfully to his Christian faith and to seek to win others to Jesus Christ; (4) to appreciate and take advantage of the training and service opportunities offered him in his church program; (5)

to learn to work unselfishly on a team by filling well the places of service in his church suited to his ability and stage of development; (6) to be a good steward of his money as an expression of his gratitude to God and as a means of supporting his church in its world missions program; (7) to show compassion for persons in need (8) to participate in group and community service projects which contribute to social welfare; (9) to accept the ideal of self-giving service as the true goal of life.

Young People

I. *Christian conversion.*—Our aim is to lead each unsaved young person to a genuine experience of the forgiving and saving grace of God through Jesus Christ. This means helping each one:

(1) to become aware of the nature and prevalence of sin and to recognize God's judgment upon it; (2) to realize his own sin and his consequent need of the salvation which God has provided in Christ; (3) to turn from sin and commit himself to Jesus Christ, the Son of God, who gives complete salvation to all who trust him; (4) to gain, after conversion, a growing sense of assurance as to the reality of that experience and its implications in terms of the lordship of Jesus.

II. *Church membership.*—Our aim is to guide each Christian young person into intelligent, active, and devoted membership in a New Testament church. This means helping each one:

(1) to unite with a church by baptism upon a personal profession of faith in Christ (if he has not already done so); (2) to grow in understanding and appreciation of the meaning, purpose, faith, and practices of his church; (3) to grow in loyalty to his church and the world program of Christ; (4) to participate wholeheartedly in Christian service in and through the channels of his church; (5) to transfer his church membership promptly when he changes his place of residence.

III. *Christian worship.*—Our aim is to help each young person make Christian worship a vital and constant part of his expanding experience. This means helping each one:

(1) to develop a deepening understanding of the meaning and values of worship; (2) to develop a growing appreciation of all the elements that make for meaningful worship, both private and corporate; (3) to develop and maintain the practice of daily individual worship, including the devotional reading of the Bible, meditation, and prayer; (4) to develop the habit of regular attendance at the public services of his church and the ability to participate in them with understanding and appreciation; (5) to encourage and to participate in experiences of family worship.

IV. *Christian knowledge and conviction.*—Our aim is to help each young person to grow toward mature Chrisian knowledge, understanding, and conviction. This means helping each one:

1. With respect to the Bible—(1) to recognize the Bible as a unique revelation from God and to accept its authority as supreme in matters of faith and conduct; (2) to gain fuller understanding of the origins of the Bible, the history of its preservation, and the significance of the many translations and versions; (3) to achieve an increasing knowledge of the content of the Bible and a growing understanding of the customs, geography, and history out of which the Bible came; (4) to acquire a growing comprehension of how Bible truths apply to personal daily living, to family life, and to community and world problems; (5) to commit choice passages to memory.

2. With respect to the great realities of the Christian faith—(1) to grow in understanding of the nature, attributes, and disposition of God; (2) to grow in understanding of the nature of man, of sin and salvation, and of the varied elements of Christian experience; (3) to grow in understanding of the Christian concepts of personal righteousness and social responsibility; (4) to develop a growing conviction about the truth and finality of the Christian faith.

3. With respect to the Christian movement—(1) to know something of the general outline of Christian history; (2) to learn some of the outstanding facts about other Christian groups and our common heritage with them; (3) to grow in understanding of present-day trends and issues in the Christian movement and to develop ability to evaluate their significance for his own life, his own church, and the cause of Christ throughout the world.

4. With respect to his church and denomination—(1) to understand something of the history of Baptists; (2) to understand the distinctive features of Baptist doctrine and polity; (3) to grow in his understanding of the program, missionary outreach, problems, and needs of his church and denomination; (4) to develop worthy convictions about the doctrines and mission of Baptists and about his personal responsibility to his denomination.

V. *Christian attitudes and appreciations.*—Our aim is to assist each young person in developing such Christian attitudes and appreciations that he will have a Christian approach to all of life. This means helping each one:

1. Regarding God—(1) to reverence God, respect his commandments, and seek to know and do his will as the supreme good; (2) to love and trust the Heavenly Father, Jesus Christ as Lord and Saviour, and the Holy Spirit as ever-present counselor and source of power; (3) to develop a sense of gratitude to God for all his goodness.

2. Regarding the meaning of existence—(1) to regard all existence as the expression of God's creative power, wisdom, and goodness; (2) to see himself in relation to all existence in such a way as to feel secure in the purpose and sovereignty of God; (3) to regard life as a trust from God to be used for his glory and the good of others; (4) to believe with confidence that the Bible and the Holy Spirit are his guides in making the best use of this life; (5) to believe that the main purposes of God for mankind are redemption and development in righteousness.

3. Regarding self—(1) to realize that as a person created in the image of God, he is of infinite worth and has marvelous possibilities; (2) to realize that he stands in continuing need for forgiveness and strength from God; (3) to recognize that he possesses spiritual needs and capacities which only God can supply; (4) to acknowledge that his body is a divine trust to be cared for, to be protected from abuse, to be disciplined in habit, and to be employed in honest labor, unselfish service, and healthful recreation; (5) to dedicate all of his God-given abilities to the pursuit and achievement of worthy aims and to test their worthiness by the teaching of Jesus; (6) to have as his personal ideal the attainment of a mature, well-balanced Christian personality.

4. Regarding others—(1) to cultivate an attitude of Christian love, the willingness to practice forgiveness, and the determination to apply Christian principles in all his relationships; (2) to accept responsibility for the influence of his life upon all people whom his life touches; (3) to develop wholesome attitudes toward other young people of the opposite sex; (4) to cultivate a sense of belonging to the human race as a whole; (5) to develop an attitude of Christian concern for the welfare of people of all cultures, social levels, and races; (6) to feel a concern for the salvation of all men everywhere and to accept the obligation to share the gospel and the blessings of the Christian faith; (7) to feel a responsibility to pass on to future generations the good in his social heritage enriched by his own contribution to it.

5. Regarding the Bible and divine institutions—(1) to develop a growing love for the Bible and an appreciation of the relevance of Bible teaching to daily life; (2) to respect the divine nature and purpose of the church and to give it a place of sacred pre-eminence over all institutions of human origin; (3) to respect the ordinances of baptism and the Lord's Supper and to seek through the right observance of them to honor Christ; (4) to regard the Lord's Day as the Christian sabbath to be used to the honor of the risen Christ; (5) to accept the standards set by Christ and the New Testament for marriage and family life; (6) to respect the institution of civil government as being of divine appointment and accept the responsibilities of good citizenship.

6. Regarding the present world—(1) to feel that the world as God made it is good and that all the resources of nature and the necessity to work are gifts of God

designed for the enrichment of life; (2) to recognize that evil is a dominant force in the world order and that the Christian, while he must live in this world, is not to share its spirit nor indulge in its sins but is to resist evil and be a positive force for morality and justice; (3) to develop a deepening consciousness of responsibility for the social order of which he is a part and a courageous purpose to work for its improvement.

VI. *Christian living.*—Our aim is to guide each young person in developing habits and skills which promote spiritual growth and in applying Christian standards of conduct in every area of life. This means helping each one: (1) to live daily in vital fellowship with Jesus Christ, seeking always to bring the whole life under the direction of the Holy Spirit; (2) to engage regularly in serious Bible study and to use the Bible as a guide for life; (3) to understand the values of prayer and to practice prayer in daily experience; (4) to pattern all of his personal conduct in accordance with the teachings, spirit, and example of Jesus Christ; (5) to do all possible to make his home life Christian; (6) to refuse to enter into relations and participate in activities which compromise or violate New Testament principles; (7) to seek to apply Christian principles and standards of conduct to all social relationships.

VII. *Christian service.*—Our aim is to lead each young person to make his maximum contribution to the cause of Christ. This means helping each one: (1) to seek and use opportunities to invest his talents and skills in Christian service; (2) to witness consistently to the truth and power of the Christian faith and to seek to win others to Jesus Christ; (3) to work faithfully for the building up of his church and to serve sacrificially in and through his church; (4) to give of his money, for worthy motives and according to biblical teachings, for the support of his church and its work; (5) to show compassion for persons in need and do deeds of helpfulness in his daily life; (6) to find God's will for his life, to prepare adequately for the vocation to which he is called, and to enter that vocation with a sense of dedication to Christian service; (7) to serve effectively as a member of a team and to serve without desire for self-glory; (8) to dedicate his total personality and resources to world missions as the means of carrying forward the redemptive undertaking of Jesus Christ; (9) to join with others in co-operative action for the improvement of social conditions, the creation of a more Christian society, and the realization of God's purpose for mankind.

Adult

I. *Christian conversion.*—Our aim is to lead each unsaved adult to a genuine experience of the forgiving and saving grace of God through Jesus Christ. This mean helping each one: (1) to become aware of God's judgment concerning sin and of his mercy; (2) to realize his own failure and inability to measure up to God's standard of righteousness and his consequent need of the salvation which God has provided in Christ; (3) to recognize the all sufficiency of Jesus Christ, working through the Holy Spirit, to give complete salvation to all who trust him (4) to turn from sin and commit himself wholeheartedly to Jesus Christ as his personal Saviour; (5) to gain after conversion, a growing sense of assurance as to the reality of that experience and its implications in terms of the lordship of Jesus.

II. *Church membership.*—Our aim is to guide each Christian adult into intelligent, active, and devoted membership in a New Testament church. This means helping each one: (1) to unite with a church by baptism upon a personal profession of faith in the Lord Jesus Christ (if he has not already done so); (2) to grow in understanding and appreciation of the meaning, purpose, faith, and practices of his church; (3) to participate in and actively cultivate the fellowship in his church; (4) to participate wholeheartedly in constructive Christian service in and through the channels of his church; (5) to grow in loyalty to his church and the world program of Christ (6) to have his membership in a church in the community where he resides.

III. *Christian worship.*—Our aim is to help each adult to make Christian worship a vital and constant part of his expanding experience. This means helping each one: (1) to develop a deepening understanding of the meaning and values of worship; (2) to develop a growing appreciation of all the elements that make for meaningful worship whether in private or in the group; (3) to develop and maintain the practice of daily individual worship, including the devotional reading of the Bible, meditation, and prayer; (4) to develop the habit of regular attendance at the worship services of his church and the ability to participate in them with understanding and appreciation; (5) to encourage, provide, and participate in experiences of family worship.

IV. *Christian knowledge and conviction.*—Our aim is to help each adult to grow toward mature Christian knowledge, understanding, and conviction. This means helping each one:
1. With respect to the Bible—(1) to recognize the Bible as a unique revelation and message from God and to accept it as authoritative in all matters of faith and conduct; (2) to understand the origin of the Bible and its history, preservation, and translation; (3) to understand the customs, geography, and historical backgrounds out of which the Bible came; (4) to gain an orderly and increasingly comprehensive grasp of the content of the Bible; (5) to acquire a growing comprehension of how Bible truths apply to personal daily

living, family life, and community and world problems;
(6) to commit choice passages to memory.

2. With respect to the great realities of the Christian faith—(1) to grow in understanding of the nature, attributes, and disposition of God; (2) to grow in understanding of the nature of man, of sin and salvation, and of the varied elements of Christian experience; (3) to grow in understanding of the Christian concepts of personal righteousness and social responsibility; (4) to develop a growing conviction about the truth and finality of the Christian faith.

3. With respect to the Christian movement—(1) to learn some of the outstanding facts of Christian history; (2) to learn some of the outstanding facts about other Christian groups and our common heritage with them; (3) to understand significant present-day trends in the Christian movement and to evaluate their meaning for his own life and the cause of Christ.

4. With respect to his church and denomination—(1) to learn some of the outstanding facts about the history of his own denomination; (2) to understand the distinctive features of Baptist doctrine and polity and to have solid convictions as to their soundness; (3) to know the organization, program, missionary outreach, problems, and needs of Southern Baptists and to understand his personal relationship to the whole of the denominational enterprise.

V. *Christian attitudes and appreciations.*—Our aim is to assist each adult in developing such Christian attitudes and appreciations that he will have a Christian approach to all of life. This means helping each one:

1. Regarding God—(1) to reverence God, respect his commandments, and seek to know and do his will as the supreme good; (2) to love and trust the Heavenly Father, Jesus Christ as Lord and Saviour, and the Holy Spirit as ever-present counselor and source of power; (3) to develop a sense of gratitude to God for all his goodness.

2. Regarding the meaning of existence—(1) to regard all existence as the expression of God's creative power, wisdom, and goodness; (2) to see himself in relation to all existence in such a way as to feel secure in the purpose and sovereignty of God; (3) to regard life as a trust from God to be used for his glory and the good of others; (4) to believe with confidence that the Bible and the Holy Spirit are his guides in making the best use of this life; (5) to believe that the main purposes of God for mankind are redemption and development in righteousness.

3. Regarding self—(1) to realize that as a person created in the image of God he is of infinite worth and has marvelous possibilities; (2) to realize that he stands in continuing need of forgiveness and strength from God; (3) to recognize that he possesses spiritual needs and capacities which only God can supply; (4) to acknowledge that his body is a divine trust to be cared for, to be protected from abuse, to be disciplined in habit, to be employed in honest labor, unselfish service, and healthful recreation; (5) to dedicate all of his God-given abilities to the pursuit and achievement of worthy aims and to test worthiness by the teachings of Jesus; (6) to have as his personal ideal the attainment of a mature, well-balanced Christian personality.

4. Regarding others—(1) to cultivate an attitude of Christian love, the willingness to practive forgiveness, and the determination to apply Christian principles in all his relationships; (2) to accept responsibility for the influence of his life upon all people whom his life touches; (3) to feel and manifest wholesome attitudes toward persons of the opposite sex; (4) to cultivate a sense of belonging to the human race as a whole; (5) to develop an attitude of Christian concern for the welfare of people of all cultures, social levels, and races; (6) to feel a concern for the salvation of all men everywhere and to accept the obligation to share the gospel and blessings of the Christian faith; (7) to feel a responsibility to pass on to future generations the good in his social heritage enriched by his own contribution to it.

5. Regarding the Bible and divine institutions—(1) to develop a growing love for the Bible and an appreciation of the relevance of Bible teaching to daily life; (2) to respect the divine nature and purpose of the church and to give it a place of sacred pre-eminence over all institutions of human origin; (3) to respect the ordinances of baptism and the Lord's Supper and to seek through the right observance of them to honor Christ; (4) to regard the Lord's Day as the Christian sabbath to be used to the honor of the risen Christ; (5) to accept the standards set by Christ and the New Testament for marriage and family life; (6) to respect the institution of civil government as being of divine appointment and accept the responsibilities of good citizenship.

6. Regarding the present world—(1) to feel that the world as God made it is good and that all the resources of nature and the necessity to work are gifts of God designed for the enrichment of life; (2) to recognize that evil is a dominant force in the world order and that the Christian, while he must live in this world, is not to share its spirit nor indulge in its sins but is to resist evil and be a positive force for morality and justice; (3) to develop a deepening consciousness of responsibility for the social order of which he is a part and a courageous purpose to work for its improvement.

VI. *Christian living.*—Our aim is to guide each adult in developing spiritual growth and in applying Christian standards of conduct in every area of life. This means helping each one:

(1) to live daily in vital fellowship with Jesus Christ, seeking always to bring the whole life under the direction of the Holy Spirit; (2) to engage regularly in serious Bible study and to use the Bible as a guide for life; (3) to learn the spirit, art, and values of prayer; (4) to pattern all of his personal conduct in accordance

with the teachings, spirit, and example of Jesus Christ;
(5) to do all possible to make his family life Christian;
(6) to refuse to enter into relations and participate in
activities which compromise or violate New Testament
principles; (7) to seek to apply Christian principles and
standards of conduct to all social relationships.

VII. *Christian service.*—Our aim is to lead each adult
to invest his talents and skills in Christian service. This
means helping each one:

(1) to witness consistently to the truth and power
of the Christian faith and to seek to win others to Jesus
Christ; (2) to work faithfully for the building up of his
church and to serve sacrificially in and through his
church; (3) to give of his money from worthy motives
and according to biblical teaching for the support of
his church and its work; (4) to show compassion for
persons in need and do deeds of helpfulness in his daily
life; (5) to find God's will for his life and to fulfil that
will in his vocation; (6) to engage in those phases of
Christian service which are best suited to his individual
capacities, environment, occupation, and social group;
(7) to serve effectively as a member of a team and
to serve without desire for self-glory; (8) to take a
worthy part as a Christian in community service projects; (9) to dedicate his total personality and resources
to world missions as the means of carrying forward the
redemptive undertaking of Jesus Christ; (10) to join
with others in co-operative action for the improvement
of social conditions, the creation of a more Christian
society, and the realization of God's purpose for mankind.

Our Educational Viewpoint

It is now in order to consider the educational viewpoint
on which the curriculum for the educational task of the
church is built. This also grows out of the nature of the
persons to be taught. They are learning beings, with individual differences. They have the capacity for perception
and understanding, for adjustment and growth. The psychology of learning leads, therefore, to a concept of teaching and training. The way persons learn gives important
guidance for curriculum building. In the following paragraphs we undertake to set forth the educational viewpoint
which gives direction in the development of curriculum
materials for use in the churches:

1. *The individual has the capacity to learn.*—In creating
man, God gave him greater intelligence than he gave to
any other creature. Man was given a central nervous sys-

tem which gives him the ability to think and reason
Because of his degree of intelligence, man can participat
creatively in his own growth by choosing goals, by dis
covering contrasts between his actual achievement an
these goals, by planning constructive change in relatio
to these contrasts, and by using his power of choice an
energies in achieving his goals. When constructive chang
takes place, it is recognized principally in the individual'
growth and in the improvement of the individual's environ
ment or his relation to it.

II. *Learning comes through experience.*—Mere activit
does not constitute experience. Experience is both doin
and undergoing; that is, we experience something when w
act, undergo, and evaluate the consequences. Thus th
purpose of Christian education is to guide individuals i
experiences which direct their growth toward accepte
goals. The curriculum includes all the experiences, activi
ties, and materials utilized by a church in seeking to reac
the objectives of Christian education. Freedom to choos
is a significant characteristic of the individual. Man is a
free moral agent. However, ignorance of possibilities o
the alternatives of a situation limits freedom of choice an
the effective functioning of intelligence. In those situation
in which attainable knowledge would make a difference
ignorance involves guilt. Worthy personal growth is base
on knowledge, but knowledge must be relevant to experi
ence. Even with regard to divine revelation, the Bibl
truth must be desired, understood, accepted, and applie
by the pupil if it is to make its maximum contribution t
his growth.

III. *Learning continues throughout life.*—Learning be
gins at birth. During infancy and early childhood, learnin
develops in proportion to the learning opportunities pro
vided by parents and the experiences the child has wit
other members of the family and with persons outside th
family. Learning continues at a high rate during childhoo
and adolescence. Although the rate of learning may de
crease during adulthood, learning continues throughou
life. In adult years the ability to learn and the rate o
learning are determined largely by the desire to learn an
the practice of good study habits.

IV. *Group experiences play an important part in th
learning process.*—Learning with others and from other
is basic to personal growth. Learning through group ex
perience begins in family life. Parents are teachers. Th
general atmosphere of the home is educative. Since th
home has the child first and during his most impression
able years, the family has a profound effect upon him
One's community offers opportunities for learning throug
group experiences. The immediate neighborhood and th
wider experiences one has in the institutions, organization
and activities of community life influence his thinking
choices, and ultimate goals. The classroom rightly con
ceived is a community of learning. In the classroom, grou
experience can contribute to learning by the encouragemen
of creative activities; the free expression of interest, ideas
and opinions; participation in group experiences related to

ife situations; and the sharing of information and experience. Group life always should enhance the individual.

V. *Teachers and other leaders exercise significant influence upon individual learners.*—In the learning process the life and example of the teacher are among the most effective and influential factors. Essentially, the learning process is one in which the teacher and members of the group become partners in the growth of one another. Freedom of expression is encouraged. Participation is anticipated and sought. The teacher seeks to know the members' problems and needs. The teacher's mastery of content is directed toward meeting the needs of the members and guiding them toward their maximum growth. He seeks to do this in an atmosphere of freedom. This freedom in learning does not mean the individual is free to do as he pleases. Any lack of interest or concern, any indication of idleness and inattention must be recognized and reconstructed.

VI. *The use of spiritual resources is necessary to maximum growth.*—Man is not restricted in his growth and development to his own finite limitations, but he has the capacity for fellowship with God and the opportunity to avail himself of unlimited spiritual resources. In regeneration one becomes a new person in Christ, experiences this fellowship with God, and gains access to these spiritual resources. This great truth makes Christian education different from all other education. It includes but goes beyond the limits of mere intellectual understanding and activity.

The Nature and Mission of the Church

Finally, the foundation of the curriculum is the nature and mission of the church. Let it be remembered that a church is a redeemed community; a fellowship of believers in Christ, a congregation of persons baptized in the name of Christ and associated together to carry forward the work of Christ to the world. A church is a living body. Its life calls for growth. Its work and witness call for instruction and training, knowledge and skill, discretion and dedication.

Let it be remembered also that the church has a divine mission. Its members are called of God to demonstrate the qualities of Christ-likeness. They are meant to be the salt of the earth and the light of the world. They are commissioned to make disciples of all nations and to be Christ's witnesses to the uttermost part of the earth. They are the servants of Christ in a world of need, and they are the disciples of the kingdom of God in a world of evil.

It should be obvious, therefore, that the life and work of the church demand that it be a teaching church. Its members must learn to live together in harmony and helpfulness if it is to be a fellowship in Christian love. They must learn the meaning of the gospel if they are to give a convincing witness to the world. They must have intelligent convictions about the doctrines of the faith if they are to be the pillar and ground of the truth. They must learn to live uprightly and courageously if they are to hold forth the word of life in the midst of a crooked and corrupt generation. They must come to know the mind of Christ in terms of the cross and the resurrection if they are to fulfil their mission as the body of Christ.

All of this is implied by Paul's matchless portrayal of the teaching church in Ephesians 4:11-16. Christ has given gifts to men. It is his will that the abilities and talents of persons be developed to the highest level of usefulness, that every person rise to the highest level of a redeemed personality. He has therefore ordained a teaching ministry in his church "for the immediate equipment of God's people for the work of service, for the ultimate building up of the body of Christ, until we all attain to unity in faith and to perfect knowledge of the Son of God, namely, to a mature manhood and to a perfect measure of Christ's moral stature; so that we may not be babies any longer, or like sailors tossed about and driven around by every wind of doctrine, by the trickery of men through their cunning in inventing new methods of error. But, on the other hand, we shall go on holding to the truth and in love growing up into perfect union with Him, that is, Christ Himself who is the Head" (Eph. 4:12-15, Williams).

A curriculum for Christian teaching and training is a necessity if the church is to be true to the New Testament. The educational task is central in its mission.

This material originally appeared in the *Curriculum Guide,* copyright 1960 by Convention Press. All rights reserved.

APPENDIX C
Sample Note Sheet for Sermon Construction

SAMPLE SERMON CONSTRUCTION PLAN SHEET

Notes to be entered direct onto a form of this nature,
where spaces are left.
Completed sheets can be taken into the pulpit as sermon notes,
and filed for further reference (see records section on final page).

SERMON PLAN
General Planning

Approach: expository; *Materials:* mature, various, Biblical, biographical. *Dynamics:* use the vital, novel, suspensive, relevant, humorous, illustrative, imaginative, and the pupil related; *Style:* with empathy, dialogue, energy, subtlety, clarity—*think back and feel back to hearers.*

Communication: watch mental images, verbal symbols, unclear objectives, irrelevant presentation. *Promote* pleasurable learning experience, and personal advantages.

Spiritual Thrust: claim Holy Spirit, acknowledge *His* work. Don't plead for a verdict, but with the authority of an involved witness testify to truth. Minister to the ministry of others; pray.

Specific Planning

N E E D (Discover, clarify, express, choose. Use own needs; meet ages and stages of hearers; meet needs for assurance, daily life, relationships to God, to Bible truth, and to progress.)

———————————————————————

———————————————————————

A I M (Brief, specific, clear; the desired sermon outcome; related to information, inspiration, motivation, or edification.)

———————————————————————

———————————————————————

(i)

SUBJECT_____

PASSAGE_____

ASPECT_____

SERMON TITLE_____

THESIS_____

_____

INTRODUCTION

a) *Point of Contact* (story, description, life-situation, quotation, problem, etc. - opening sentences in full)

_____

_____

_____

_____

_____

_____

_____

_____

b) *Transition* (from contact point to Biblical relevance)

_____

_____

c) *Thesis* (chosen central idea; a timelss truth expressed as a proposition)

_____

d) *Interrogative (one* of *how, when, where, why, who, which,* or *what)*

_____

e) *Keyword* (plural noun following *these, in these, at these, because of these, etc.)*

_____

DIVISIONS

Mutually exclusive, parallel form, from other truth in the passage. See notes on back page for extra facts, etc., that cannot be committed to this page. Use as many divisions as desired, but with a maximum of five, plus a maximum of three subpoints (plus illustrations) for each main division. The keyword should be implied, if not expressed, in every division of the thesis, and each division should be supporting or illustrating the thesis.

(I to V: number as needed)_____

_____

_____

_____

_____

_____

_____

_____

_____

_____

_____

_____

_____

_____

CONCLUSION

Repeat divisions and thesis. Ask, "So what?" Answer, "then we ought to . . . ." Present definite hearer benefit; appeal for specific "conduct response."

Final Sentences _____

_____

_____

Notes (segments to be committed to memory; facts for illustration detail; quotations; statistics)

_____

_____

_____

_____

_____

_____

_____

_____

_____

_____

_____

_____

_____

_____

DATE	WHERE PREACHED	REMARKS

Craig Skinner ©

(iv)

BIBLIOGRAPHY

Bibliography

Abbey, Merrill R. *Preaching to the Contemporary Mind.* New York: Abingdon, 1963.

———. *Living Doctrine in a Vital Pulpit.* New York: Abingdon, 1964.

———. *The Word Interprets Us.* New York: Abingdon, 1967.

Albright, Raymond W. *Focus on Infinity: A Life of Phillips Brooks.* New York: Macmillan, 1961.

Anderson, Robert. *The Silence of God.* London: Pickering and Inglis, n.d.

Asquith, Glen H. *Preaching According to Plan.* Valley Forge, Pa.: Judson, 1968.

Autrey, C. E. *Basic Evangelism.* Grand Rapids: Zondervan, 1959.

Bader, Jesse M. *Evangelism in a Changing America.* St. Louis: Bethany Press, 1957.

Baird, John E. *Preparing for Platform and Pulpit.* New York: Abingdon, 1969.

Barclay, William. *The Mind of St. Paul.* New York: Harper, 1959.

———. *Train Up a Child.* Philadelphia: Westminster, 1959.

Barnette, J. N. *The Place of the Sunday School in Evangelism.* Nashville: Baptist Sunday School Board, 1945.

Barrett, Ethyl. *Story-Telling: It's Easy!* Los Angeles: Cowman, 1960.

Barth, Karl. *Evangelical Theology: An Introduction.* New York: Holt, Rinehart, and Winston, 1963.

———. *God in Action.* New York: Round Table Press, 1963.

Bass, George M. *The Renewal of Liturgical Preaching.* Minneapolis: Augsburg, 1967.

Baxter, B. B. *The Heart of the Yale Lectures.* New York: Macmillan, 1947.

Bernays, Edward L. *The Engineering of Consent.* Norman: University of Oklahoma Press, n.d.

Blackwood, A. W. *Preaching from the Bible.* New York: Abingdon, 1941.

———. *Planning a Year's Pulpit Work.* New York: Abingdon, 1942.

———. *The Fine Art of Preaching.* New York: Macmillan, 1945.

———. *The Preparation of Sermons.* New York: Abingdon, 1948.

———. *Expository Preaching for Today.* New York: Abingdon, 1953.

———. *Biographical Preaching for Today.* New York: Abingdon, 1954.

———. *Doctrinal Preaching for Today.* New York: Abingdon, 1956.

Bohren, Rudolph. *Preaching and Community.* Translated by D. E. Green. Richmond: John Knox, 1966.

Bonhoeffer, Dietrich. *Life Together.* Translated by John W. Doberstein. New York: Harper, 1954.

Booth, John Nicholls. *The Quest for Preaching Power.* New York: Macmillan, 1943.

Brack, Harold A. *Effective Oral Interpretation for Religious Leaders.* New York: Prentice-Hall, 1964.

Brack, Harold A. and Hance, Kenneth G. *Public Speaking and Discussion for Religious Leaders.* Englewood Cliffs, N.J.: Prentice-Hall, 1961.

Bradley, Martin E., ed. *The Quarterly Review.* Nashville: Sunday School Board of the Southern Baptist Convention, July 1969, 29:3.

Brister, C. W. *Pastoral Care in the Church.* New York: Harper, 1964.

Broadhurst, Allan R. *He Speaks the Word of God: A Study of the Sermons of Norman Vincent Peale.* Englewood Cliffs, N.J.: Prentice-Hall, 1963.

Broadus, John A. *On the Preparation and Delivery of Sermons.* Rev. ed. New York: Harper, 1944.

Brown, Elijah P. *Point and Purpose in Preaching.* New York: Revell, 1917.

Brown, H. C., Jr., ed. *Southern Baptist Preaching.* Nashville: Broadman, 1959.

———. *More Southern Baptist Preaching.* Nashville: Broadman, 1964.

Brown, H. C., Jr.; Clinard, H. Gordon; and Northcutt, Jesse J. *Steps to the Sermon.* Nashville: Broadman, 1963.

Brown, Henry, Jr. *A Quest for Reformation in Preaching.* Waco, Tex.: Word Books, 1968.

Burns, James. *Revivals: Their Laws and Leaders.* Revised ed. edited by A. W. Blackwood. Grand Rapids: Baker, 1960.

Butler, J. Donald. *Four Philosophies and Their Practice in Religious Education.* Rev. ed. New York: Harper, 1957.

———. *Religious Education.* New York: Harper, 1962.

Buttrick, George A. *Christ and History.* New York: Abingdon, 1963.

Cairncross, T. S. *The Steps of the Pulpit.* London: Hodder and Stoughton, 1910.

Campbell-Wycoff, D. *The Gospel and Christian Education.* Philadelphia: Westminster, 1959.

Chave, Ernest J. *A Functional Approach to Christian Education.* Chicago: University of Chicago Press, 1947.

Christian Century. Chicago: 4 March 1964.

Christianity Today. Washington, D.C.: 1 February 1963; and 5 June 1959.

Church Program Guidebook. Nashville: Sunday School Board of the Southern Baptist Convention, 1965, appendix on "Theological Foundations of the Curriculum."

Clarke, James W. *Dynamic Preaching.* New York: Revell, 1960.

Cleland, James T. *Preaching to Be Understood.* New York: Abingdon, 1965.

Come, Arnold B. *An Introduction to Barth's Dogmatics for Preachers.* Philadelphia: Westminster, 1963.

Cordasco, Frensesco. *A Brief History of Education.* Totowa, N.J.: Littlefield, Adams, and Co., 1967.

Crocker, Lionel. *Public Speaking for College Students.* New York: American Book Co., 1941.

Crusader. Valley Forge, Pa.: American Baptist Convention newsmagazine, March 1963.

Dale, R. W. *Nine Lectures on Preaching.* New York: Geo. H. Doran, n.d., lectures delivered at Yale in 1878.

Dargan, E. C. *The Art of Preaching in the Light of Its History.* Nashville: Sunday School Board of the Southern Baptist Convention, 1922.

———. *A History of Preaching.* Reprint ed., 2 vols. Grand Rapids: Baker, 1954.

Davidson, W. T. *The Indwelling Spirit.* London: Hodder and Stoughton, 1911.

Davis, H. Grady. *Design for Preaching.* Philadelphia: Westminster, 1949.

Dewey, John. *The Child and the Curriculum: The School and Society.* Chicago: University of Chicago Press, 1956.

Dillistone, F. W. *Christianity and Communication.* New York: Scribner's, 1956.

Dobbins, Gaines S. *The Improvement of Teaching in the Sunday School.* Nashville: Convention Press, Baptist Sunday School Board, 1943.

———. *A Ministering Church.* Nashville: Broadman, 1960.

Dodd, C. H. *The Apostolic Preaching and Its Development.* Cambridge: University Press, 1935.

Drakeford, John W. *Psychology in Search of a Soul.* Nashville: Broadman, 1964.

Easton, B. S., and Robins, H. C. *The Eternal Word in the Modern World.* New York: Scribner's, 1937.

Edge, Findley B. *Teaching for Results.* Nashville: Broadman, 1956.

———. *Helping the Teacher.* Nashville: Broadman, 1959.

Ellison, J. M. *They Who Preach.* Nashville: Broadman, 1956.

Encyclopaedia Britannica. Chicago: Encyclopaedia Britannica, 1960 ed.

Encyclopedia of Southern Baptists. 2 vols. Nashville: Broadman, 1958.

Evans, William. *How to Prepare Sermons.* Chicago: Moody, 1964.

Fairchild, Roy W., and Winn, John Charles. *Families in the Church: A Protestant Survey.* New York: Association Press, 1961.

Farmer, H. H. *The Servant of the Word.* New York: Scribner's, 1942.

Faw, Chalmer E. *A Guide to Biblical Preaching.* Nashville: Broadman, 1962.

Filson, Floyd V. *Three Crucial Decades: Studies in the Book of Acts.* Richmond: John Knox Press, 1963.

Fosdick, Harry Emerson. *The Living of These Days.* New York: Harper, 1956.

Foulkes, Francis. *The Epistle of Paul to the Ephesians.* In *Tyndale Bible Commentaries,* ed. by R. V. Tasker. Grand Rapids: Eerdmans, 1963.

Freeman, Roger Maclement. *The Inviability of Two Basic Principles in the Christian Faith and Life Curriculum.* Cambridge, Mass.: unpublished Ph.D. thesis, Divinity School, Harvard University, 1963.

French, E. A., ed. *Evangelism—A Re-interpretation.* London: Epworth, 1921.

Garrison, Webb B. *The Preacher and His Audience.* New York: Revell, 1954.

———. *Creative Imagination in Preaching.* New York: Abingdon, 1960.

Gibb, J. R.; Platts, Grace N.; and Miller, Lorraine F. *Dynamics of Participative Groups.* St. Louis: John Swift, 1951.

Grimes, Howard. *The Church Redemptive.* New York: Abingdon, 1958.

———. *The Rebirth of the Laity.* New York: Abingdon, 1962.

Gwynne, Price H., Jr. *Leadership Education in the Local Church.* Philadelphia: Westminster, 1952.

Hakes, J. Edward, ed. *An Introduction to Evangelical Christian Education.* Chicago: Moody, 1964.

Henderson, Stella V. *Introduction to Philosophy of Education.* Chicago: University of Chicago Press, 1947.

Henry, Carl F. H., ed. *Revelation and the Bible.* Grand Rapids: Baker, 1958.

———. *Basic Christian Doctrines.* New York: Holt, Rinehart, and Winston, 1962.

Henry, Nelson B., ed. *Social Forces Influencing American Education.* 41st yearbook of the National Society for the Study of Education, Part II. Chicago: University of Chicago Press, 1942.

———. *Mass Media and Education.* 54th yearbook of the National Society for the Study of Education, Part I. Chicago: University of Chicago Press, 1955.

Highet, Gilbert. *The Art of Teaching.* Vintage Books ed. New York: Random House, 1950.

Hilgard, Ernest R. *Introduction to Psychology.* 2nd ed. New York: Harcourt, Brace, and Co., 1957.

Hiltner, Seward. *Self-Understanding: Through Psychology and Religion.* New York: Scribner's, 1951; also in Abingdon Apex Paperback edition.

Hoffman, Hans, ed. *Making the Ministry Relevant.* New York: Scribner's, 1960.

Hoiland, Richard, ed. *Planning Christian Education in the Local Church.* Rev. ed. Valley Forge, Pa.: Judson Press, 1962.

Hoppin, James M. *Homiletics.* New York: Dodd, Mead, and Co., 1881.

Manson, T. E. *Ministry and Priesthood, Christ's and Ours.* London: Epworth, 1958.

Marcel, Pierre Ch. *The Relevance of Preaching.* Translated by Rob Roy McGregor. Grand Rapids: Baker, 1963.

Marty, Martin E. *The New Shape of American Religion,* New York: Harper, 1958.

Mead, Frank S. *Reaching Beyond Your Pulpit.* Westwood, N.J.: Revell, 1962.

Miller, Donald. *Fire in Thy Mouth.* New York: Abingdon, 1954.

Miller, Paul. *Group Dynamics in Evangelism.* Scottsdale, Pa.: Herald Press, 1958.

Moody, Dale. *Christ and the Church.* Grand Rapids: Eerdmans, 1963.

Moore, William J. *The New Testament Concept of the Ministry.* St. Louis: Bethany Press, 1956.

Morgan, G. Campbell. *The Ministry of the Word.* New York: Revell, 1919.

Morris, Leon. *The Apostolic Preaching of the Cross.* Grand Rapids: Eerdmans, 1955.

Mounce, Robert L. *The Essential Nature of New Testament Preaching.* Grand Rapids: Eerdmans, 1960

Myers, Frederick W. H. *St. Paul.* London: Samuel Bagster and Sons, n.d.

Narramore, Clyde M. *This Way to Happiness.* Grand Rapids: Zondervan, 1958.

Nichols, Sue. *Words on Target, For Better Communication.* Richmond: John Knox Press, 1963.

Nida, Eugene A. *Message and Mission: The Communication of the Christian Faith.* New York: Harper, 1960.

Nizer, Louis. *My Life in Court.* New York: Pyramid Publications, 1963.

Oates, Wayne E. *The Christian Pastor.* Philadelphia: Westminster, 1951.

————. ed. *Introduction to Pastoral Counseling.* Nashville: Broadman, 1959.

Oliver, Robert T. *The Psychology of Persuasive Speech.* New York: Longmans, Green, and Co., 1942.

Olmsted, Michael. *The Small Group.* New York: Random House, Studies in Psychology Series, 1959.

Olson, Bessie G. *George Whitefield: A Great Orator.* Philadelphia: Walfred Publishing Co., 1955.

Orr, James. *A Christian View of God and the World.* New York: Scribner's, 1892.

————. ed. *The International Standard Bible Encyclopedia.* Chicago: Howard Severance Co., 1930.

Orr, J. Edwin. *The Second Evangelical Awakening.* London: Marshall, Morgan, and Scott, 1955.

Packard, Vance. *The Hidden Persuaders.* New York: David McKay, 1957.

Packer, J. A. *Fundamentalism and the Word of God.* London: Inter-Varsity Fellowship, 1960.

———. *Evangelism and the Sovereignty of God.* Chicago: Inter-Varsity Press, 1961.

Pearce, J. Winston. *Planning Your Preaching.* Nashville: Broadman, 1967.

Pearson, Roy. *The Ministry of Preaching.* New York: Harper, 1959.

———. *The Preacher: His Purpose and Practice.* Philadelphia: Westminster, 1962.

Perry, Lloyd M., and Whitesell, Faris D. *Variety in Your Preaching.* Westwood, N.J.: Revell, 1954.

———. *Preaching with Purpose.* Beverly Farms, Mass.: Gordon College Press, 1961.

Perry, Lloyd M., and Strickland, Bruce L. *Variety in Biblical Preaching.* Peabody, Mass.: Powell Publishing Co., 1959.

Phelps, Austin. *The Theory of Preaching.* Rev. ed. edited by Faris D. Whitesell. Grand Rapids: Eerdmans, 1947.

Phillips, J. B. *The New Testament in Modern English.* London: Bles, 1959.

Randolph, David J. *The Renewal of Preaching.* Philadelphia: Fortress Press, 1969.

Reid, Clyde. *The Empty Pulpit.* New York: Harper, 1969.

———. *Two-Way Communication Through Small Groups in Relation to Preaching.* Boston: Boston University School of Theology, unpublished Ph.D. thesis, 1960.

Richardson, Alan, ed. *A Theological Word Book of the Bible.* New York: Macmillan, 1962.

Ridderbos, Herman N. *When the Time Had Fully Come.* Grand Rapids: Eerdmans, 1957.

Riley, W. B. *The Preacher and His Preaching.* Wheaton, Ill.: Sword of the Lord, 1948.

Ritschl, Dietrich. *A Theology of Proclamation.* Richmond: John Knox Press, 1960.

Robertson, Archibald T. *The Glory of the Ministry.* Reprint ed. Grand Rapids: Baker, 1967.

Roddy, Clarence Stonelyn. *We Prepare and Preach.* Chicago: Moody, 1959.

Rogers, Carl. *Client-Centered Therapy.* Boston: Houghton-Mifflin Co., 1951.

Sahlin, Clarence J. *A Comparison Between the Pragmatic and Conservative Christian Approach to Education.* Chicago: unpublished Th.M. thesis, Northern Baptist Theological Seminary, 1956.

Sangster, P. E. *Speech in the Pulpit.* New York: Philosophical Library, 1958.

Sangster, W. E. *The Craft of Sermon Construction.* London: Epworth, 1949.
————. *The Approach to Preaching.* Philadelphia: Westminster, 1952.
————. *Give God a Chance.* Wyvern ed. London: Epworth, 1951.
————. *Let Me Commend.* Wyvern ed. London: Epworth, 1961.
————. *Power in Preaching.* London: Epworth, 1958.

Sargent, Leslie W. "Communicating and the Spirit," in *Christianity Today,* 1 February 1963.

Schloerb, Rolland W. *The Preaching Ministry Today.* New York: Harper, 1946.

Schroeder, F. W. *Preaching the Word with Authority.* Philadelphia: Westminster, 1954.

Segler, Franklin M. *A Theology of Church and Ministry.* Nashville: Broadman, 1960.

Sellers, James. *The Outsider and the Word of God.* New York: Abingdon, 1961.

Sellers, James Earl. *The Church and Mass Communication.* Nashville: unpublished Ph.D. thesis, Vanderbilt University, 1958.

Sherril, Lewis Joseph. *The Struggle of the Soul.* New York: Macmillan, 1951.

Shoemaker, Samuel. *With the Holy Spirit and with Fire.* New York: Harper, 1960.

Sizoo, Joseph R. *Preaching Unashamed.* New York: Abingdon, 1949.

Skinner, Craig. *Gospel Communication—The Life of the Church: A Study in Age-Relevant Evangelism.* Chicago: unpublished Th.M. thesis, Northern Baptist Theological Seminary, 1963.

Sleeth, Roland E. *Persuasive Preaching.* New York: Harper, 1956.
————. *Proclaiming the Word.* New York: Abingdon, 1964.

Smart, James D. *Basic Principles: Christian Faith and Life: A Program for Church and Home.* Philadelphia: Board of Christian Education, Presbyterian Church in the U.S.A., 1948.
————. *The Teaching Ministry of the Church.* Philadelphia: Westminster, 1954.
————. *The Rebirth of Ministry.* Philadelphia: Westminster, 1960.
————. *The Old Testament in Dialogue with Modern Man.* Philadelphia: Westminster, 1964.

Smith, Charles W. F. *Biblical Authority for Modern Preaching.* Philadelphia: Westminster, 1949.

Smith, Henry P. *Psychology in Teaching.* New York: Prentice-Hall, 1954.

Southard, Samuel. *Pastoral Evangelism.* Nashville: Broadman, 1962.

Southern Baptist Handbook. Nashville: Baptist Sunday School Board of the Southern Baptist Convention, Research and Statistics Department, 1965.

Spurgeon, Charles Haddon. *The Soul-Winner*, reprint. Grand Rapids, Eerd-
  mans, 1963.
Stevenson, Dwight D. *In the Biblical Preacher's Workshop*. New York:
  Abingdon, 1967.
Stewart, Donald Gordon. *Christian Education and Evangelism*. Philadelphia:
  Westminster, 1963.
Sweazey, George E. *Effective Evangelism*. New York: Harper, 1953.
Sweet, W. W. *The Story of Religion in America*. New York: Harper, 1930.

Taylor, Marvin J., ed. *Religious Education*. New York: Abingdon, 1960.
Teikmanis, Arthur L. *Preaching and Pastoral Care*. Philadelphia: Fortress
  Press, 1968.
Thelen, Herbert A. *Dynamics of Groups at Work*. Chicago: University of
  Chicago Press, 1954.
Thielicke, Helmut. *How the World Began*. Philadelphia: Muhlenberg Press,
  1961.
———. *Encounter with Spurgeon*. Philadelphia: Fortress Press, 1963.
Thompson, Claude H. *Theology of the Kerygma*. Englewood Cliffs, N.J.:
  Prentice-Hall, 1962.
Thompson, W. D. *Listener's Guide to Preaching*. New York: Abingdon, 1966.
Thompson, W. D., and Bennet, Gordon C. *Dialogue Preaching: The Shared
  Sermon*. Valley Forge, Pa.: Judson Press, 1969.
Turnbull, Ralph G. *Baker's Dictionary of Practical Theology*. Grand Rapids:
  Baker, 1967.
———. *The Preacher's Heritage, Task, and Resources*. Grand Rapids: Baker,
  1968.

Vieth, Paul H. *The Church School*. Philadelphia: Christian Education Press,
  1957.
Vos, Geerhardus. *The Pauline Eschatology*. Grand Rapids: Eerdmans, 1957.
Weatherhead, Leslie D. *Psychology, Religion, and Healing*. New York:
  Abingdon, 1952.
Webber, F. R. *A History of Preaching in Britain and America*. Part III—
  "America." Milwaukee: Northwest Publishing House, 1957.
Wesley, John. *The Works of John Wesley*, A.M. Vol. 10. London:
  Wesleyan-Methodist Bookroom, 1872.
Westphal, Edward P. *The Church's Opportunity in Adult Education*.
  Philadelphia: Westminster, 1941.
Whitesell, Faris Daniel. *Basic New Testament Evangelism*. Grand Rapids:
  Zondervan, 1949.
———. *The Art of Biblical Preaching*. Grand Rapids: Zondervan, 1950.
———. *Power in Expository Preaching*. Westwood, N.J.: Revell, 1963.

Whitney, Frederick Lamson. *The Elements of Research.* 3rd. ed. New York: Prentice-Hall, 1950.

Yohn, David W. *The Contemporary Preacher and His Task.* Grand Rapids: Eerdmans, 1969.

Young, Warren C. *A Christian Approach to Philosophy.* Grand Rapids: Baker, 1962.

INDEX

Index of Subjects

See also *Table of Contents,* page 7; *List of Illustrations,* page 16; and *Index of Persons,* which follows.

Index of Persons

*See also bibliography, and
list of significant preachers, pages 35-38.*